# Teaching the New English

Series Editor
Ben Knights
Teesside University
Middlesbrough, UK

Teaching the New English is an innovative series primarily concerned with the teaching of the English degree in the context of the modern university. The series is simultaneously concerned with addressing exciting new areas that have developed in the curriculum in recent years and those more traditional areas that have reformed in new contexts. It is grounded in an intellectual or theoretical concept of the curriculum, yet is largely concerned with the practicalities of the curriculum's manifestation in the classroom. Volumes will be invaluable for new and more experienced teachers alike.

More information about this series at
http://www.palgrave.com/gp/series/14458

Richard Jacobs
Editor

# Teaching Narrative

*Editor*
Richard Jacobs
School of Humanities
University of Brighton
Brighton, UK

Teaching the New English
ISBN 978-3-319-70677-1     ISBN 978-3-319-71829-3  (eBook)
https://doi.org/10.1007/978-3-319-71829-3

Library of Congress Control Number: 2018935237

© The Editor(s) (if applicable) and The Author(s) 2018
This work is subject to copyright. All rights are solely and exclusively licensed by the Publisher, whether the whole or part of the material is concerned, specifically the rights of translation, reprinting, reuse of illustrations, recitation, broadcasting, reproduction on microfilms or in any other physical way, and transmission or information storage and retrieval, electronic adaptation, computer software, or by similar or dissimilar methodology now known or hereafter developed.
The use of general descriptive names, registered names, trademarks, service marks, etc. in this publication does not imply, even in the absence of a specific statement, that such names are exempt from the relevant protective laws and regulations and therefore free for general use.
The publisher, the authors and the editors are safe to assume that the advice and information in this book are believed to be true and accurate at the date of publication. Neither the publisher nor the authors or the editors give a warranty, express or implied, with respect to the material contained herein or for any errors or omissions that may have been made. The publisher remains neutral with regard to jurisdictional claims in published maps and institutional affiliations.

Printed on acid-free paper

This Palgrave Macmillan imprint is published by the registered company Springer International Publishing AG part of Springer Nature
The registered company address is: Gewerbestrasse 11, 6330 Cham, Switzerland

# Series Editor's Preface

One of the many exciting achievements of the early years of the UK English Subject Centre was the agreement with Palgrave Macmillan to initiate the series 'Teaching the New English'. The intention of Philip Martin, the then Centre Director, was to create a series of short and accessible books which would focus on curriculum fields (or themes) and develop the connections between scholarly knowledge and the demands of teaching.

Since its inception as a university subject, 'English' has been committed to what is now known by the portmanteau phrase 'learning and teaching'. The subject grew up in a dialogue between scholars, critics, and their students inside and outside the university. Yet university teachers of English often struggle to make their own tacit pedagogic knowledge conscious, or to bring it up to a level where it might be shared, developed, or critiqued. In the experience of the English Subject Centre, colleagues found it relatively easy to talk about curriculum, but far harder to talk about the success or failure of seminars, how to vary modes of assessment, or to make imaginative use of virtual learning environments or web tools. Too often, this reticence meant falling back on received assumptions about how students learn, about how to teach or create assessment tasks. At the same time, we found, colleagues were generally suspicious of the insights and methods arising from generic educational research. The challenge for the extended group of English disciplines has been to articulate ways in which our own subject knowledge and forms of enquiry might themselves refresh debates about pedagogy. The need becomes all the more pressing in the era of rising fees, student loans, the National Student Survey, and the characterisation of the student as a demanding consumer of an educational product. The implicit invitation of the present series is to take fields of knowledge and survey them through a pedagogic lens.

'Teachers', people used to say, 'are born, not made'. There may be some tenuous truth in this. There may perhaps be generosities of spirit (or, alternatively, drives for didactic control) laid down in early childhood. But the implication that you cannot train or develop teachers is dubious. Why should we assume that even 'born' teachers should not need to learn or review the skills of their trade? Amateurishness about teaching has far more to do with the mystique of university status than with evidence about how people learn. This series of books is dedicated to the development of the craft of teaching within university English Studies.

Emeritus Professor of English and Cultural Studies            Ben Knights
Teesside University
Middlesbrough, UK

Visiting Fellow
UCL Institute of Education, London, UK

# Acknowledgements

I would like to thank the editorial team at Palgrave, Ben Doyle and Milly Davies: their help was always patiently available. The book has enjoyed the unstinting support of Ben Knights, the Series Editor, who gave so much of his time in answering queries and proffering advice and helpful feedback. I want to express my warmest thanks to him. It's been a real pleasure to work with the contributors who have all been willing, eager and timely with their work and enthusiastic about the volume. In choosing the contributors I benefited from recommendations offered by Robyn Warhol, Dino Felluga and Will Norman, and the latter also kindly suggested improvements to the Introduction. I'm very grateful to them.

Suzanne Keen would like to thank Kate Higgins, Assistant Archivist at the Library, the London School of Economics and Political Science, for her guidance in reproduction of images from Charles Booth's poverty maps.

# Contents

| | | |
|---|---|---|
| 1 | **Introduction**<br>Richard Jacobs | 1 |
| 2 | **Time, Narrative and Culture**<br>Mark Currie | 23 |
| 3 | **Talking Race and Narrative with Undergraduate Students in the USA**<br>Sue J. Kim | 39 |
| 4 | **The Ethics of Teaching Tragic Narratives**<br>Sean McEvoy | 55 |
| 5 | **Teaching Comic Narratives**<br>Rachel Trousdale | 71 |
| 6 | **Teaching Crime Narratives: Historicizing Genre and the Politics of Form**<br>Will Norman | 87 |

| 7 | Teaching Historical Fiction: Hilary Mantel and the Protestant Reformation<br>Mark Eaton | 103 |
|---|---|---|
| 8 | Text and Context: Using Wikis to Teach Victorian Novels<br>Ellen Rosenman | 123 |
| 9 | Digital Humanities in the Teaching of Narrative<br>Suzanne Keen | 139 |
| 10 | The Work of Narrative in the Age of Digital Interaction: Revolutions in Practice and Pedagogy<br>Alec Charles | 155 |
| 11 | Empowering Students as Researchers: Teaching and Learning Autoethnography and the Value of Self-Narratives<br>Jess Moriarty | 175 |
| 12 | Narrative and Narratives: Designing and Delivering a First-Year Undergraduate Narrative Module<br>Richard Jacobs | 191 |

Index   211

# Notes on Contributors

**Alec Charles** is Professor and Dean of the Faculty of Arts at the University of Winchester. He has worked as a print journalist and a BBC radio programme-maker, and has taught at universities in Estonia, Japan, Cornwall, Chester, Luton and Hull. He is the author of *Interactivity*, *Interactivity 2*, *Out of Time* and *Political Animals*, co-editor of *The End of Journalism*, and editor of *The End of Journalism 2*, *Media/Democracy* and *Media in the Enlarged Europe*. He serves as co-convenor of the Political Studies Association's Media and Politics Group.

**Mark Currie** is Professor of Contemporary Literature at Queen Mary, University of London. His research is focused on theories of narrative and culture, particularly in relation to time. He is the author of *Postmodern Narrative Theory* (1998; second edition 2011), *Difference* (2004), *About Time: Narrative Fiction and the Philosophy of Time* (2007), *The Unexpected: Narrative Temporality and the Philosophy of Surprise* (2013) and *The Invention of Deconstruction* (2013). His recent work is focused on the relation between fictional narrative and philosophical writings about time, and more generally, on questions of futurity in intellectual history. He is currently writing a book called *Absolute Uncertainty*, which explores the relationship between narrative and contingency.

**Mark Eaton** is Professor of English and Director of Graduate Studies at Azusa Pacific University, where he teaches American literature and film studies. He is co-editor of *The Gift of Story: Narrating Hope in a Postmodern World* (Baylor UP, 2006) and a contributor to *A Companion to the Modern*

*American Novel, 1900–1950* (Wiley-Blackwell, 2009); *A Companion to Film Comedy* (Wiley-Blackwell, 2012); *Screenwriting* (Rutgers UP, 2014); and *The Routledge Companion to Literature & Religion* (Routledge, 2015).

**Richard Jacobs** is Principal Lecturer in Literature at the University of Brighton. His publications include *A Beginner's Guide to Critical Reading: An Anthology of Literary Texts* (Routledge), chapters in *Reassessing the Twentieth Century Canon* (Palgrave) and *The Twentieth Century* (Penguin History of Literature), editions of *Vile Bodies* and *The Ordeal of Gilbert Pinfold* (Penguin Classics), materials for teachers on post-16 literature teaching, and several articles and reviews.

**Suzanne Keen** writes about narrative empathy. Her affective and cognitive narrative studies combine expertise in the novel and narrative theory with interests in emotion science and psychology. Her books include *Thomas Hardy's Brains*, *Empathy and the Novel*, *Romances of the Archive in Contemporary British Fiction*, *Victorian Renovations of the Novel* and a volume of poetry. She serves as Thomas H. Broadus Professor of English and Dean of the College at Washington and Lee University, where she started a collaborative Digital Humanities Initiative in 2013.

**Sue J. Kim** is Professor of English and Co-Director of the Centre for Asian American Studies at the University of Massachusetts Lowell. She is the author of *On Anger: Race, Cognition, Narrative* (2013) and *Critiquing Postmodernism in Contemporary Discourses of Race* (2009), and co-edited *Rethinking Empathy through Literature* (2014). She has served on the Association for Asian American Studies Board of Directors and the Executive Committee of the International Society for the Study of Narrative.

**Sean McEvoy** is currently a visiting lecturer at Murray Edwards College, Cambridge. For many years he taught literature at Varndean College, Brighton. His publications include *Shakespeare: The Basics* (Routledge, third edition, 2012), *William Shakespeare's 'Hamlet': A Sourcebook* (Routledge, 2006), *Ben Jonson, Renaissance Dramatist* (Edinburgh UP, 2008) and *Tragedy: The Basics* (Routledge, 2017). His book *Theatrical Unrest: Ten Riots in the History of the Stage, 1603–2004* (Routledge, 2016) was shortlisted for the 2016 Theatre Book Prize.

**Jess Moriarty** is course leader for the Creative Writing MA and English Literature and Creative Writing BA at the University of Brighton. She is the co-editor of *Self-narrative and Pedagogy: Stories of Experience within Teaching and Learning* (2017) and the author of *Analytical Autoethnodrama* (2015). Her research focuses on auto-ethnography, writing as a craft and community engagement. Her doctorate explored her autobiographical experiences with teaching in higher education and in particular the effect of the audit culture on how we teach and how we live.

**Will Norman** is a senior lecturer in American literature at the University of Kent. He has also been a Fulbright scholar in American Studies at Yale University. He is the author of the monographs *Nabokov, History and the Texture of Time* (2012) and *Transatlantic Aliens: Modernism, Exile and Culture in Midcentury America* (2016), and co-editor of the essay collection *Transitional Nabokov* (2009). His essays on crime fiction have appeared in *Modernism/modernity*, *Journal of Modern Literature* and *Post-45*.

**Ellen Rosenman** is a Provost's Distinguished Service Professor in the English Department at the University of Kentucky. She is the author of *Unauthorized Pleasures: Accounts of Victorian Erotic Experience* (Cornell UP, 2003), co-editor with Claudia Klaver of *Other Mothers: Beyond the Maternal Ideal* (Ohio State UP, 2008), and co-editor with Susan Bordo and Cristina Alcalde of *Provocations: A Transnational History of Feminist Thought* (U California Press, 2015). She has published articles about Victorian gender, sexuality and social class in edited collections and journals, including *Victorian Studies*, *Journal of the History of Sexuality*, *Studies in the Novel* and *Journal of Victorian Literature and Culture*.

**Rachel Trousdale** is an assistant professor of English at Framingham State University. She is the author of *Nabokov, Rushdie, and the Transnational Imagination: Novels of Exile and Alternate Worlds* (Palgrave Macmillan, 2010), *The Joking Voice: Humour in Twentieth-Century American Poetry* (Oxford, forthcoming) and a poetry chapbook, *Antiphonal Fugue for Marx Brothers, Elephant, and Slide Trombone* (Finishing Line Press, 2015). More information is available at www.racheltrousdale.com

# LIST OF FIGURES

| | | |
|---|---|---|
| Fig. 9.1 | Legend for color-coding streets by degrees of affluence or poverty. *Charles Booth Online Archive*, http://booth.lse.ac.uk/static/a/4.html | 149 |
| Fig. 9.2 | Hyde Park Corner, a wealthy neighborhood, from *Charles Booth Online Archive*. ('Printed Map Descriptive of London Poverty 1898–1899.' Sheet 7. Inner Western District. Covering: Pimlico, Westminster, Brompton, Chelsea, Mayfair, Marylebone, Paddington, Bayswater, Notting Hill, Kensington, Knightsbridge, Pimlico and Belgravia. LSE reference no. BOOTH/E/1/7.) | 150 |
| Fig. 11.1 | Triangulation of practice | 181 |

## CHAPTER 1

# Introduction

*Richard Jacobs*

### ENCHANTMENT/DISENCHANTMENT; CLOSURE/NARRATABILITY

Narrative is everywhere: and its pervasiveness makes it, in a sense, harder rather than easier to teach. Defamiliarizing what is so familiar, in students' lives and in the texts they've consumed, all the way from bedtime infancy to 'set texts' for exams, can be an unsettling experience. In addition, for a lecturer to convey and gauge the power of narratives, especially over his students' own lives (as well as his own: in teaching narrative, I make this very clear and personal) can seem intrusive. Fiction is fictive but narratives can occlude their own fictiveness so seductively as to seem true. This isn't just the trivial matter, say, of early readers of *Gulliver's Travels* indignantly complaining that they didn't believe a word about those little and big people (presumably such readers gave up before they got to the talking horses); it's serious.

I'm writing this in July 2017 not long after a momentous general election in the UK in which, to everyone's astonishment, a narrative of hope, communality and desire for a fairer society was at least as much listened to and believed (especially by students and other young people) than the narrative of fear, cynical inequality and hatred of others, a narrative relentlessly elaborated by the 'free' world's most aggressively partisan newspapers, that have poisoned British politics for so long. Earlier we had Brexit and Trump. Narratives swung both those results. The coerciveness of narrative—its power to lie, oppress and enslave—is just as significant as its more widely acclaimed and more benevolent powers: narrative being (in H. Porter Abbott's words) 'the principal way our species organises its understanding of time' (Abbott 2002: 3) and, through that, the way we come to terms with mortality; its power to make sense of our world, our lives and ourselves; and its power to give us an infinitely enriched understanding of alternative worlds and lives—and of a better future. Students can more readily accept the plausibility of the latter life-enhancing powers rather than the former coercive ones. Enchantment with narrative is more easily taught than disenchantment.

The balance between enchantment and disenchantment also operates differently across the student's educational experience. It may be one way of distinguishing what happens in university teaching from what comes before it that the balance there tips sharply towards the disenchantment pole, as we teach the application of critical literacy, with its attendant and necessary scepticisms, to the reading of narrative, whereas, at the other extreme, in childhood, enchantment with narrative very much has its 'uses' (Bettelheim 1976).

But students also come to see that what is involved in their later reading of narrative is an oscillation between enchantment and disenchantment, in their experience not just of different sorts or genres of texts, or as to the liberating or oppressive nature of the narrative, but even within the same text. The narrative enchants us and simultaneously we are aware of, and meant to be aware of and meant to resist, that enchantment. It would be conventional to map this process or oscillation, and to assess the balance between the two processes, on to and in terms of the differences, or alleged differences, between realist and modernist narratives, with their sharply divergent allegiances to notions of coherence, wholeness, plausibility, dimensionality and hierarchies of discourse.

Students of literature at university are encouraged to see those differences in terms of linear chronology as they move from the great nineteenth-century realist narratives of, say, Jane Austen, Dickens and George Eliot to the high modernist post-war experiments of, say, Joyce, Woolf and Ford. These would conventionally be taught on separate modules. But this cleanly demarcated linear development should be destabilized and I give some examples of that process in the last chapter of this book, in relation to 'Bartleby' and to the 'Alice' books in dialogue with Freud's 'Dora'. And it's very pertinent that D. A. Miller observes that the standard account of the realist novel serving 'the repressive order of the nineteenth century bourgeoisie' whereas the modernist novel 'registers an implicit protest against this repression' (Miller 1981: 281) is too simple. He doesn't say it but one complicating point would be to note that when realism was being heralded as a new breed of narrative fiction, in the form of *Madame Bovary*, Flaubert's novel and realism itself (though Flaubert hated and rejected the term) were being defined by reviewers as the politics of 'discontented democracy' and 'implacable equality' (Heath 1992: 51). Miller draws on Fredric Jameson to argue that modernist fiction can be 'suspiciously consonant, not to say complicitous, with aspects of the social order that provides its own context' (Miller 1981: 281).

Even more telling, however, is for students to come to see that single texts in the so-called realist or modernist traditions can be read as containing unstable compounds of the two traditions—both, in Barthes' famous terms, 'readerly and 'writerly' (Barthes 1990: v), that reading them is a matter of negotiating between enchantment and disenchantment, and that it's less a matter of modernism being a chronological development from and break with realism and more that the two represent a tension in narrative texts that has been with us from the start (from at least Cervantes) and is still with us today (see Josipovici 2010). The 'realist/modernist' dynamic can be traced in manifold ways and places: students on a first-year 'Re-Viewing Shakespeare' module have been stimulated to notice the shifting proportions of 'realist' and 'modernist' narratives in the proto-realist *Hamlet* and the proto-modernist *King Lear*. As suggested above, it's a tension that's inherent in the very fictiveness of narrative.

Teaching nineteenth-century 'realist' novels to students who have been introduced to the critical approaches to narrative fiction pioneered by Peter Brooks and D. A. Miller has proved a very fruitful and bracing experience, whether working with second-year undergraduates on a 19th century module that takes in some of the usual landmarks or an MA module on rhetoric that pays close attention to Jane Austen (and, as we'll see, Mary Shelley). And we might relate the enchantment/disenchantment dynamic to the crucial feature that Miller (who is at his dazzling best on Jane Austen) identifies in narrative fiction as the permanent tension between closure and narratability: closure can only 'work' by abolishing the possibilities of what can be narrated, a process that involves the 'discontents' of Miller's title (Miller 1981). For Miller closure depends on 'a suppression, a simplification, a sort of blindness' (Miller: 89), and is 'an act of "make-believe", a postulation that closure is possible', a postulation of 'self-betraying inadequacy' (267). There is, writes Miller, 'no more fundamental assumption of the traditional novel than [the] opposition between the narratable and closure' (267) and 'what discontents the traditional novel is its own condition of possibility' (265).

To put it another way, closure is defined, only made possible, by the elements that refuse closure. When closure in narrative means happy love, that happy love may only be achieved because it chooses to forget the price of its happiness. That narrative closure is guiltily aware of exclusion (the coercions dictating who gets left out of the final happinesses, like Hetty Sorrel in *Adam Bede*) accounts for the sense of exasperation that students can hear as accompanying closure itself. The narrator, in the very act of managing the married couples, can suddenly betray an exasperated note as if aware of what has to be left out in novelistic management or housekeeping. We can hear this with varying degrees of intensity in Jane Austen, notably so in the chillingly bitter treatment (which students are invariably shocked by) handed out to the adulterous Maria at the end of *Mansfield Park*, condemned to live in a purgatorial misery with Austen's least 'liveable with' character, Mrs Norris:

> ...where, shut up together with little society, on one side no affection, on the other no judgment, it may be reasonably supposed that their tempers became their mutual punishment. (Vol. 3, Ch. 17)

In an equivalent way, students are taken aback by the implausible (exasperated?) ending of *Bleak House*, which they find difficult to take seriously. This only 'works' by what Dickens himself must have realized was the staginess of superimposing an identikit new but happier Bleak House upon the old (bleak) one, so that Jarndyce can give Esther the appropriately grounded happiness. This is designed to justify the way Dickens simultaneously superimposes Woodcourt as Esther's 'new' husband (as-if her brother) upon the old one, Jarndyce himself (as-if her father).

## TEACHING CONFLICTED NOVELS

Miller's analysis of the dynamics of narrative in the realist novel is developed, in a more obviously Foucauldian direction, in his *The Novel and the Police* (Miller 1988). Here the narratives of Victorian realism are shown to be complicit in a process by which readers, deluded by the image of private power offered by the narrative, are blinded to the operation of more pressingly real social and public power in which they are caught up, the narratives 'enlisting the consciousness of its subject in the work of supervision'. The effect is that the reader, the liberal subject, can only recognize himself fully 'when he forgets or disavows his functional implication' in a system of 'restraints or disciplinary injunctions' (Miller 1988; Hale 2006: 554, 543). The enchantments of narrative, in this respect, are the necessary occlusions of disenchantment, precisely in not knowing that by reading you have become your own policeman.

David Musselwhite, in an often brilliant and under-rated book that anticipates Miller's arguments, shows how in the classic realist novel, from Jane Austen to Dickens, the 'exuberance and threat' of revolutionary forces are 'steadily but ineluctably worked within a new axiomatic, a new set of rules and constraints, of prescribed places and possibilities that made them both manageable and self-monitoring', while at the same time 'the potential of desire, which should be social and productive' is 'slowly asphyxiated' (Musselwhite 1987: 9).

These ideas have usefully informed discussions in university seminar classrooms during the MA rhetoric module when I've brought together two novels written within a few years of each other—years in the period between 1811 and 1819 when 'the possibility of a violent revolution in England was greater than at almost any other time and was contained, with ever increasing difficulty, by the resort to force alone' (Musselwhite 1987: 31). The two novels are startlingly different but share submerged structural anxieties: *Emma* and *Frankenstein*. (They also share an early recourse to doubling and othering, much more subtly so in *Emma*.) The asphyxiation of potentially social and productive desire is one way of describing what happens to Shelley's Creature, whose last words (deriving from Milton's Satan as he first observes the embracing Adam and Eve) register the agony of 'wasting in impotent passions' and permanently unsatisfied desires (1818, ed., Vol. 3, Ch. 7). Musselwhite notes that in these last pages the Creature pointedly refers (twice, actually) to his life not as a narrative but as the 'series of my being': as if he and he alone belongs to the non-narratable (despite his being the most eloquent narrator in the novel), with his plea to be 'linked to the chain of existence and events' (Vol. 2, Ch. 9), as if in a narrative signifying system, so cruelly denied.

But students recognize something similar about the structure of *Emma* in which marriage brings an end, but in a sense an arbitrary (discontented) end, to what has characterized Emma's life hitherto—a 'series of being' lived as an arbitrarily strung together series of match-makings (driven in Harriet's case by the displacements of narcissistic pseudo-homosexual desire), a kind of anti-narrative or what Miller calls 'radical picaresque: an endless flirtation with a potentially infinite parade of possibilities' (Miller 1981: 15). And this match-making is like a 'bad' or 'othered' version of the novel's marriage-orientated dominant narrative: Emma's match-making (as 'bad novelist') is in effect positioned to empty the master-narrative of its ideological purposes, to naturalize and legitimize it.

Emma's desire to live through and in that picaresque 'series' must be bound up ('corrected') in closure, in effect asphyxiated in hetero-normative marriage. Students regularly see the radical feminist potential in what Emma desires to be and to do, to assert and exercise control and power, in effect to usurp power in a patriarchal world, to be the subject of her sentence, and students connect that desire with Frank Churchill's more obviously subversive undermining of social protocol—and they are very alive to the sharp irony of Emma discovering that it's Frank of all people whose power games have exposed the weakness of her supposed autonomy, that she's all along been a pawn in his game, the object of his sentence, in a feigned relationship, and then of Mr Knightley's, in marriage.

And students are richly exercised when we come to discuss the multiple ironies of the novel's version of 'closure', in which the married Emma and Mr Knightley will live chastely and as if childishly together with the tyrant-baby Mr Woodhouse—and as if forever: I've found that students feel that Mr Woodhouse will as it were 'live forever' when they project beyond the last pages (after all, as they say, there's nothing actually wrong with his health). In effect, and absurdly, the married couple will never be released into fulfilled desire in Donwell Abbey but instead will live suspended in Hartfield, which early in the novel is significantly mentioned as 'but a sort of notch in the Donwell Abbey estate to which all the rest of Highbury belonged' (Vol. 1, Ch. 16). We leave Emma and Mr Knightley living in a notch, she still mistress in her own home and he displaced and emasculated.

Marilyn Butler famously identified the political 'war of ideas' in the inner workings of Austen's novels (Butler 1975) and students can see in both these novels conflicting elements of conservative and Jacobin ideas and the way both texts have thereby generated contested critical readings. Chris Baldick in his indispensable study (Baldick 1990) makes it very clear that the Burke–Paine post-revolutionary pamphlet-war shaped the intrinsic and internal debate that Mary Shelley articulated in the conflicted presentation of the Creature, especially in the poignancies of his demands for love and to be loved, and in the recognition that his murders were a direct result of the cruelty of his several rejections, most painfully by his 'father' Frankenstein. Baldick's careful assessment is that Shelley's own response is 'an uneasy combination of fearful revulsion and cautious sympathy' for the Creature, an 'anxious liberalism' (Baldick 1990: 55). My students usually read Shelley's sympathies for the Creature and the novel's radical politics more forcefully than that.

Both novels have at their centres a conservative message about the dangers of playing God (Emma with Harriet who, Creature-like, turns on her 'maker' by aspiring to marry Mr Knightley) and of seeking to undermine given hierarchies of gender (Frankenstein appropriating the maternal role) and class (Emma's plans for Harriet). But many students are startled to discover that Frank Churchill, that great opener of windows and fierce advocate of the class-dissolving opportunities of balls, is rewarded (especially after he treats her at Box Hill with such callow cruelty) with the most desirable and 'perfect' of all Austen's young women, Jane Fairfax, in sharp contrast with how Austen handles those other deceptive charmers Willoughby, Wickham and Henry Crawford.

This may be a measure of Austen's critical scepticism about the values of landed conservatism, what D. W. Harding long ago called her 'regulated hatred' (Harding 1940) of much that sentimental Janeites (and makers of costume-drama films, and students who have only seen those films before reading the novels) profess or assume to see in her, as well as her not quite suppressed sympathies for and attractions to those pseudo-revolutionaries who come in, like the Crawfords, from outside to undermine and even destroy it. (Miller and Musselwhite in different ways are excellent on what Austen had to fight against in herself when dealing with the contradictory forces in *Mansfield Park*.)

Emma uses very strongly worded, indeed for her unusually politicized language (again evoking Satan) when condemning Frank (and Jane) after hearing of their secret engagement. She describes him as deploying 'espionage and treachery—to come among us with professions of openness and simplicity' (Vol. 3, Ch. 10). This is Jane Austen's sole use of 'espionage', a word that only entered the English language in 1793. French words like this and 'finesse' are associated with Frank and add to the sense of his allegiance with Jacobin ideas. But it remains the case that the Frank–Jane relationship, though breaking all courtship protocols, has an intensity of process and outcome that marks it out as unique in all of Jane Austen. Students regularly find that Frank and Jane coming together is more credible and moving (and closer to later Victorian novels) than Emma and Mr Knightley doing so, about whose future they're often sharply sceptical (even allowing for the death of Mr Woodhouse), and some of them even suspect that Jane Austen, in another and final subversion of conservative values, intended her readers to respond in just that way.

When I ask students to assess the different 'weightings' the novel accords to the married couples, they recognize and quite properly question the narrative coercion involved in the way the novel privileges Emma and Mr Knightley's love as ontologically more 'real' than Frank and Jane's ('being' in love rather than 'falling' in love). This is because the former is positioned as an 'in-built', secreted feature of their relationship since she was a teenager, only activated and made visible to them both when dramatized in Girardian triangular jealousy (his love made 'real' when he thinks Frank is in love with her; hers when she thinks he's in love with Harriet), whereas Frank and Jane are as it were 'only' lovers brought together in casual (holiday) intimacy.

This is a coercive opposition, one drawing on what I encourage students to see as a 'depth-effect' illusion in narrative fiction whereby the 'revelation' of hidden 'truth' (that Emma and Mr Knightley have 'always' loved each other without knowing it) aims to persuade us of a 'deeper' reality attendant on some relations and characters at the expense of others. Students debunk this readily enough when we discuss the fact that the novel itself openly jokes with the notion of Emma and Mr Knightley being in effect brother and sister and is silent with the notion of their being in effect (with the sixteen-year age difference) father and daughter.

## NARRATIVE AND THE EROTICS OF READING

The discontented conflict between the narratable and closure that Miller identifies connects powerfully with the no-less exemplary work of Peter Brooks in his brilliant and influential study *Reading for the Plot* (Brooks 1984). This is very evident in his chapter on *Great Expectations* where Brooks argues that, quite against the usual traditions of revelation through plot and its applications for happiness (in marriage), Pip in effect moves beyond plot and at the end his life has 'outlived plot, renounced plot, been cured of it' (Brooks 1992, ed.: 138). This is because, having at last, like a novelist or detective himself, solved the mystery of Estella's true parentage, he can do absolutely nothing with that revelation, least of all use it to marry her. Steven Connor reads Pip's situation at the end in a way that parallels Brooks' comments, in an analysis drawing on Lacan and Marx that students find compelling. He argues that the novel 'displays progressively Pip's alienation from himself' in so far as the novel's principal revelations are merely 'revelations of Pip's marginality in his own life... Pip is forced to recognise that not only are the objects of his desire unattainable, but also that his desires are not even really his own' (Connor 1985: 138).

This moving beyond plot, as if in proto-modernist rejection of plot itself, informs the notorious and itself unresolvable question of Dickens' two endings to the novel. Brooks is right to say that the choice between them is 'somewhat arbitrary and unimportant' (Brooks 1992, ed.: 136), given that Pip is already cured of plot. Nevertheless, when I teach the novel to undergraduates on their second-year 19th century module, and they read for the first time the original ending (having already got used to the famous later ending), the clear majority of them invariably prefer it. This must be because there is a muted melancholy in two potential lovers parting in solitary lonelinesses (and, in the saddest of all the novel's misrecognitions, with Estella thinking that Pip is little-Pip's father), a melancholy corresponding not just to the air of disenchanted retrospection pervading the entire novel but specifically to the discontentment with narrative itself that is such a radical feature of this apparently classic-realist novel.

But it is Brooks' early theoretical chapters in his book that have had the most far-reaching influence on the teaching and understanding of narrative (though he hasn't gone unchallenged: see Hale 2006: 275–279), above all through his determination to move away from a static or structuralist reading of narrative to a dynamic and, crucially, psychoanalytically informed reading, one which attends above all to the processes of reading itself. Of the theorists sampled on a first-year undergraduate narrative module that I teach (described in detail in the last chapter of this volume) it's Peter Brooks who speaks most eloquently and powerfully to the students and this is because he engages directly with, and helps them theorize, their experiences of reading narrative fiction, in his Freudian analysis of the erotics of reading. That is, Brooks is interested not just in what makes a plot move forward (and backward), why plots work the way they do, but also why and how we read on, what impels us to negotiate the dilations and digressions of the long 'middle' of novels, how we are driven (forward and backward) by what Brooks calls 'anticipation of retrospection' (Brooks 1992, ed.: 23). If the focus for Miller (once Brooks' student) is on the discontented novel, for Brooks it is the erotically charged reader.

Brooks' innovation is to apply the struggle that Freud identified as at the heart of our psychic lives, between the pleasure principle and the death drive (Eros and Thanatos), to the unfolding and our reading of plot. From the initiation of desire at the start of plot to the satisfied quiescence of closure, plot moves through the amassing and binding of materials (plot-strands, subplots, seemingly diverse characters, all to be revealed later as coherently connected) in a process analogous to the totalizing drive of desire, seeking to bind more and more material into larger, fuller and more completed wholes—as in the erotics of love. And at narrative closure we are granted what we seek for ourselves in vain, a retrospectively cohesive and totalizing (and illusionary) understanding of our lives, at the moment of death.

We could develop Brooks' argument about the erotics of reading in relation to teaching in two ways. First, teaching literary narratives in higher education involves asking students to be self-reflective about their reading experiences and, teaching the long realist novel, I ask my second-year undergraduate and MA students to reflect on how the reading of those narratives is different from the reading of lyric poetry and attendance in a theatre audience. Students quickly identify two pairs of paradoxes. Reading the novel is, on the one hand, though principally a solitary experience, one formed and shadowed by the communal: the community of novel readers is self-evidently 'there', if only felt as materially present in, for instance, lecture-halls and seminars, though it's also the case that most readers, and not just teachers, feel the impulse to share and talk about their experiences with other novel readers. On the other hand, the reading of long novels is both charged in the moment and also protracted, spread over time (days and weeks) and thus often to ever more erotically charged effect, through interruptions to reading, with the added and necessary involvement of memory in the psychics and mechanics of reading (following or 'losing' the plot). The relationship between the reader and the text, when reading takes so long, is both more distant (because mediated by non-reading time) and more intense (because such reading soaks into 'living').

I could put it this way. The subject matter of the realist novel privileges the individual destinies of the protagonists but shows those destinies as formed and shadowed by the communities in which the protagonists' narratives are activated and shaped (what David Musselwhite calls the novel's 'determination to both "homogenise" and "individualise" the occupants of the social space' (Musselwhite 1987: 8)). At the same time, the realist novel oscillates between the intensities of dramatic moments and the protractions of felt time and history. What students realize is that those two notions are duplicated in the reading experience in the way that isn't true for the reading of lyric poetry or being in a theatre audience.

Another crucial difference that we discuss involves the degree of activity and passivity in the reading experience of the realist novel. At the simplest level, the ability and indeed (because of the sheer length of novels) the necessity of interrupting the reading, positions the reader in a unique kind of involvement/detachment or activity/passivity paradox. All texts, and especially all narrative texts, are predicated, as Brooks shows, on the paradox of reading that is both forward and backward looking. The drive towards closure is always retrospective in its powers and illuminations. Not for nothing is the detective narrative so often cited as definitive for the novel: its unfolding forwards is by necessity an unfolding-reconstruction backwards.

The fact that readers of realist fiction, often under the implicit direction of the text (often explicit in the case of the modernist text), can and often have to stop reading forwards and can or have to literally turn the pages back to confirm or learn (or be misled about) something earlier in the narrative (or just to enjoy and savour something again, or to delay further the revelation of plot) suggests a suspended, active/passive, there/not-there kind of reading experience, one which (again unlike in the reading of the lyric or the watching of a play) involves a kind of blurring of the roles of primary consumption and secondary or critical reflection into a heightened and quite different experience. At the very moment (impossible in the theatre) at which we lift our eyes from the page—for momentary relief, in pleasurable reflection, extending an erotic foreplay, before returning to the text—we dramatize a scenario, itself a mini-narrative, of gain and loss, there and not-there, active and passive—a Freudian fort-da narrative (Miller also connects his narratable/closure analysis to Freud's fort-da game: see Miller 1981: 266).

Students also come to realize that there is something qualitatively different about the relations felt between the solitary reader and novelistic characters as opposed to an audience's relations with characters in drama, or the evoked consciousness of the lyric poem's 'voice' with which the reader communicates only as a privileged eavesdropper. This must partly be due to the equally obvious fact that the stage-character is always structured and mediated by the performative (the bodily presence of the actor acts as a limit, a literal barrier, to the spectator's investment in felt relations with character) but more important is the sense that the narrator of realist narrative is the necessary agent, catalyst or go-between in allowing for the free-play of the reader's erotic involvement, necessary to allow and activate and provide the sacred space for such erotic involvement—and that the activation of those erotic feelings on the reader's part are a duplication of a felt erotics of feeling between the narrator (author) and his or her characters, a sense that doesn't seem to obtain for the felt relations between the playwright and his characters, because the crucial mediating voice of narrative is absent.

The free-play of the reader's erotic involvement in novelistic narrative creates a fictive space in which normal moral or ethical concerns can be suspended or at least bracketed off. This must account for transgressive adultery in the novel being not only necessary as motor to the plot (as argued by Rene Girard (1966) and Tony Tanner (1979)) but also why readers so willingly want to read about it and even identify with it. This issue is inescapable when teaching *Madame Bovary*, which features at my university on a third-year undergraduate module called 'Victorian Sexualities', and students easily see the way this ethically ambivalent fictive space connects with Flaubertian impersonality and free indirect style (and with both sides of the argument put forward in the *Bovary* trial). When students identify with Emma Bovary, or at least feel intense sympathy for her, it is not just a function of her being the centrally narrated consciousness of the novel but also because it answers to the vicarious need we feel, in the erotics of reading, to experience change without its responsibilities, change being the prime motor behind all realist plots.

Another idea we discuss is this. Plenty of evidence shows that the experience of being in the audience during a particularly charged and powerful theatrical event can lead to spontaneous demonstrations of something close to mass hysteria or mass catharsis where the communality of the experience breaks down usual reticencies (for a fascinating account of actual theatre riots, see McEvoy 2016). That is, the individual response becomes overtaken by the communal response. But students come to see that the emotional intensities offered by the realist novel can be of the same power, though rather than issuing as communal response, in which the individual response is subsumed, the individual reader is returned to communal life in a more complex, more provisional but also more conscious and thus more long-lasting way. I discuss with students the feeling, which they too recognize, when moved to tears in the theatre or cinema that my tears are somehow not quite mine, and even that I resent being manipulated into shedding them, whereas, moved to tears by reading the end of a realist novel, alone, those tears are intensified by the sheer pain of their being shed, precisely, alone, in the presence (which, in terms of their power to evoke the communities in my solitude, is now an inconsolable absence) of just words on a page.

In an ideal university world, with unlimited time and insatiable students, we would then turn to Proust.

## Narrative, Teaching and Desire

The other way I'd like to develop some ideas from Brooks (and to end this part of the Introduction) is with very brief and tentatively offered thoughts about how his model can be applied to the teaching of narrative, how we might theorize the relations between teaching, desire and narrative in higher education.

I start with the dynamics of desire. Rene Girard (1966) argued that desire is imitative and that processes of identification precede desire. As in Brooks' point that the protagonist's desire needs to be activated (by the pleasure principle) in order for plots to begin and that this is duplicated or mapped on to the reader's desire to read on, so an activation of desire is vital for literature teaching to thrive.

Narrative texts desire to be read. That is, they desire to be alive and not museum pieces, and to that end they need to be activated, made present and real in the lecture and seminar space. In this sense all narrative texts are performative and desire to be 'performed'. Their desire is a desire to be awakened, an erotic desire that can be mapped onto the protagonist's desire and the teacher/students' desire. The teacher's and the students' desires for the text are in an imitative, re-energizing and mutually identifying relationship, forming a kind of virtuous circle (< >text< >teacher< >student< >text< >), across which desire flows in all directions, enriching the text, the student and the teacher in what is in effect an erotically charged totality where the three elements merge.

And this activation or awakening of the text, the binding of its desire to the students' and the teacher's desire in the classroom's virtuous circle, happens in a space that is both richly democratic, where all voices are equal and students feel safe to voice ideas that can't be dismissed as 'wrong', and in an alternative 'narrative time' where the 90 minutes of the seminar create a paradoxical 'free time' or unwritten and unwriteable narrative which only ends by arbitrary fiat.

Brooks' argument can be developed to show the importance of narrative as a model for the teaching of literature. We could think of a dynamic process in three parts, beginning in the personal (the student reading the text in advance), moving to a communal experience shared in the lecture and seminar, and ultimately returning, with new insight, to the text. These correspond to Brooks' notion of how we negotiate plot as we read novels, the middle sections of which are where the pleasure principle totalizes the divagations and digressions that mediate between the linear beginnings and eventually endings where the death instinct as well as the pleasure principle are gratified.

If the experience of the literature lecture and seminar can be seen, taken together, as analogous to the desire involved in reading the extended 'middle' of novels, then we can also chart the lecture and seminar, seen separately, as a narrative beginning, middle and end. The (largely) univocal and linear lecture gives way to the populated field of the communally voiced seminar where 'plot' diverges and dilates, and then both student and teacher are returned to linearity—another book, better reading, better teaching.

## THE CHAPTERS THAT COMPRISE THIS VOLUME

The chapters that follow are from ten distinguished specialists in narrative, all of them recognized for the quality of their teaching, and each contributor was invited to reflect on and describe the way their specialist academic knowledge translated into pedagogical practice in their university teaching. Wherever possible the chapters are tied to actual units of work taught by the contributors and, again, wherever possible the chapters allow space for the students' actual experiences in the teaching/learning processes (including in collaborative experiences with fellow students and with the lecturer) to be articulated and reflected on. The arrangement of chapters moves from, in the first group of six, considerations of teaching narrative by topic and genre—time, race, tragedy, comedy, crime-fiction, historical-fiction—to a group drawing on innovative applications of digital technologies, the third of which connects well with the following chapter on the important field of auto-ethnography, and the volume ends with a description of a deliberately introductory and simply theorized first-year narrative module aimed at easing students' transition to university.

The paragraphs that follow are summaries of the contributors' own abstracts.

- Mark Currie's focus is on the experience of teaching narrative in the context of philosophical and social theories of time. Most critical writing about time and narrative is focused on the question of memory, but Professor Currie argues that expectation, anticipation and surprise are equally fruitful concepts for teaching narrative. He looks at the notion of 'epochal temporality', or the claim that different historical epochs have distinct and describable experiences of time, and asks what this might mean for an understanding of narrative time in the contemporary novel. He explores the idea that, in the historical present, there is a preoccupation with the unforeseeable, which differs significantly from predominant conceptions of time in the second half of the twentieth century. His teaching also aims to set out a range of useful narratological concepts, particularly related to the notion of narrative tense, which are useful for the description of time structures in epochal temporality and for the teaching of time experiments in contemporary fiction. The chapter is closely tied to a third-year undergraduate module in which students work on a range of modern novels.

- Sue J. Kim starts from the observation that students often have difficulty talking critically about race and narrative—particularly fictional narratives—because they seem so familiar and, therefore, have become naturalized. Students often take race and narrative as givens, rather than multifaceted constructions and ongoing processes arising from long, complex histories. Professor Kim reflects on her experiences using two short stories to teach narrative theory and racialization to undergraduate students: Toni Morrison's 'Recitatif' and Ted Chiang's science fiction 'Story of Your Life'. While students are more willing to believe that race is a central structuring element in Morrison's famous story featuring protagonists of unspecific race, they are more ambivalent about Chiang's story because it does not overtly deal with race and/or ethnicity as we generally understand it. But through discussions of narratological concepts, such as Gerard Genette's focalization, order and anachrony and David Herman's concept of story world, Chiang's 'Story' can become a way to talk about the logics and processes of racial formation, as theorized by Michael Omi, Howard Winant and others. In other words, 'Story of Your Life' defamiliarizes some key elements of narrative and racialization in ways that can enable students—sometimes—to recognize how they are inextricably intertwined.
- Sean McEvoy asks whether we should not reflect more on the ethical consequences of taking narratives of violent death, mutilation, pain and degradation—often with no sense of redemption—into a room full of impressionable young people. In the ancient world, Plato and

Aristotle clashed over the issue of the moral effects of tragedy upon its readers and audiences. Having considered their arguments, Dr McEvoy goes on to discuss how effective (and ethical) modes of teaching tragedy may be where role-play and distancing techniques are employed. He surveys political critiques of the genre, including some contemporary claims that certain texts can cause psychological harm to students. He concludes that when we teach tragedy we are actually conducting a philosophical exploration into the nature of value itself in an open-eyed, honest way which can only be of benefit to us all.

- Rachel Trousdale examines the challenges and rewards peculiar to teaching comic narrative. Readers frequently respond to humour as trivial, so students who expect readings in university courses to be 'important' often fail to recognize when a text is also funny. Instead, they find these texts confusing: why do the characters behave so illogically and say such contradictory things? Recognizing humour can be even more difficult when a text's comic elements depend on unfamiliar references, or when the subject matter is shocking. But jokes often provide the focal point for a text's thematic components, and are often where apparently contradictory ideas are brought into productive conflict. Using examples from Tom Stoppard, Sterling Brown and Virginia Woolf, and drawing on theories of humour from Plato to Bergson, Professor Trousdale examines ways to help students see how comic narratives construct substantive philosophical and political arguments.
- Will Norman examines the teaching of crime narratives in the context of an undergraduate module on American Crime Fiction. Dr Norman's purpose is to elucidate how the study of crime fiction can be a way of helping students understand the politics of narrative form. As such he traces the progression of the module from the reading of Poe's detective stories through the narrative disruptions of mid-century hardboiled crime fiction to more contemporary noir fiction by authors such as Sara Paretsky and Attica Locke. He discusses how students become accustomed to historicizing shifts in the ways crime narratives are constructed. Todorov's classic essay on 'The Typology of Detective Fiction' serves as an accessible Formalist introduction to the spectrum of crime narratives, distinguished by their various configurations of the relationship between *fabula* and *sjuzhet*. Dr Norman helps students to begin asking narratological

questions about their reading, but one of the objectives of the module is to encourage students to discover the limitations of Todorov's ahistorical perspective. In discussing the transition from the classic whodunit narrative structure to the disorientating and tangled narratives of Chandler and his successors, students find their own ways of recuperating some of the historical content of the form, which has been evacuated from purely Formalist analysis. Using Franco Moretti's Marxist analysis of detective fiction as a corrective, the module moves into more sophisticated discussions of how readers undertake structural and functional analyses simultaneously, and thereby of how hardboiled and contemporary noir narratives represent entanglement with society and politics.

- Mark Eaton analyses Hilary Mantel's Wolf Hall Trilogy as a case study for what historical fiction can contribute to our understanding of history. In particular, Professor Eaton attends to what her novels reveal about the complex processes of historical and religious change that occurred during the Protestant Reformation. Guided by his experience teaching Mantel's fiction in courses on contemporary British fiction and historical fiction, he examines the ways that literary narratives offer a unique perspective on major historical developments in religion and theology, especially by giving students, of whatever background or belief, an opportunity to encounter, and indeed inhabit, religious interiority. By showing how new religious ideas and sensibilities develop, how they come into conflict with older viewpoints, and how they are by turns absorbed, adopted, challenged, resisted or rejected, Mantel discloses how religion is subject to the same historical contingencies as anything else. Far from being timeless and unchanging, it is contextual and more often than not syncretistic. The Wolf Hall Trilogy offers students one example of how a writer can take even a period as thoroughly documented as the Tudor dynasty, or a movement as widely studied as the Protestant Reformation, and somehow defamiliarize them, or make them seem fresh. In turn, students are invited to reflect on their own methods of reading and interpreting literature. Reading historical fiction necessarily involves us in multiple temporalities: the time period when the work is set, when it was written, and when we are reading it. Students are led to reconsider their own beliefs, whether or not they are religious, in light of an earlier period of momentous historical change.

- Ellen Rosenman, who admits to having personally fallen victim to the romance of the archive, starts from her love of introducing students to primary sources that help them navigate the distant world of Victorian novels. Without contextual knowledge, they often find themselves puzzled or frustrated—why don't ill-suited spouses just divorce each other? Why are aristocrats so clueless about the Stock Exchange? Hoping to improve upon conventional assignments, Professor Rosenman tasked students with creating a wiki. To an online version of the novel, they attached their own essays, which they keyed to points of conflict or confusion in order to help future student readers understand the issues at stake. Students investigated the novelty of investment capitalism, attitudes towards Jews, the contested nature of the term 'gentleman', the history of medical reform, and domestic violence, among other topics. Students also came to see that their primary sources did not establish facts about Victorian beliefs but were no more authoritative than the novels. Moreover, certain genres, such as advice literature, attempted to stabilize social meanings, while the novels were more interested in opening up areas of ambiguity or change. Students traced the dynamic interrelationships among texts, as novels, conduct books, newspaper accounts and memoirs vied for authority over social meanings. They also noted the ways in which the novel itself registered competing values and ideas. In doing so, they became more sensitive to the features of different narratives and different kinds of narratives, developing a special appreciation for the heteroglossia of the novel.
- Suzanne Keen distils some of the benefits that can be realized in the undergraduate literature classroom by replacing one or more traditional writing assignments with group (crowd-sourced) or individual projects employing Digital Humanities (DH) techniques of analysis, visualization and interpretation of narrative. Professor Keen describes a modest mapping exercise in a course about London novels, with a frank account of the start-up effort required and the surprising cognitive gains realized by its incorporation into a traditional English syllabus. In a brief account of a pedagogically focused DH initiative at a small liberal arts college, she shows how undergraduates gain a digital skill set and more acute engagement with narrative texts by participating in the Text Encoding Initiative mark-up of a digital edition of a medieval epic poem. She refers to colleagues' DH projects,

for example involving undergraduate students in research that maps characters' movements in space, leading to new interpretations of canonical texts. The centrepiece of the chapter shares an original discovery about the sources and influences on Joseph Conrad's *The Secret Agent* that came out of DH pedagogy.
- Alec Charles notes that there are three main challenges in the teaching of narrative development in the area of new media: (1) the interactive, multilinear and ludic natures of new media platforms do not necessarily lend themselves to traditional narrative structures; (2) the emphasis which these media put upon users' otherwise unmediated forms of self-expression is not necessarily conducive to classical structures of narrative communication; and (3) many of the promises which these media forms have made in relation to narrative advances not only have not been realized and are perhaps unrealizable, but are also not always entirely desirable. Bolter and Grusin's scepticism as to the potential of introducing 'interactivity to the novel' is, for example, echoed by Koskinen's rebuttal of 'interactive narratives'— 'no one in his right mind can write an alternative ending to the story of Jesus Christ'. Yet Professor Charles argues that these challenges also represent opportunities. The questions which these technologies pose as to how we teach narrative open up possibilities as to the development of narrative structures, practices and modes of reception—beyond blogging and citizen journalism, beyond Wikipedia, social media, virtual worlds and video games: not amateurish 'produsage' but a late postmodern incarnation of Roland Barthes' notion of *scriptibilité*. Such opportunities may promote ways to teach writing which themselves underpin the development of cultural identity and critical thought.
- Jess Moriarty argues that helping students to connect their academic research with their creative writing processes can often be a challenge but, when achieved, can provide valuable pathways between their personal experiences and the social world under study. Dr Moriarty identifies supporting this connection as a potentially powerful teaching and learning tool, helping undergraduates to make the leap from student to writer and researcher. She identifies possible ways in which the writing and sharing of autobiographical narratives can inform and enhance pedagogy in creative writing workshops with undergraduate students. Auto-ethnography is shown to be an evolving methodology that values and legitimizes personal stories

and evocative academic work, and can facilitate recovery from personal events that have been difficult or traumatic. The chapter explores how the study of self-narrative can empower students to make explicit links between these personal experiences and their academic research. This chapter will be of interest to teachers and students carrying out research in education and to those trying to develop their own teaching practice to incorporate student-focused approaches to creative writing. Dr Moriarty suggests that an auto-ethnographic approach can contribute to an increased confidence in students' sense of their place within the discipline of creative writing and the place of their discipline within the wider world.

- In the final chapter, I describe the background, development and delivery of a first-year undergraduate narrative module. Designed partly as a module helping students in their transition from school and college work to undergraduate study, the module starts with fairy tales and folktales (drawing on Zipes, Bettelheim and Propp), myths (Frye, Eliade and Barthes), examines the central importance, as well as the potential coercions, of narrative in our culture (at one point the module brings together the 'Alice' books and Freud's case study of Dora), and moves on to the analysis of short novels or novellas (by Melville, James, Conrad, Joyce, Mann, Mansfield, Rhys and detective stories) that demonstrate some of the narrative techniques and issues—including the realist/modernist narrative 'divide'—that the module explores in narratological theory (Walter Benjamin and Peter Brooks among others). The module concludes with a debate around 'Disneyfication'.

## Works Cited

Abbott, H. Porter. 2002. *The Cambridge Introduction to Narrative*. Cambridge: CUP.
Baldick, Chris. 1990. *In Frankenstein's Shadow*. Oxford: OUP.
Barthes, Roland. 1990. *S/Z*. Translated by Richard Miller. Oxford: Blackwell.
Bettelheim, Bruno. 1976. *The Uses of Enchantment*. New York: Knopf.
Brooks, Peter. (1984) 1992. *Reading for the Plot*. Cambridge, MA: Harvard University Press.
Butler, Marilyn. 1975. *Jane Austen and the War of Ideas*. Oxford: OUP.
Connor, Steven. 1985. *Charles Dickens (Re-Reading Literature)*. Oxford: Basil Blackwell.

Girard, Rene. 1966. *Desire, Deceit and the Novel*. Translated by Yvonne Freccero. Baltimore: Johns Hopkins University Press.
Hale, Dorothy J., ed. 2006. *The Novel: An Anthology of Criticism and Theory 1900–2000*. Oxford: Blackwell Publishing.
Harding, D.W. 1940. Regulated Hatred: An Aspect of the Work of Jane Austen. *Scrutiny* VIII: 346–362.
Heath, Stephen. 1992. *Flaubert: Madame Bovary*. Cambridge: CUP.
Josipovici, Gabriel. 2010. *What Ever Happened to Modernism?* New Haven: Yale University Press.
McEvoy, Sean. 2016. *Theatrical Unrest*. Abingdon: Routledge.
Miller, D.A. 1981. *The Novel and Its Discontents*. Princeton: Princeton University Press.
———. 1988. *The Novel and the Police*. Berkeley: University of California Press.
Musselwhite, David. 1987. *Partings Welded Together*. London: Methuen.
Tanner, Tony. 1979. *Adultery and the Novel*. Baltimore: Johns Hopkins University Press.

CHAPTER 2

# Time, Narrative and Culture

*Mark Currie*

The triangle of time, narrative and culture has been the basis on which I have taught contemporary fiction for many years, most recently in a third-year module at Queen Mary in London. *Time, Narrative and Culture* is a course that gives the student three related frameworks through which to think about contemporary novels: the theory of narrative, the philosophy of time and theories of contemporary society or culture. The three frameworks are made to connect directly with each other; so, for example, the narrative theory that we study is mostly theory about time structures and temporality, and the social theory is largely about what we call 'epochal temporality'. In what follows I am going to try to show how these frameworks operate and cooperate on the module, and how the teaching tries to produce a certain kind of written work on narrative fiction. Third-year modules in this degree are options based closely on the research interests of the staff who deliver them, and in this case, the module closely reflects my own research on time structures in narrative. Towards the end of the discussion I will turn to the question of surprise as a phenomenon in narrative and to the importance of uncertainty and the unforeseen event in our contemporary cultural self-understandings—topics which are at the centre of my current research and writing. Though we talk about modules

M. Currie (✉)
Queen Mary University, London, UK

at this level as examples of 'research-led teaching', I would like to dedicate this discussion to the opposite idea, of 'teaching-led research', and the proposition that university research interests are often developed and deepened by what happens in the classroom. This is certainly the direction of influence between this course and my own written work, a module whose evolution has actually led the changing direction of my research from a kind of tense-based narratology, to work focused on questions of uncertainty, contingency and surprise. I am going to start with an exposition of the concept of 'epochal temporality' because it is the point of departure for the module, and an effective way to get students talking about some complex issues about narrative in a social context.

# 1

We begin with the topic of globalization, from a well-known diagram that comes from David Harvey's *The Condition of Postmodernity* (1989: 241) which represents the phenomenon that he calls 'time–space compression'. The diagram represents the decreasing size of the globe relative to epochal travel speeds across periods of history, the largest of which depicts a world in which the fastest available speed is that of the horse-drawn cart or the sailing ship (10 mph; 1500–1840), and the smallest, the age of the jet (500–700 mph; the 1960s). Between the two, globes decreasing in size represent the age of steam locomotives and ships (35 mph; 1850–1930) and the propeller-driven aircraft (300–400 mph; 1950s). It is worth noting that, as the world contracts towards the condition of a global village, so too the time spans shorten from centuries to decades, so that the process of *time–space compression* exists in a condition of acceleration, in the sense that the speed of contraction increases with modernity. The diagram is helpful because it raises problems that are foundational for the social theory that we progress to: it proposes that there is something epochal about our experience of time, and that some change in temporal experience follows from newly attainable travel speeds. Increased travel speeds mean that places once separated by months of travel are, metaphorically at least, closer together in the modern age. Harvey argues that the process of contraction is partly a representational issue—a question of trying to represent the whole world in a single frame—and that the first photographs taken by astronauts of the globe in its totality represented the culmination of this tendency to comprehend the world as a simultaneity. The underlying principle is endlessly productive for a module on narrative—that modernity is about perceiving as a simultaneity that which was once strung out in time, or to use Bernard Stiegler's phrase, that modern epochal temporality is about the *elimination of delay* (Stiegler 2010: 79).

There are a number of steps into cultural theory that can follow from the elimination of delay. The idea that we reach our destination sooner is easily connected to the many other ways in which we wait less for our food, for news reports, for purchases, information, personal communications, films, television programmes and almost everything else in the contemporary world. One step that can follow usefully from the time–space compression that results from travel speeds is the enhanced simultaneity—perhaps the globe without dimensions that can be imagined at the bottom of Harvey's diagram—that arises in the context of digital culture. As well as being a topic which enlivens seminar discussion, the question of the internet, of new media and digital technologies is, I would claim, by far the most important context available to us for contemporary fiction. I don't think it is controversial to argue, in the context of teaching, that the very continuation of the novel in a contemporary setting has to be theorized alongside this fundamental change in the technology of representing, recording and narrating events. This is one of the routes that can be followed from the elimination of delay: that the internet represents a phase of globalization that establishes simultaneity, or accelerates the becoming simultaneous of that which was strung out in time, to a degree unattainable by mere speed.

Stiegler and Derrida are thinkers that I have used to link the notion of an epochal temporality specifically to digital cultures. There are two easily graspable concepts in particular that can do this work: the phenomenon that Derrida describes as *archive fever* (Derrida 1998) and the question that Stiegler discusses as the delegation of human memory to machines (Stiegler 2010). For Derrida, archive fever is a kind of psychic illness that frantically archives and preserves everything that happens for the future. We might once have been able to think that events and their representations were sequenced, that an event happens first and is represented later, or that a happening and its archivization were strung out in time. For Derrida, the temporality is backwards, in the sense that the archive produces the event that it purports to record. Though Derrida says this in the context of news media, the idea of an event which would not happen but for the fact that it is represented in an archive is immediately recognizable to any user of social media. For both Derrida and Stiegler, this is a basic psychic condition for all memory, but it has an epochal dimension because the technology of the memory device and the internet as a representational medium so significantly encourage and universalize an experience of the present as the object of a future memory. Technology makes the archiving of everything feverish, by turning envisaged memories into the cause of what happens in the present. This too must be established at the beginning of *Time, Narrative and Culture* because its basic time structure, the anticipation of retrospect, has a broad significance for our discussions of contemporary fiction, and for the comprehension of narrative more generally.

One final framework for the description of epochal temporality acts as a kind of counterpart to the anticipation of retrospection, and can be given the name *accelerated recontextualization*. If archive fever seems to incorporate some future moment of recollection in the present, recontextualization does the opposite, in the sense that it resurrects some past form or style in the present, as a kind of repetition or citation. Recontextualization is a kind of recycling of things from the past in the present, and points to the acquisition of new meanings that such repetition often involves. So, for example, the return to flared jeans in the 1990s represents, in the fashion industry, a kind of repetition of, or quotation from, a former epoch, and new meanings of the original style arise from the new context—perhaps to do with nostalgia, with the rejection of modernity in favour of 'retro', or with the generation of irony. Recontextualization is often thought of as fundamentally ironic in the sense that the new context doubles the meaning of the original, so that the kipper tie from the 1970s is worn again in the 1990s as an ironic citation of bad taste. Accelerated recontextualization simply refers to the drastic reduction in the delay between an original occurrence and its repetition, or even to the elimination of delay altogether. If we think of Renaissance architecture as a return to and recycling of classical forms, we recognize the repetition in the domain of style, of cultural forms that have been absent for about a thousand years. In the change-driven fashion industry of the late twentieth and twenty-first centuries, the gap between an original style and its repetition is much shorter, in the sense that we recycle not only the distant but also the increasingly recent past, repeating clothing styles of twenty years ago, and too quickly moving on from the 1970s to the 1980s. The complete elimination of this delay apparently results in an absurdity, where we might be recycling the 1990s in the 1990s, or the present in the present, and it is my experience that this absurdity is immediately recognized as a time structure which is at work in contemporary commerce and culture. In

*Time, Narrative and Culture* I have usually spent the first week discussing these aspects of epochal temporality—of time–space compression, archive fever and accelerated recontextualization—as social frameworks, and move on, in the second, to more philosophical ways of approaching these questions about time.

## 2

The question of the historical present, of its temporal rhythms and its commercial logic, is easily mapped onto philosophical approaches to time, and to the notion of the present as the foundational concept for time. I have always used Augustine of Hippo, and his fabulous discussion of the present in Book XI of *Confessions* (Augustine 1961) to make this link. Here, the focus of the module moves markedly away from theories of postmodernity and the temporal logic of digital cultures, towards classical frameworks for thinking about time. Augustine's problem, often referred to as the 'vanishing present', analyses an intriguing and intuitive conundrum about the ungraspability of the present. The present, Augustine claims, is the only thing that exists. The past does not exist: it used to exist, but it is now the domain of that which is no longer. Symmetrically, the future is that which will be, that which will exist, but which, from the point of view of the present, is the domain of the not yet. It is helpful to take note of the tense structures that are at work in this discussion: of the relationship on which it all hinges, between the time of an utterance (the present) and the time to which it refers. A certain conspiracy, perhaps circularity, is visible in this relation, between the concepts of presence and existence, which allow us to see the tense structure as a double structure made up of the present, which exists, and the past or future (which don't). The notion of tense structure, seen here in its most philosophical context, is crucial for discussion to come on the module about double structures in Todorov (2000), the tense framework in Genette (1980) and the analysis of narrative time in Ricoeur (1985). As a starting point, this idea that tense might in some way be bound up with a philosophical question about existence, is an effective way of connecting the philosophical framework of this module with a set of questions in narrative theory and narratology.

Augustine's vanishing present is basically a problem about the duration of the present. The problem, he decides, is that the present seems to lack extension, since it passes away in the very moment that it comes into being, and therefore cannot be grasped. To exist at all, the present must have some duration, but of course if it does have any duration whatever, another problem arises, namely that it can then be divided into the bits of the present that are still ahead and the bits that have already been. The divisibility of the present introduces into it the very elements of non-existence and non-presence against which it is defined, since its duration introduces bits of past and future into the present moment. In fact, this account of what Augustine calls the threefold present can be used as a basic introduction to much of the modern tradition of thinking about time, and can be directly linked to Edmund Husserl's description (Husserl 1964), at the end of the nineteenth century, of the present as a crossed structure of protentions and retentions (or those parts of the present that are orientated towards the future and those that retain the past). In Husserl, as in Augustine, there is an acknowledgement that there is something inherently illogical about the present as time's foundational concept—that is it seems to be constituted by the very things that it is not. The common ground here between Augustine and Husserl is essentially that they are turning the whole question of time into an issue for the way that time appears to the mind, rather than unfolds in the universe. These are both, fundamentally, psychological accounts of time, or of the present as a phenomenon of human consciousness. Indeed, thinking about these things as aspects of the human mind is, for Augustine, the solution to the problem of the vanishing present, since the mind can provide the extension, a kind of imagined duration, which the present moment cannot logically possess. A significant and easily grasped distinction can be reached by way of the vanishing present: the distinction between objective time and subjective time, where the former is measured by the clock, at work in the universe and mind-independent, where the latter is time as it appears to human consciousness. The distinction can serve as a portable dictum which proposes that this is in fact a way of understanding narrative in general and the novel in particular in its dealings with time: that the novel has special resources for exploring the dynamic interaction between subjective and objective time, or as Paul Ricoeur puts it, 'for following the subtle variations between the time of consciousness and chronological time' (Ricoeur 1985: 61). It is also one of the constant elements of the module's assessment that students are encouraged to analyse what it is that narrative can explore about the nature of time that might lie beyond the analytical powers of philosophy, and one approach to an answer is to foreground this dynamic in narrative between the time that passes on the clock and the way that it is experienced in the head.

The idea that the present is made up of traces of the past and traces of the future corresponds directly to the social theories of time that were introduced in the first week. Just as the historical present can be comprised of traces of the future, such as the anticipations of future retrospection in archive fever, and traces of the past, such as the repetitions of past styles involved in recontextualization, so the present moment can be understood in general terms, we might say in existential terms, as a composite of past and future orientations. I also said above that the purpose of Harvey's diagram is partly to understand the difference between succession (things being sequenced or strung out in time) and simultaneity (or the co-presence of that which used to be separated in time). In fact that difference between sequence and simultaneity is well established, even for Augustine, who inherited the distinction between *nunc movens* and *nunc stans* from the ancient philosophers, where the former, the moving now, is the human apprehension of presence as succession, and its opposite, the standing now, is a divine perspective in which all moments coincide in the stasis of eternity. The ancient distinction is useful for the student of narrative for two reasons. First, it describes something about the narrative structure of Augustine's *Confessions*, which moves from the distant recollection of past events towards a kind of proximity to God. Beginning as it does in babyhood, *Confessions* narrates Augustine's own life at first from a position of considerable temporal distance, and in the course of the narration, that distance is reduced to the point that it becomes not only a proximity with God, but a position in which the gap between the narrator and the narrated is reduced and eventually eliminated. When narrated events catch up with the time of narration, and there is no story left to tell except the story of narration itself, the narrative erupts with philosophical problems about the nature of time, and this convergence tells us something about the function of temporal distance in first-person storytelling: that narrative is, in its default settings, a recapitulation of past events, and that a kind of crisis ensues when the sequence transforms into simultaneity. On the other hand the distinction between *nunc movens* and *nunc stans*, as well as being the difference between human and divine perspectives, represents two approaches to the act of reading a narrative in book form. On one hand we move though a sequence of narrated events, as we move from left to right, and on the other we hold the whole sequence in our hand, as a spatial object, and therefore as a simultaneity, as if, like the globe represented in a single frame, it can be apprehended as a whole.

Many of the module's philosophical perspectives, and their relevance to narrative, can be approached through this nexus of succession and simultaneity and its connection to the human and divine. Gary Saul Morson, in his wonderful book on time and narrative, helps to make sense of this constellation in his discussion of *Oedipus*:

> One the one hand, we contemplate the structure of the whole, and we see signs of it as the action unfolds. On the other, we also identify with Oedipus and his experience, which, like our own, is lived without knowledge of the future. Lacking such identification with the hero, we would probably lose interest in the play.
>
> Our experience of time in *Oedipus* is therefore double: we can imagine what each act feels like, and we also see what it 'really' is. (Morson 1994: 61)

This description focuses on the experience of watching *Oedipus* in the theatre, and in particular, on the duality that results from both knowing what is going to happen and imagining what it is like not to know. The 'structure of the whole' is available to us in *Oedipus* because we know the story in advance, but our interest in the play, according to Morson, is produced in our identification with someone who cannot know. Our perspective is doubled in the sense that we stand astride human and divine perspective, apprehending at the same time what each act feels like and what it really is, and part of the value of this insight for our module lies in the idea that narrative might always, to different degrees, be implicated in this dynamic between human temporal becoming and some godlike comprehension of what our actions really are. For Morson, the duality is fundamentally a dynamic between freedom and fate, since what appears to Oedipus as a sequence of contingent acts susceptible to his efforts of will appears to us, with the benefit of foreknowledge or hindsight, as an unalterable and scripted fate. One of the reasons that this description of *Oedipus* can be generalized in this way as a condition for all narrative is exactly this idea that the gods are not actually required for this duality of freedom and predestination. The connotations of the word *scripted* are an indication that the written-ness of written narrative is itself the thing that guarantees a certain dynamic between the open future of human temporality and the predestined or unalterable future that lies ahead in the act of reading. Just as the gods are not required for this double time to operate, so too, we might add, foreknowledge of outcomes is not required, since the written-ness of the future is itself the fatalism that we know to be at work whenever we follow a protagonist through a written sequence of events.

# 3

It has always been my aim in seminars, when discussing time and narrative, to steer students away from the merely thematic consideration of novels and narratives. Philosophical frameworks about the present, and what it might mean for a reader, point the discussion away from the notion of time as a topic of novels, or a thematic intention of novelists. Time, this module insists, is a topic for all narratives because it is inherent in the sequential nature of writing. It is critical to distinguish two meanings of sequence here, so that on one hand there is a sequence of words on a page and on the other a sequence of events to which those words refer: there is the sequence of the linguistic chain, of words and sentences and pages in a book, and the sequence of events that happen in the depicted story world. It is not an exaggeration to say that the narrative theory and the readings of novels that follow on the course all addresses this core question: how do these notions of sequence interact? This is a more basic, and perhaps intelligible, framework than the traditional narratological distinctions between *fabula* and *sjuzhet*, or between story and discourse, both of which are founded in the difference between the chronological order of events and the arrangement of those events in a particular act of telling. It brings the book forward in its full objecthood, and asks students to think about writing, at a maximal distance from thematic analysis, as graphic marks on a page.

This assumption, that thematic criticism is not the module's central interest, requires some elaboration. The fact is that the literary texts we study on *Time, Narrative and Culture* are all in some way engaged with the topic of time, or contain some kind of time experiment. Our literary seminars begin with the *prolepsis*, or the use of narrative flash-forward, in Muriel Spark's *The Driver's Seat* (Spark 1974). We move from that to questions about history and narrative order, first in Graham Swift's *Waterland* (Swift 2002) and then to the question of backward narration in Martin Amis's *Time's Arrow* (Amis, 2003). In this section of the module, the question of what we know and when is in the foreground. We make use of two theoretical sources, the first being the discussion of the double time of detective fiction in Todorov, and the second, Genette's categories of *order*, *duration* and *frequency*. By playing with order, these texts produce a very formal kind of engagement with the topic of time, by which I mean that they do not openly discuss time, but rather perform their interests in relation to conventions and structures of narrative representation. The category of *prolepsis* is of special interest in these discussions because it develops two of the theoretical arguments from the beginning of the module: (1) the idea of an epochal temporality which lives the present in anticipation of retrospection; and (2) Morson's idea of the importance of foreknowledge in the double time of *Oedipus*. Prolepsis can be thought of as the provision of foreknowledge that changes the suspenseful orientation of narrative sequences, or as the installation of retrospect within the present. Though we think of *prolepsis* as flash-forward, it contains a kind of backward glance on the present by virtue of its posteriority to the narrative present. All three of these texts bring something interesting into view about the relationship between forwards and backwards movement in narration, or between prospection and retrospection, and they do so through formal arrangement rather than thematic elaboration. We might say that they explore the topic of time through the temporal logic of storytelling, and it is therefore the module's principal tenet in this section that the analysis of the novels must be an analysis of temporal structures rather than abstract ideas.

The tense framework proposed by Genette in *Narrative Discourse*, and in particular the discussion of the 'anachronies' of *prolepsis* and *analepsis*, is the most valuable analytical resource for these novels, but the argument about detective fiction in Todorov's 'The Typology of Detective Fiction' comes a close second. This essay argues that detective fiction can be distinguished from the thriller on the grounds that it tells two stories, or narrates two sequences simultaneously: one which begins with the crime and proceeds through the sequence of events that comprise the investigation, and another which reconstructs events that lead up to the crime. The value of this argument is that it illustrates so clearly the imbrication of forward and backward directions on the narrative timeline—that progress through the narrative entails the acquisition of a back story, and that any surprises we encounter as readers on the way through the investigation are in fact disclosures of an unexplained past. The argument works particularly well alongside *Waterland*, which develops an extended analogy between the methods of historical explanation and the investigations of a detective. *Prolepsis* in *Waterland* is used to install some knowledge of future events in the narrative present, but the explanation of those events is achieved only by patient reconstructions of the personal and social histories in which they are embedded. *Waterland* moves forwards by moving backwards, openly theorizing on the topic of historical explanation at the same time as it corroborates those speculations with temporal loops and digressions. The core proposition of the novel seems to be that every moment is structured by a relation to the past, and at the same time that it bears the trace of an unforeseeable future which comes into view in narrative retrospect. Moments of presence which cannot be articulated in this way to the 'always already' and the 'not yet' are represented in the story as a kind of void, a nothingness that narrative fills by providing exactly these links with past and future events. A number of our philosophical frameworks come back into view in relation to *Waterland*, and none more obviously than the discussion of presence as trace structure, comprised of retentions of the past and protentions of the future. The novel sets itself on a lock on a tributary of the river Ouse, and the introductory mini-lecture for this session spends some time on the prominence, in the philosophy of time, of the river as a metaphor for the unidirectional flow of time. A lock on a river represents the attempt to arrest this flow, or presence itself, and everything that happens in the story follows from objects, including the dead body of Freddie Parr, that are caught in this lock. Such events are unintelligible in the stasis of the lock, and their explanation emerges only when they are restored to their sequence of cause and effect, or strung out in time by narrative. *Waterland* is the novel that most openly discusses time, not only in its metaphors, of rivers, water, land, lines and circles, but openly in relation to the progress of history. As such, it encourages the kind of thematic paraphrase that the module tries at all times to discourage, but because it also practices what it preaches, in its network of backstories and proleptic flashes, it also supports the proposition that novels explore the topic of time through the temporal logic of storytelling, and it is this relation that any written work must analyse.

The encouragement of formal analysis can of course be addressed by essay questions themselves, but there are also clear ways in which the primary texts themselves prevent or render problematic the kind of thematic paraphrase that I am seeking to exclude. The clearest examples are texts which place graphic, rather than referential, properties of writing in the foreground, and so offer a perspective on time more concerned with the linguistic chain itself than with the events to which it refers. Ali Smith's *Hotel World* and J. M. Coetzee's *Slow Man* (Coetzee 2005) introduce the second half of the module with exactly this emphasis on the materiality and objectivity of the book, and its constituent parts—pages, sentences, words and letters. *Hotel World*, for example, sustains a sense throughout that the enquiry into time is in fact inseparable from an enquiry into writing, and the novel develops an extended analogy between death and the blank page that begins in Sara Wilby's exuberant narration in the first section and ends in her sister Clair's melancholic comparisons between writing and life in her closing monologue. These are themes that connect back to questions about writing and fate, and Morson's ideas of freedom and predestination in narrative, but they also very creatively exploit the graphic dimension of the novel. *Hotel World* is, above all, obsessed with letters, which fall out of words just as Sara Wilby, who dies in an accident in the novel's opening, has fallen out of the world. In the following example, Sara Wilby's language is breaking down as she finally disappears from the world:

> I will miss mist. I will miss leaf. I will miss the, the. What's the word? Lost, I've, the word. The word for. You know. I don't mean a house. I don't mean a room. I mean the way of the. Dead to the. Out of this. Word. (Smith 2002: 30)

The missing word here is of course the word 'world', but the letter 'l' has fallen out of 'world' (just as letters fall out of words, and words fall out of sentences throughout the novel) to leave the word 'word' in its place. In this transformation of the word 'world' to the word 'word', we have an illustration of the novel's core dynamic between the story world and the linguistic chain, or between the sequence of events referred to in the novel and the graphic chain of letters, words, sentences and pages that make up the novel's sequence at the most literal level. Indeed, Ali Smith's novel takes a vigorous interest in the word 'literal' itself, the literal meaning of which is, of course, 'pertaining to letters'. Smith's novel is full of this kind of playful interaction between the time of the story and the time of material language, and its presence on the module helps to pose questions about time that relate to the graphic materiality of writing and the idea of the book as an object.

Coetzee's *Slow Man* has a similar interest in the written, scripted quality of the life it portrays, and extends our enquiry into the relationship between written narrative and fate. *Slow Man*, like *Hotel World*, begins with an accident, and then with the protagonist, Paul Rayment, coming back to consciousness after an operation to remove his leg. As he comes round, the letters Q-W-E-R-T-Y appear to him on the inside of his eyelid, so that the period of his consciousness, after the accident, which the novel represents is associated with typing and writing. Coetzee's novel has an interesting relation with the first novel on the module, Muriel Spark's *The Driver's Seat*, which features a protagonist who goes to Italy to find someone to kill her. In an inversion of the holiday romance narrative, this quest for death involves finding her 'type', and it is clear throughout the novel that the word 'type' evokes both the commonplace notion of romantic suitability and the protagonist's condition as a piece of writing. In Coetzee's novel, the type or print of the novel is central to the plot, which begins with an accident the description of which is cited verbatim in italic print thirteen chapters later, when the novel's author, Elizabeth Costello, turns up at the protagonist's door. Paul Rayment is, it would seem, authored by Costello, and in this sense he lacks any of the freedom that we impute to him as a character. The novel, from this point onwards, enacts this tension between the scriptedness of his condition as a narrative representation and his freedom as a quasi-person. These novels all have ways of bringing writing into the foreground and making readers think about the graphic dimension of time sequences in fiction. It is not, in such cases, that the theme of time is exterminated by the graphic dimension of words, but rather that the enquiry into time as a theme is inextricable from questions about fate and freedom that inhere in the medium of writing itself. These are, emphatically, novels that explore the theme of time through the temporal logic of writing at the most material level.

## 4

The novels that we read in the second half of *Time, Narrative and Culture* are *Hotel World* and *Slow Man*, followed by Kazuo Ishiguro's *Never Let Me Go* (Ishiguro 2006) and Julian Barnes' *The Sense of an Ending* (Barnes 2011). These all in different ways develop this tension between lived and written time, but they have another purpose on the module: they represent, in different ways, the phenomenon of narrative surprise. Coetzee and Smith, as I have mentioned, begin their novels with accidents—a young woman falling to her death down the shaft of a dumb waiter, and an older man being knocked off his bicycle by a speeding car. These are sudden moments—contingent and surprising events that change everything—of a kind that would normally, in Aristotle's scheme, take their place in the middle of a narrative as a reversal of fortune or expectation, which he called *peripeteia*. *Never Let Me Go* and *The Sense of an Ending* also contain surprising moments, but they are in the nature of slow recognitions or disclosures, and have more to do with the distribution of information in a novel than contingent events such as accidents. These disclosures are more akin to what Aristotle called *anagnorisis*, which we usually translate as 'recognition', and the distinction between *peripeteia* and *anagnorisis* structures our discussion in the last weeks. The question of narrative surprise and how it works is one of my own central research interests in narrative theory, and it overlaps with a broader interest in the topic of uncertainty, which I consider to be the emergent concept and core idea in our new epochal temporality. I would like to finish this account of the module with a short explanation of the role that surprise plays at the end of the module, and the challenges it presents to the concept of cultural time that has been a key strand in the discussion. When I described the three topics of epochal temporality at the outset—*time-space compression, archive fever* and *accelerated recontextualization*—I was selecting what I consider to be the most useful concepts from a range of arguments about time in postmodern literary and cultural theory. These are ideas, I would argue, that characterize a period of intellectual history which was deeply convinced that the future was somehow blocked. The 'blocked future' is a recognizable attitude which characterizes the postmodern epoch as a kind of repetition: as a citational culture in which the very concept of originality is under suspicion, where all that remains open to us is to endlessly repeat, recycle and reconstrue the cultural forms of the past. It was, for Frederic Jameson (1991), a perpetual present, and, according to Francis Fukuyama (1992), the end of history, and the novels of the period often represent protagonists who are culturally stuck in this kind of futureless present. But in the new millennium, prominent surprising events like the terrorist attacks on September 11th 2001 and the global financial crisis of 2008 seem to have displaced this influential account of the blocked future and have, as Terry Eagleton puts it (Eagleton 2011), broken history open again. One of the advantages of the prominence of surprise in this closing section of our module is that it poses an epochal question that everyone wants to talk about: what comes after postmodernity? It is my own conviction in the classroom that the ideas of contingency and uncertainty are the core characteristics of the new epoch, and that they are as observable in the new philosophical approaches to time that emerged after Derrida's death in 2004, in the work of Badiou (2006), Žižek (2012) and Meillassoux (2006), as they are in our most popular cultural self-understandings. We finish *Time, Narrative and Culture* by studying storytelling in print journalism, by reading the newspapers from the day of the final seminar, and I have yet to encounter any real difficulty in showing that the epoch is popularly understood as an age of uncertainty, of unforeseeable happenings and of constant surprise. Our attention, at the module's ending, is turned towards the question of the opacity of the future, and the discussion is informed by the narrative versions of unforeseeability, fate, reversal and disclosure that we have engaged with in narrative form.

## WORKS CITED

Amis, Martin. 2003. *Time's Arrow or the Nature of the Offence*. London: Vintage. First published by Jonathan Cape (1999).
Augustine. 1961. *Confessions*. Translated by R.S. Pine-Coffin. Harmondsworth: Penguin Books.
Badiou, Alain. 2006. *Being and Event*. Translated by Oliver Feltham. London: Continuum.
Barnes, Julian. 2011. *The Sense of an Ending*. London: Jonathan Cape.
Coetzee, J.M. 2005. *Slow Man*. London: Vintage.
Derrida, Jacques. 1998. *Archive Fever: A Freudian Impression*. Translated by Eric Prenowitz. Chicago: University of Chicago Press.
Eagleton, Terry. 2011. *Why Marx Was Right*. New Haven and London: Yale University Press.
Fukuyama, Francis. 1992. *The End of History and the Last Man*. New York: Avon Books.
Genette, Gerard. 1980. *Narrative Discourse*. Translated by Jane Lewin. Oxford: Basil Blackwell.
Harvey, David. 1989. *The Condition of Postmodernity*. Oxford: Blackwell.
Husserl, Edmund. 1964. *The Phenomenology of Internal Time Consciousness*. Translated by James Churchill. Bloomington: Indiana University Press.
Ishiguro, Kazuo. 2006. *Never Let Me Go*. London and New York: Vintage.
Jameson, Frederic. 1991. *Postmodernism, or the Cultural Logic of Late Capitalism*. London: Verso.
Meillassoux, Quentin. 2006. *After Finitude: An Essay on the Necessity of Contingency*. London and New York: Continuum.
Morson, Gary Saul. 1994. *Narrative and Freedom: The Shadows of Time*. New Haven and London: Yale University Press.
Ricoeur, Paul. 1985. *Time and Narrative*. Translated by Kathleen Blamey and David Pellauer. Chicago: University of Chicago Press.
Smith, Ali. 2002. *Hotel World*. London: Penguin.
Spark, Muriel. 1974. *The Driver's Seat*. Harmondsworth: Penguin.
Stiegler, Bernard. 2010. Memory. In *Critical Terms for Media Studies*, ed. Mark B.N. Hansen and W.J.T. Mitchell. Chicago: University of Chicago Press.
Swift, Graham. 2002. *Waterland*. London: Picador.
Todorov, Tzvetan. 2000. The Typology of Detective Fiction. In *Modern Criticism and Theory: A Reader*, ed. D. Lodge and N. Wood, 2nd ed. London and New York: Longman.
Žižek, Slavoj. 2012. *Less Than Nothing: Hegel and the Shadow of Dialectical Materialism*. London and New York: Verso.

CHAPTER 3

# Talking Race and Narrative with Undergraduate Students in the USA

*Sue J. Kim*

> *Art removes objects from the automatism of perception in several ways.*
> —Victor Shklovsky (2007)

With American undergraduate students, two of the most difficult things to defamiliarize are race and prose fiction. Because both are so familiar, it can be a challenge to help students understand that race and narrative are actually multifaceted constructions and ongoing processes arising from long, complex histories. As teachers of literature well know, students often want to talk about fictional characters as if they are real and plots as if they are inevitable. In discussing race, students often rely on various problematic ideas that are common in public discourse: race is an essential identity (for good or for ill); or race is a 'social construction', by which they mean a wholly voluntarist and unreal phenomenon; or race is no longer relevant because we live in a 'post-racial' era. Even students who do not read a lot of novels or deal with race explicitly have imbibed many commonplace ideas of each, or what have become our unmarked norms. Contemporary racial formations and experiences of reading fiction only seem natural because they are familiar. Students are often

S. J. Kim (✉)
University of Massachusetts Lowell, Lowell, MA, USA

© The Author(s) 2018
R. Jacobs (ed.), *Teaching Narrative*, Teaching the New English, https://doi.org/10.1007/978-3-319-71829-3_3

willing to acknowledge this basic concept, but have trouble really digesting and applying it, and of course they are not alone in this. Therefore, grappling with the actual complexities of narratives and race can be challenging but rewarding.

This chapter reflects on my experiences using two short stories to teach narrative theory and theories of racialization to undergraduate students: Toni Morrison's famous short story 'Recitatif' (1983) and Ted Chiang's science fiction 'Story of Your Life' (2002). Morrison's text seeks explicitly to examine with racial codes. Chiang's story does not overtly deal with race and/or ethnicity as we generally understand it, but nevertheless like many science fiction narratives it explores race in other ways. I want students to understand that race is not just a matter of bodies or individual identity, but also ideological and material. Through deployments of narratological concepts, such as focalization, order and anachrony, both stories can become a way to talk about the logics and processes of racial formation, as theorized by Michael Omi, Howard Winant and others. In other words, using narrative theory can help students understand theories of race, and vice versa.

I have taught these texts at two public universities, one in the South and one in New England. Despite regional differences, the institutions had much in common, particularly in having large numbers of first-generation college students who must work and/or have significant family obligations. Students at these both institutions have had little to no experience with either theories of race or theories of narrative, and they have generally been receptive. In order to minimize the cost of textbooks, I have used Ismail Talib's website *Narrative Theory: A Brief Introduction* (2010), alongside specific reading assignments and guiding questions. This essay draws from my experiences in an introductory foundations course for English majors as well as mid- and upper-level courses on contemporary American literature.

## RACIAL DISCOURSES AND HISTORIES OF RACE

Most students come into the classroom sharing the depressingly limited and problematic discourses on race prevalent in the USA. As evidenced by the 2016 US presidential election, essentialism or 'biological racism', or the notion that identity is inherent ethnically or racially, is alive and well; white supremacists are one of the most tenacious forms of essentialism. Allied to biological racism is 'cultural racism', which locates characteristics and stereotypes based in culture instead of biology; examples of cultural racism include the model minority myth and Islamophobia.

More common today in the USA, however, is the bizarre phenomenon of 'postracialism', which asserts that we are 'beyond' race, or that racism no longer exists. On the left and center, the requisite discourse of diversity and 'tolerance' is generally present in (almost) every university, corporation, institution and so on. But many critics have shown how such liberal or corporate multiculturalism is problematic for a slew of reasons: it assumes the homogeneity of cultures and groups; it ignores structural, systemic inequalities between and within groups (i.e. income, education, cultural capital, actual capital that has grown out of a long history of uneven capital accumulation within and across nations); it most often does not seek solutions to structural and systemic problems. Unfortunately, liberal multiculturalism can go happily hand in hand with elitism. No one in educated polite society—so it goes—is actually a racist; only those ignorant, premodern, violent 'Others' are racists.

On the right, postracialism has taken a mind-boggling form: any discussion of race—including and especially antiracist struggles—is itself a form of racism. David Theo Goldberg discusses this form of postracialism as 'antiracialism', or rejection of racial categories altogether. He distinguishes antiracialism from antiracism; while antiracism requires 'remembering and recalling', antiracialism advocates 'forgetting, getting over, moving on, wiping away the terms of reference' and 'at best (or worst) a commercial memorializing' (Goldberg 2009: 21). Antiracialism denies continuing structures of inequality and exploitation, hampering our ability to recognize 'institutionalized inequality' and change the systems in which racial categories continue to constitute a repressed (and sometimes not-so-repressed) term (Goldberg 2009: 23). Somehow, in some arenas of contemporary public discourse, antiracialism has become confused with or superseded antiracism.

Adding to these confusions is the limited definition of 'racism' in the public. It usually goes as follows: (1) racism is an individual feeling or attitude; (2) it is irrational; (3) it is based on ignorance, and (4) it is expressed as overt racial animosity. As George W. Bush stated in his address to the NAACP, 'I understand that racism still lingers in America… It's a lot easier to change a law than to change a human heart.' This may very well be true, but the problem with this formulation is that it poses racism purely as an individual attitude, rather than as institutional, historical, systemic and rational. While individual, affective racism obviously still exists, it can by no means explain the complexity of race in the USA.

The challenge, then, is to get students to think beyond identity or overly narrow formulations of postracialism; race is neither an expression of a primordial self, nor a freely chosen performance, nor completely dictated by 'society', as students may put it. Rather, the goal is to help them understand that race is constituted by a host of social, political, legal and discursive systems and processes, sometimes in contention with one another. Our identities and actions in these structures are both agentive and dictated, imposed from above and produced from below, socially constructed yet very real in shaping our lives and our world. Students are often initially puzzled by this complex formulation, or—as happens often—they may grasp the idea but find it challenging to articulate or to apply.

In order to help students navigate these complexities, I supply them with theories of race, depending on the level of the course. Michael Omi and Howard Winant's classic *Racial Formations in the US* (Omi and Winant 1994) theorizes racial formations as socio-historical concepts of race that are tied to political projects. Thus, rather than only thinking in terms of 'racism' and identifying individual racists, they argue that the project of racial critique seeks to understand how race—like gender—has shaped the cultural and political dimensions of the world we live in, in ways we often do not recognize. Ian F. Haney Lopez's essay 'The Social Construction of Race' (Haney Lopez 1999) is also a useful essay for introducing concepts of race as socially embedded constructions. Such texts, which are fairly readable for undergraduates, seek to de-essentialize race. They discuss how race is a historical construct and *not* biological, but also delineate specific ways that race constitutes real social/political forces.

In discussing race—or any nexus of identities, power and structures—I want students to understand three concepts: racial discourse, history (or 'material history', as some might put it) and the complex negotiation between agency and power. While 'discourse' is a commonly used concept in literary and cultural studies, students are usually not familiar with its uses in our field. Our use tends to range from a set of codes, representations and other signifiers that is historically situated, to a binding together of knowledge and power, after Foucault. Discourse analysis entails teasing out the various codes and signifiers and how they function with power. Discourse analysis, however, must go hand in hand with an understanding of material histories, which are never wholly extricable from discourse but may sometimes conflict with certain discourses. In other words, as I tell students, we also have to know the histories beyond the predominant discourses.

The third concept is the idea that subjectivity, including actions and thoughts, in a racialized society is both the product of freedom and dictation, of individual agency as well as subject to scripted sets of norms. This concept is usually the most difficult to convey: that we are both free and not free. As Anne Cheng writes in *The Melancholy of Race*,

> [W]e need a more nuanced sense of agency that goes beyond volunteerism or a positivism blind to performative constraints. We need to imagine a form of agency that recognizes *competition* between performance and performativity, between historicity and reenactment. Only then can we understand the coexistence of coercion and agency in any act of cultural performance. Only then can we see the performances of citizenship and nationalism as a continuous navigation between a scripting history and individual response. (Cheng 2001: 59, original emphasis)

With all of these basic concepts—discourse, history and circumscribed agency—narratives of all kinds play a crucial role. So the tools of narrative theory can help students to unpack the complex racial dynamics laid out in prose fiction, and the ways that racial formations are integral to how we read narratives.

## 'RECITATIF'

Toni Morrison's only published short story focuses on the relationship between two female protagonists, Twyla and Roberta. The narrator, Twyla, describes the two girls' first meeting in a shelter, St. Bonaventura, presumably sometime in the 1950s, and then four more times through the next few decades. While we are told that they are different races, the story never explicitly identifies the race of either character. The story becomes a way to reflect on the characters' and readers' stereotypes and preconceptions about race, class and gender. Narrative concepts such as types of narrators, focalization, degrees of reliability and irony can help students unpack the racial processes at work in this story. While students can readily apply the concepts to the story and identify some of the various processes of racial formation, students will often revert to the idea each character is an expression of some more-or-less homogeneous group, and then try to 'decode' each character according to that group. The struggle in teaching this story is to get them past the concept of identity as expressive of an individual or collective essence, rather than an ongoing negotiation within various discourses and histories that everyone navigates, even if they are positioned differently.

In this unit, I want students to understand focalization and limited narration as textual strategies, and to understand that race is not simply a matter of inner essence and that the dynamics of racial attitudes go beyond issues of stereotype (versus truth), or expressions of internal bigotry, although these do come into play. Rather, discourses about race are also, to paraphrase Bakhtin (1981), partly our words and partly someone else's. Exploring how a character sees the world—to inhabit their internal discourse—is a way to unpack these various discourses, and focalization helps us understand this process. Gerald Prince defines focalization as 'the perspective in terms of which the narrated situations and events are presented; the perceptual or conceptual position in terms of which they are rendered' (Prince 2003: 31). 'Recitatif' presents an excellent example because, although the narrator's voice seems perfectly reasonable, the text constantly puts pressure on us to question Twyla's, Roberta's and our own assumptions, or, in a sense, our own focalizations. The focalizer of 'Recitatif', the limited first-person narrator Twyla, demonstrates how race is constantly produced by navigating discourses that not only belong to Twyla, Roberta or the reader ('opinions', as students sometimes like to put it), but also are beyond any one person. Racial discourses exceed individuals, are accepted as fact by some and rejected by others, and are real but not easily demarcated or defined. Moreover, the text provides many subtle historical clues that point to material histories and process—informed by discourses yet not reducible to them—that interact complexly with discourses. The characters' interactions with one another through the years demonstrate how racialized beings operate within multiple discourses and material histories of race and class, but not in any simple or obvious way.

The surprisingly difficult task sometimes is to get the students to question the focalizer, even when the text implies unreliability. So another goal is for students to understand that narrators are formal choices among various possible kinds of narrators, including first-person participant, third-person limited, omniscient and so on, with varying degrees of reliability. To this end, the students read section 7, 'The Narrator', of the *Narrative Theory* website, and I ask them to focus on sections on focalization and types of narrators. After discussing the various options outlined by Talib (2010), students readily identify Twyla as a first-person participant narrator as well as the focalizer. But while students readily acknowledge this textbook definition, unpacking and grappling with the implications of focalization and limited narration are more challenging.

I try to stave off embarrassing or unfortunate discussions by telling students up front about Morrison's intentions with this story. While students should be engaging with the racial 'clues' in the story, I do not want the class to devolve into an argument in which students try to prove who is which race and why. Rather, I want them to focus on the racial codes and scripts invoked in the story, which Morrison seeks to denaturalize. In *Playing in the Dark*, she writes,

> The kind of work I have always wanted to do requires me to learn how to maneuver ways to free up the language from its sometimes sinister, frequently lazy, almost always predictable employment of racially informed and determined chains. (The only short story I have ever written, 'Recitatif', was an experiment in the removal of all racial codes from a narrative about two characters of different races for whom racial identity is crucial.) (Morrison 1992: xi)

Armed with this awareness—that the author is intentionally playing with racial codes and social constructions of race—I have the students read 'Recitatif' with the guiding question, 'What are some of the discourses of race and/or class used by (or applied to) Twyla and Roberta? What discourses as well as material histories does the story draw on?' I ask them to identify at least two specific examples in the text, including page numbers and paragraph numbers.

The ensuing discussions are always illuminating. Often I have to get the conversation started because students can be shy or nervous about talking about race in any capacity. The story's five sections are intentionally laden with thoughts, words and actions that can be attributed to race or class in a variety of combinations. As Elizabeth Abel notes, while her own reading of the story focused on 'body types, degrees of social cool, or modes of mothering' (Abel 1993: 474), her black feminist colleague read the story more in terms of politics and 'economic status' (475), given the historically disadvantaged status of African Americans.

The first two sections feature the young protagonists parroting and/or reproducing racial discourses. The third and fourth sections show rising degrees of bitterness over race and class, while the fifth section encapsulates the difficulty of answers through the uncertainty of the two women.

The first section is set sometime in the 1950s; although they have mothers, both girls temporarily find themselves in a state home for children. The story makes clear from the outset that the girls are different races, and that these races are probably black and white. Twyla notes that Roberta is 'a girl from a whole other race' (Morrison 1983: 3541), and while they are ignored by 'New York City Puerto Ricans and upstate Indians' and 'two Koreans', 'we looked like salt and pepper' (3542). Twyla is at the home because her mother, Mary, 'danced all night' (3541); other clues in the story indicate that she is young, pretty and poor. Roberta is there because her mother is 'sick' (3541), the nature of which the story never clarifies, although some critics speculate mental health (Abel 1993: 474).

As eight-year-olds, they replicate the discourses they have learned from their parents and others, but it is unclear whether these attitudes are based in class or race. There are the physical markers noted by Abel; for instance, Twyla thinks of her mother, 'Every now and then she would stop dancing long enough to tell me something important and one of the things she said was that they never washed their hair and they smelled funny. Roberta sure did. Smell funny, I mean' (3541). It is often a revelation for students that many ethnic and racial groups have their own lore, or discourse, that other groups—which can include the poor—'smell funny'. Both girls are also poor, indicated by their very being in the state home as well as their learning deficits; Twyla cannot remember anything and Roberta cannot read. The text invokes multiple fraught, overdetermined images to provoke thought. Twyla is embarrassed by Mary's 'ugly green slacks that made her behind stick out' and 'fur jacket with the pocket linings so ripped she had to pull to get her hands out of them' (3544). While this image may indicate the tradition of hypersexualization of black women's bodies, this disapproval of gaudy or revealing attire is also a hallmark of bourgeois morality, which can be shared by a member of any racial group.

The ambiguous markers accumulate. Twyla describes Roberta's mother as '[b]igger than any man and on her chest was the biggest cross I'd ever seen. I swear it was six inches long each way. And in the crook of her arm was the biggest Bible ever made' (3544). This image draws on a tradition of mammy stereotypes as well as the prominent history of the African American church. On the other hand, some readers see Roberta's mother as a white religious fundamentalist and racist who refuses to shake Twyla's mother's hand (3542). Yet Roberta's mother might refuse to shake Mary's hand because of class-based moral disapproval. Class and racial codes of mothering also come into play; Twyla tells us that 'Mary's idea of supper was popcorn and a can of Yoo-Hoo' (3542), while Roberta's mother brings 'chicken legs and ham sandwiches and oranges and a whole box of chocolate-covered grahams. Roberta drank milk from a thermos while her mother read the Bible to her' (3545).

Along with these racial and class signifiers, however, are historical indicators that indicate that racial attitudes are not simply free-floating. For instance, Mary wears Lady Esther's dusting powder (3544), which was used primarily by white women in the early to mid-twentieth century and still does not create products for women of color (Collecting 2016; *Lady Esther* 2016). Moreover, despite the stereotype of fried chicken, many African Americans are lactose intolerant or believe themselves to be lactose intolerant (Goldstein-Shirley 1997: 78; Brown-Riggs 2013). That is, even seemingly straightforward, simple phrases such as 'chicken legs' or 'green slacks' are embedded in racial discourses and histories.

A similar contrast between the student's expectations, the focalizer's point of view and historical contexts comes into play in the next section. A teenage Twyla is working as a waitress at Howard Johnson's and runs across Roberta with 'big and wild hair' and two male friends. They inform her that they are on their way to 'the Coast. He's got an appointment with Hendrix' (3546), of whom Twyla has never heard. Again, there are multiple ways to read this. On one hand, Hendrix is black and the fact that Twyla has never heard of him suggests that she is a working-class white woman. On the other hand, Hendrix is often thought of as a breakthrough artist who appealed primarily to white audiences, particularly white hippies who were children of middle-class families.

The next two sections highlight increasing bitterness between the two as social tensions grow. In the third section, set in the 1970s, Twyla has married James Benson, a fireman who lives in Newburgh, NY, a primarily working-class town. She runs into Roberta, who works for IBM, and lives in Annandale, a wealthier suburb (3548). The working-class Twyla thinks, '[Roberta] got from Jimi Hendrix to Annandale, a neighborhood full of doctors and IBM executives. Easy, I thought. Everything is so easy for them. They think they own the world' (3548). In the fourth section, set in roughly the same period, Roberta and Twyla clash over school bussing as a means to integration; Twyla supports her son attending a richer school, while Roberta opposes her children being sent to another school 'out of the neighborhood' (3551).

The immediate reaction of many students is to read Roberta as white because she is wealthier and opposes bussing. But working-class Newburgh is 39% white and 30% black, with a significant population living in poverty. Moreover, the specific historical setting provides contexts beyond the characters' attitudes. I share with them this excerpt from Elizabeth Abel's important essay,

> Morrison explained that her project in this story was to substitute class for racial codes in order to drive a wedge between these typically elided categories. Both eliciting and foiling our assumption that Roberta's middle-class marriage and politics, and Twyla's working-class perspective, are reliable racial clues, Morrison incorporated details about their husbands' occupations that encourage an alternative conclusion. If we are familiar (as I was not) with IBM's efforts to recruit black executives and with the racial exclusiveness of the Firemen's union in upstate New York, where the story is set, we read Roberta as middle-class black and Twyla as working-class white. Roberta's resistance to bussing, then, is based on class rather than racial loyalties: she doesn't want her (middle-class black) stepchildren bussed to a school in a (white) working-class neighborhood; Twyla, conversely, wants her (white) working-class child bussed to a middle-class school (regardless of that school's racial composition). (Abel 1993: 476)

The issue here is not whether resistance to bussing is justified or not (this may arise in class discussions). Rather, the devolution of Twyla and Roberta's hostility into a battle of signs that makes no sense to anyone else is, as Morganstern notes, an excellent example of how signifiers are 'purely relational and differential and therefore arbitrary in Saussure's sense' (Morganstern 2005: 817–819). That is, racial discourses are very real—they determine both characters and their experiences—but they are not essential, predetermined or free-floating. Racial and class discourse are fundamentally relational within systems of power and material histories. Our job as close readers is to help analyze, identify and hopefully combat not just 'stereotypes', but also larger discourses and histories in which we live.

## 'STORY OF YOUR LIFE'

With 'Story of Your Life', the learning objectives are to understand the distinction between *fabula* and *sjuzhet*, concepts of order (anachrony, analepsis, prolepsis) and the difference between temporal succession and causality. As with characters, students will often treat the plot as given, or natural cause and effect. As a long tradition of avant-garde artists have pointed out, naturalizing fictional narratives runs the risk of translating into our extratextual lives; we may accept our plots as given. Thus, discussion of plot can be an innovative—if challenging—way to approach a more complex understanding of racialization as neither wholly voluntary nor wholly scripted, but as an ongoing performance that is in-between free will and determination. In other words, Chiang's story helps illustrate agency within the confines of multiple social constraints and prescriptions, particularly race but also other social roles. In introducing this story, I note that the genre of science fiction often uses aliens as a metaphor for race, delinking concepts from specific racialized bodies in order to examine our ideas about those bodies. 'Story of Your Life' helps denaturalize racial formations not only in terms of aliens, but also in the very construction of language, agency and power. In other words, 'Story of Your Life' denaturalizes some key elements of narrative and racialization in ways that can enable students—sometimes—to recognize how they are inextricably intertwined.

Alongside the story, students are assigned sections five ('Events') and six ('Plot') of Talib's *Narrative Theory*. I ask them to focus particularly on the basic distinction between story (*fabula*) and discourse (*sjuzhet*); the distinction between temporal succession and causality; and the concepts of order, anachrony, analepsis and prolepsis. I also provide them with Dino Franco Felluga's succinct definition of *fabula* vs. *sjuzhet*: '*Fabula* refers to the chronological sequence of events in a narrative; *sjuzhet* is the re-presentation of those events (through narration, metaphor, camera angles, the re-ordering of the temporal sequence, and so on)' (Felluga 2011). I ask students several questions to guide their reading. Given that 'Story of Your Life' does not present a strictly temporal *or* causal succession of events, how would they describe the *fabula* ('actual' order of events) and *sjuzhet*, or presented order of events? What is the effect of presenting the events in this non-chronological way? I also ask them to locate at least one *specific* place in the text, including page and paragraph number, that shows an achronological progression, through either analepsis or prolepsis. Then I ask them to identify how 'Story of Your Life' deals with concepts of time thematically as well. In other words, I ask them to consider ways that the text deals formally and thematically with time, and to identify specific places in the text that provide an example of how the story works.

'Story of Your Life' is ideal for teaching concepts of *fabula* and *sjuzhet* because, in this text, the two are so distinct and yet inextricably linked. The *fabula* goes as follows: The narrator Louise Banks is a linguist who is tasked by the military to learn the language of an alien species, the heptapods. They're described as looking like barrels with seven 'radially symmetric' limbs, hence their nickname. They have 'seven lidless eyes' that 'ring the top' of their bodies. Louise is assigned to work with Gary Donnelly, a physicist, and teams of other scientists and linguists to learn about the heptapods. She is initially puzzled by their language, but once she learns it, it radically changes her consciousness. The Heptapods suddenly leave with no explanation, and Louise resumes her teaching career. She marries Gary and they have a daughter together—who is the narratee, the 'you' of the title. Eventually, they divorce and move on with their lives, becoming estranged. When their daughter is 25, she is killed in a mountain climbing accident and Louise and Gary must identify her body.

The *sjuzhet*, however, is what gives the text its initially disorienting form. On the last page we learn that the 'now' of the telling is some moment in the middle of the story, when Louise is with her daughter. The narrative then jumps backward and forward in time. This narrative progressive, we learn, is not simply artistic experimentation; rather, it reflects how Louise's acquisition of the heptapod language has radically changed her consciousness in relation to time. This process—how she learns and how that changes her relationship to time and free will—is really the heart of the story.

After Louise and the other linguists learn how to communicate verbally with the heptapods ('Heptapod A'), they are puzzled by the heptapods' written language, or what they call 'Heptapod B'. Lacking punctuation, its grammar rules and logic of composition puzzle the linguists: 'its syntax was indicated in the way the semagrams were combined, and there was no need to indicate the cadence of speech… A "sentence" seemed to be whatever number of semagrams a heptapod wanted to join together; the only difference between a sentence and a paragraph, or a page, was size' (Chiang 2002: 111–112). Writing the equivalent of long sentences requires the writer to know the entirety of what will be written before writing it:

> The heptapods didn't write a sentence one semagram at a time; they built it out of strokes irrespective of individual semagrams. I had seen a similarly high degree of integration before in calligraphic designs, particularly those employing the Arabic alphabet. But those designs had required careful planning by expert calligraphers. No one could lay out such an intricate design at the speed needed for holding a conversation. At least, no human could. (123)

Eventually, Louise comes to the realization that the mystery of the heptapods stems from the fact that they experience time as simultaneous:

> I understood why the heptapods had evolved a semasiographic writing system like Heptapod B; it was better suited for a species with a simultaneous

mode of consciousness. For them, speech was a bottleneck because it required that one word follow another sequentially. With writing, on the other hand, every mark on a page was visible simultaneously... Semasiographic writing naturally took advantage of the page's two-dimensionality; instead of doling out morphemes one at a time, it offered an entire page full of them all at once. (135)

This realization has profound implications not only for the humans' understanding of the heptapods, but for Louise's own relation to time, language and free will. She thinks, 'Before I learned how to think in Heptapod B, my memories grew like a column of cigarette ash, laid down by the infinitesimal sliver of combustion that was my consciousness, marking the sequential present' (140). But afterwards, she has brief moments of truly experiencing existence in Heptapod B, 'and I experience past and future all at once; my consciousness becomes a half-century-long ember burning outside time. I perceive—during those glimpses—that entire epoch as a simultaneity' (140–141).

If one experiences time simultaneously—in essence, one knows the future—what is the point of speech or action? Everything is predetermined. But, as Louise explains, for heptapods, this question is the wrong one to ask:

> If I could have described this to someone who didn't already know, she might ask, if the heptapods already knew everything that they would ever say or hear, what was the point of their using language at all? A reasonable question. But language wasn't only for communication: it was also a form of action. According to speech act theory, statements like 'You're under arrest', 'I christen this vessel', or 'I promise' were all performative: a speaker could perform the action only by uttering the words. For such acts, knowing what would be said didn't change anything. Everyone at a wedding anticipated the words 'I now pronounce you husband and wife', but until the minister actually said them, the ceremony didn't count. With performative language, saying equaled doing.
>
> For the heptapods, all language was performative. Instead of using language to inform, they used language to actualize. Sure, heptapods already knew what would be said in any conversation; but in order for their knowledge to be true, the conversation would have to take place. (138)

Rather than a model of language in which atomized individuals communicate with one another from intention to transmission to reception along a linear causal axis, here language is presented as performative in the sense of J. L. Austin and Judith Butler. Language is not only an expression of some internal thought on a linear axis of communication from sender to receiver, but it is also a social act that creates a new reality. For Louise, because she is not fully heptapod, language is neither wholly individual free performance nor wholly predetermined; as a hybrid being, for her language is a mix of agency and scriptedness.

It is here that we can see the ways in which the tension between *fabula* and *sjuzhet* of the narrative—or rather, the interaction of the two—can help us understand how racial discourses and histories work. As Christopher Fan has noted about 'Story of Your Life',

> [Louise] undergoes a racial transformation from human to human-heptapod hybrid that proceeds by language learning, not biology... [W]e now understand that what we have thus far been reading as Louise's prosopopoeic address to her daughter has in fact been taking place in the tenseless, performative address of Heptapod B. The story's narration becomes, from the standpoint of this realization, a representation of Heptapod B, and thus of Louise's racial difference. This racialized mode of narration...[moves] *away from a mimetic economy of racial representation to a narrative one.* (Fan, 2014, emphasis added)

That is, while Chiang's story may not represent race in an immediately visible referential way in the form of racialized bodies, it does demonstrate the process of how race and other identities are narratively lived. Race is constituted by us in a mix of agency and social determination. Racism is not simply a matter of internal intention, although it may also be that; rather, we are all continuously creating this complex system of discourses and histories that we label the shorthand of 'race'. The tension in the story between, on one hand, the doling out of individual words in spoken heptapod, and, on the other hand, the instant recognition of interconnection in written heptapod reflects the tension between performance and performativity, agency and compulsion, tied together in racial subjectivity. As Judith Butler argued, performative gender is an ongoing imitation that presents itself as an expression of authentic, internal and/or essential gender. The anachrony of 'Story of Your Life', which reflects Louise's shifted consciousness, stages this contradiction, which gets to the heart of what students (and narratology) should understand about how race and other complex ideological forces work in our world.

In discussing ideology and power, undergraduate students often struggle with questions of interpellation and agency; they will revert to the binary of free will versus determination. But the reality is much more complex, and the conceptual leap or transition invoked by 'Story of Your Life' can help students grasp this complexity. Moreover, Louise's struggle may resonate with young people who are struggling themselves with questions of their pasts, presents and futures, and with questions of freedom and control.

My goal for both of these units is to help students understand that literary narratives are important for understanding the world beyond the text. Narratives are particularly critical to unpacking how race works, and there are tools in narrative theory that can help us talk in more detail about how these narratives work. Literary narratives can help lay bare the mechanics of racial discourses and the intertwined material histories of race, and can show how we negotiate between power and agency.

## WORKS CITED

Abel, Elizabeth. 1993. Black Writing, White Reading: Race and the Politics of Feminist Interpretation. *Critical Inquiry* 19: 470–498. Accessed October 20, 2016. http://www.jstor.org.libproxy.uml.edu/stable/1343961

Bakhtin, M.M. 1981. *The Dialogic Imagination: Four Essays*. Translated by Caryl Emerson and Michael Holquist. Austin: University of Texas Press.

Brown-Riggs, Constance. 2013. Got Milk? Maybe Not If You're African-American. *The Grio*. Accessed November 5, 2016. https://thegrio.com/2013/09/18/got-milk-maybe-not-if-youre-african-american/

Cheng, Anne Anlin. 2001. *The Melancholy of Race: Psychoanalysis, Assimilation, and Hidden Grief*. Oxford: Oxford University Press.

Chiang, Ted. 2002. *Stories of Your Life and Others*. New York: Tor.

Collecting Vintage Compacts. 2016. *The History of The Lady Esther Company—Once The Most Popular Face Powder in America*. Accessed November 5, 2016. http://collectingvintagecompacts.blogspot.com/2013/05/lady-esther-once-most-popular-face.html

Fan, Christopher T. 2014. Melancholy Transcendence: Ted Chiang and Asian American Postracial Form. *Post45*. Accessed June 15, 2016. http://post45.research.yale.edu/2014/11/melancholy-transcendence-ted-chiang-and-asian-american-postracial-form/

Felluga, Dino Franco. 2011. 'Fabula and Sjuzhet'. *Introductory Guide to Critical Theory*. Accessed January 15, 2016. https://www.cla.purdue.edu/english/theory/narratology/terms/fabula.html

Goldberg, David Theo. 2009. *The Threat of Race: Reflections on Racial Neoliberalism*. Malden: Blackwell.

Goldstein-Shirley, David. 1997. Race and Response: Toni Morrison's 'Recitatif'. *Short Story* 5 (1): 77–86. Available from: Literature Resource Center. Accessed October 28, 2016.

Haney López, Ian F. 1999. The Social Construction of Race. In *Critical Race Theory: The Cutting Edge*, ed. Richard Delgado, 1st ed., 191–203. Philadelphia: Temple University Press.

*Lady Esther Cosmetics.* 2016. Lady Esther Kosmetik. Accessed January 15, 2016. http://www.ladyesther.com/

Morganstern, Naomi. 2005. Literature Reads Theory: Remarks on Teaching with Toni Morrison. *University of Toronto Quarterly* 74 (3): 816–828. Available from: Project Muse. Accessed November 1, 2016.

Morrison, Toni. 1983. Recitatif. In *The Heath Anthology of American Literature*, ed. Paul Lauter, vol. E., 7th ed., 3538–3555. Boston: Wadsworth, 2014. (Original work published in 1983)

———. 1992. *Playing in the Dark: Whiteness and the Literary Imagination.* Cambridge: Harvard University Press.

Omi, Michael, and Howard Winant. 1994. *Racial Formation in the United States: From the 1960s to the 1990s.* 2nd ed. New York: Routledge.

Prince, Gerald. 2003. *A Dictionary of Narratology.* Lincoln: University of Nebraska Press.

Shklovsky, Victor. 2007. Art as Technique. In *The Critical Tradition: Classic Texts and Contemporary Trends*, ed. David H. Richter, 774–784. Boston: Bedford St. Martin. (Original work published in 1917)

Talib, Ismail S. 2010. *Narrative Theory: A Brief Introduction.* Accessed June 10, 2016. https://courses.nus.edu.sg/course/ellibst/NarrativeTheory/

CHAPTER 4

# The Ethics of Teaching Tragic Narratives

*Sean McEvoy*

In the literature classroom there are always moral issues, to some degree or other, concerned with what we choose to teach and how we teach it. These issues are perhaps most acute when it comes to teaching tragedy, 'the art form created to confront the most difficult experiences we face: death, loss, injustice, thwarted passion, despair' (Wallace 2007: 1). How sensitive do we need to be, from a moral point of view, about what we introduce into the classroom when the texts we choose are concerned with these 'most difficult experiences'? There seems to be a renewed awareness of the performative power of texts to affect students. I want to consider some arguments and principles germane to this matter, but also go on to propose that rather than being a potentially morally hazardous activity, the teaching of texts which deal with human pain, degradation and death can and should be a valid part of educating students in the nature of morality itself and of the possibility of virtue.

Although the principal focus of this chapter will be on plays, tragic narratives are also prevalent in novels and poems. My own experience of teaching tragedy is at secondary, sixth-form, undergraduate and postgraduate level. The students whose views I will refer to are seventeen- and eighteen-year-olds following the International Baccalaureate Diploma

S. McEvoy (✉)
Varndean College, Brighton, UK

© The Author(s) 2018
R. Jacobs (ed.), *Teaching Narrative*, Teaching the New English,
https://doi.org/10.1007/978-3-319-71829-3_4

Programme at my college, where the study of English and world literature is a compulsory component.

Any discussion of the ethics of teaching tragedy inevitably begins with Plato's famous strictures in the *Republic*. In the ancient debates on this issue there is a curious foreshadowing of some contemporary arguments. Plato wanted dramatic poetry—by which is clearly meant tragedy—to be banned from his ideal state. Plato wrote that poets, who evoke feelings and appeal to the imagination, stand accused of representing and stimulating 'the lower elements of the mind to the detriment of reason, which is like giving power and political control to the worse elements of the state and ruining the better elements'. The typically anti-democratic Platonic analogy immediately stretches to the 'dramatic poet' who 'produces a similarly bad state of affairs in the mind of the individual, by encouraging the unreasoning part of it, which cannot distinguish greater and less … and by creating images far removed from the truth' (Plato 1974: 435) [605 b–c]. Tragedy aims to produce an outpouring of the emotions, the inferior element of the human mind, which can only subvert the dominance of the superior element, rationality. There is clearly something in common here with some contemporary arguments that certain tragic texts can bring to the surface anxieties and issues better left undisturbed in the non-therapeutic environment of the classroom; as with Plato, there can be a cost to the psychic health of some individuals, but, in contrast to Plato, it has been suggested that the cost is often to the psychic health of those most damaged by our society's injustices and inequalities.

The defence of tragedy offered by Plato's former pupil Aristotle in his *Poetics* seems rather to be that on the contrary, tragedy can teach us the proper use of emotion and the ability to distinguish between what is worthy of our feelings and what is not (I say 'seems' because there remains scholarly dispute about the exact meaning of the famous and disputed passage about *catharsis* (Aristotle 2013: 23 [1449b 23–28]; see Nuttall 1996: 5–16). Anthony Kenny puts it this way: 'watching tragedy helps us to put our own sorrows and worries into proportion, when we observe the catastrophes that have overtaken people who were far superior to the likes of ourselves' (Aristotle 2013: xiv). Aristotle believes that exposure to tragedy can make us better people, since virtue resides in observing the 'happy mean' in everything, and showing the appropriate amount of emotion in any given circumstance is part of virtue (Aristotle 2013: xiv). This Aristotelian view of the value of tragedy also finds its contemporary analogue in the idea that there is a distinct moral benefit to be gained from the watching, and more pertinently, from the study of tragedy. This is also the view to which I am more sympathetic, as I shall explain.

The American philosopher Paul Woodruff offers a modern voice which argues for the efficacious moral significance of theatre in its many forms in our lives. But in terms of moral impact he makes the point—directly relevant to what follows—that the literary study of drama texts is a different matter to the experience of live theatre. For Woodruff, theatre, broadly defined (to include spectator sport, for example), is necessary to what it is to be human:

> There is an art to watching and being watched, and that is one of the few arts on which all human living depends. If we are unwatched we diminish, and we cannot be entirely as we would wish to be. If we never stop to watch, we will only know how it feels to be us, never know how it might feel to be another ... Watching well, together, and being watched well, with limits on both sides, we grow and grow together. (Woodruff 2008: 10)

This importance of limits, and of the distance between watcher and watched is I think important to the moral value of tragedy in the classroom, but Woodruff is also right when he points out that theatre is not just an enactment of a written text, since theatre does not require the presence of a written text. We're doing something different from theatre when we teach a play in class: 'teaching literature is not a specifically theatrical goal' (Woodruff 2008: 43).

But if anything the way in which theatrical tragedy is experienced in education can enhance the kind of intellectual benefit gained in terms of moral education, as Aristotle would wish, and potentially diminish the capacity for unreflective emotional excess which Plato claimed to be morally damaging. There is a continuum of ways of encountering tragic theatrical texts in the classroom with the maximum emotional affect at one end of the scale and the most relatively dispassionate, reflective response at the other. At one end I would place the experience of a class watching a two-dimensional, on-screen performance in full of a tragic text, since the resources of film and video are best equipped to manipulate emotion (not always usefully) and to encourage immersive spectator experience. Next I would put the watching of a live theatrical performance of the whole text, where a more reflective and individual response is more likely. Next in the continuum would be the acting out of parts of the play by the students themselves, the experience of the text interrupted and framed by discussion and analysis by the class and the teacher (or the use of other practical, rehearsal-based or workshop-based methods). Next would come the reading aloud (or listening to a radio version) of the text, again interrupted by analytical discussion. Finally there would be encountering of the dramatic text as silent readers prior to classroom discussion and analysis. All of these methods of approaching the text have their benefits, but there is an emotionally distancing effect produced at the more classroom-based end of the spectrum by the framing and disrupting of the dramatic flow of the play in classroom teaching which is crucial in enabling students to bracket off the potentially powerful emotional impact of tragedy. It must be stressed, of course, that an approach to a play which somehow deprived the class of any sort of encounter with the emotional power of the tragic text would not be teaching the play as a tragedy in the first place. The teacher's task is to make available to the students the aesthetic and affective power of the text as well as to develop their critical and reflective intellectual response, which will require the consideration of issues and ideas beyond the text itself. The balance between the two in the methods chosen during the teaching of the text will vary depending upon the text, the course and the class, but both must be present.

There are some aspects of tragedy as a narrative genre which can engender resistance on the part of students. If the whole text has not been read in advance of the first lesson—and this will of course be the case if the first encounter occurs when the play is read aloud in class—then some students can genuinely object to later details of the plot, and particularly the ending, being revealed in discussion before they have read them. This is not just the case with tragedies, of course, but in the overwhelming majority of tragic texts[1] the mode, at least of the ending, is clear from the start. I try to show sympathy to these objections since uncertainty of outcome for the characters with whom one sympathizes is clearly one of the delights of reading a novel or of watching a play or other dramatic work. I usually take such pleas into account when possible, but not without a slightly tongue-in-cheek admonition of their disingenuousness. Given their thorough familiarity with the narrative conventions of their favourite popular genres, do they really not know how the story will end? And why do they get pleasure from watching a film of a book they know, or from reading a novel several times, if genuine suspense is so important? Their response is often that having picked up the generic clues—or just having been told the genre—they do know whether the ending will be 'happy' or not, but they still don't want to know in advance how the narrative ends.

One of the reasons why I nevertheless have some sympathy with student demands for narrative 'spoiler alerts' when teaching tragic narratives is that the possibility of catastrophe being avoided seems to be part of what tragedy requires for its effect. A totally fatalistic tragedy, where even the thoughts and feelings of the tragedy are part of a grand deterministic scheme is not a tragedy at all. The power of Racine's *Phèdre* or Sophocles' *Oedipus the King* lies partly in the struggle between the free consciousness of the protagonist and their divinely pre-ordained external fates. We, as well as those suffering on stage, need to have a sense of how things could have turned out differently, and for the better. It is useful at the end of teaching a tragic text to get students to consider their response if tragedy had been averted: if Tess and Angel had evaded their pursuers, got to Southampton and travelled to Canada and to live and farm on the prairies; if the giants of Britain really did arrive in response to Johnny Byron's drumming at the end of Butterworth's *Jerusalem*; if Emilia had let Othello know at the end of Act Four that she had found the handkerchief and given it to her husband Iago. I cannot recall a student ever feeling that these would be 'better' endings, and in getting them to reflect upon why this is the case they can gain considerable insights into the nature of tragedy.

So many of the narratives in popular culture and beyond with which my students have grown up have their origins in the pervasive Protestant providentialism of American culture that to confront a high-status literary genre which is basically anti-providentialist can cause some unease. But in that confrontation they have to think about the reality of death and suffering (including their own) which can't necessarily be explained away as part of a bigger story with an ultimate happy ending. They can also confront questions of the causes of suffering and of where, in the face of death and pain, value may reside in human actions, as I consider below. When they consider why the 'happy' ending wouldn't be the 'better' ending they are learning to live more at home in the world as it is (without accepting it as unchangeable). There has to be the sense in a tragedy that things could have turned out differently, and this feeling is I think partly there when students express resistance to knowing the narrative's outcome before its time.

There are some other opponents of tragedy at large beyond those who simply want a happy ending. Since Plato the emotional power of tragedy has always made it a suspect art form for some. It has been suggested that tragedy is inherently politically reactionary. One critique, which derives from Brecht's writings, sees tragedy as serving the interests of the political status quo, by being pessimistic about 'human nature', and also by presenting human suffering as inevitable and mysterious, rather than revealing the contingent human actions which produce it. In 1928 Brecht wrote that he was one of those people who 'believe humanity is well on the way to getting rid of the tragic entirely, merely by taking civilizing measures' (Brecht 2015: 43). What he called 'bourgeois' tragedy—middle-class orientated, realist drama—was in fact 'crude and shallow' because it never revealed the 'deeper contexts' (Brecht 2015: 52), the causes of human suffering which we are capable of changing through our own actions. This is a narrow, reductive view of the genre which fails to take into account the blatant political critique which is hard-wired into Greek, early modern and much twentieth-century and contemporary tragedy. The stereotypical hero of Romantic or 'bourgeois' tragedy, to which he refers, is only one kind of tragic protagonist. As Raymond Williams showed, there is no universal tragic theory:

> Tragedy is … not a single and permanent kind of fact, but a series of experiences and conventions and institutions. [Furthermore] It is not a case of interpreting this series by reference to a permanent and unchanging human nature. Rather, the varieties of tragic experience are to be interpreted by reference to the changing conventions and institutions. (Williams 1979: 45–46)

Another critique has condemned tragedy since it is focused on the fall of a 'great man' and relegates women to the condition of either passive victims of the hero's actions or of malign influences who bring about his fall. But this is again a narrow and reductive generalization. Rita Felski points out that 'such a description may have a limited purchase in the case of Shakespearean tragedy, but it fails utterly in explaining Greek texts that are thickly plotted with internecine strife and familial intrigue' (Felski 2008: 3). It also ignores the presence of contemporary feminist tragedy in the work of, for example, Caryl Churchill and Sarah Kane (see McEvoy 2017: 162–169).

But if such political critiques are misplaced, what of the specific psychological consequences of tragic narratives? Is there a danger we should be aware of that the violence and suffering which students will encounter can damage them emotionally? Should a teacher of tragedy offer 'trigger warnings' if the material is going to cause distress? It would certainly seem to be a humane and proper thing to excuse a student from class (when possible) if a teacher knew that part of the text they were about to teach might evoke distress for a particular student because of a recent or not so recent event in a particular student's life. On a particularly dreadful occasion one of my students was killed in a car crash the day before his class were to see a set play, *Henry V*, at the Barbican in London. I excused many of the class from attending and during the performance I felt I should have cancelled the whole trip when I saw students weeping as the King surveyed the bodies of young men littering the stage after Agincourt. But afterwards, I must say, it seemed that the performance marked and comprehended the death of their classmate in a way that was difficult but significant for them.

Excusing particular students in this way—when the teacher knows specific circumstances—may seem simply kind and sensible. But should more general warnings about the distressing content of tragic texts be given? Joanna Williams has written about just such a thing occurring in some American colleges, in a culture of postmodernity where 'the notion that words and images were pre-eminently important in shaping reality and could inflict mental harm upon people' has been influential (Joanna Williams 2016: 172). She traces the source of this idea to a 'postmodernism that assumed discourse constructed not just perceptions of reality but often reality itself' (171). This is of course a rather crude reductive notion of the ideology of the artwork in particular. In the work of Theodor Adorno, for example, our relationship to the work of art, to tragic art is at an important level non-conceptual, a bodily, physical apprehension (Gritzner 2015: 163); it is fleetingly, excitingly outside the web of language in which the postmodernists claim we are trapped and dissolved. But meanwhile, Joanna Williams reports that

> Students have demanded 'trigger warnings' or advance notifications if their course is to include content that might be considered racist, sexist, classist, homophobic or in any other way offensive or potentially capable of triggering post-traumatic stress disorder. Such demands are inherently censorious: at Oberlin College in America in 2014, faculty were asked to remove 'triggering' material when it did not directly contribute to course goals. (Williams 2016: 173)

Williams argues that the idea that students can be harmed by the content of the text that they are studying arises from what is actually a fundamentally conservative conception of the self rooted in identity politics; as Frank

Furedi puts it, 'people whose identity is defined by their biology, emotional disposition, history and culture have as their focus what they are rather than what they could be' (Furedi 2014: 172, cited in Williams 2016: 186). The student is constructed as a victim of an oppressive culture rather than as the 'rational, autonomous individual that had traditionally been assumed to have been the creator of, and audience for, academic work' (187). The assumption made is that students are incapable of distancing themselves emotionally from the material and that teachers cannot expect them to do so. Consequently, she writes,

> The more the inclusive university prioritizes sensitivity to feelings and respect for individuals, the more difficult the formation of criticism becomes. Criticism is either avoided altogether or couched in provisos or presented as just a different understanding by an alternative identity group. The prevention of offence requires the silencing of critics and potential offenders. It requires that dissenting voices be suppressed. The effect of this is to make existing understandings of the world more difficult to challenge. Without criticism it is simply impossible for knowledge to advance. (187–188)

Williams goes on to quote the American liberal commentator Jonathan Rauch in what might seem to be a bold justification for tragedy in the classroom and the theatre: 'to advance knowledge, we must all sometimes suffer. Worse than that, we must inflict suffering on others' (Rauch 2014: 19, cited in Williams 2016: 188).

Joanna Williams' argument is concerned with the teaching of the humanities in general. It would not do to overstate the scale of the phenomenon here. Though she mentions one teacher's self-censorship (187) she doesn't document any instances of the silencing of tragic narratives in particular and presents the issue as part of the wider culture wars within the American academy and beyond, where the issue is live. As an extreme example, Jonathan Bromwich records

> a letter to the *New York Times* on 31 July from an administrator in the city's Education Department [which] denounces a reading-skills exam that used an extract from Edith Wharton's *Age of Innocence*; the passage in question begins, 'It was generally agreed in New York that the Countess Olenska had "lost her looks"'; the complaint is that 'any girl taking the exam' will experience the mention of losing your looks as a 'psychic punch' that impairs concentration on the rest of the exam. (Bromwich 2016)

But Bromwich also refers to an article in a Columbia University students' newspaper which argues that events in texts such as the rape of Philomela in Ovid's *Metamorphoses* are 'wrought with histories and narratives of exclusion or oppression, [and] can be difficult to read and discuss as a survivor' (Bromwich 2016).

Joanna Williams' central point about the importance of the freedom of expression in education remains valid (always bearing in mind the kind of sensible and tactful action mentioned above to spare students feelings in particular circumstances), especially since, as Aristotle identified, it is in the nature of tragedy that through the vicarious experience of suffering we can advance a particular kind of knowledge, to adapt Rauch's words.

In any case, when teaching a literary text whose content might be distressing, or which even in its depiction of a distressing world appears to validate the oppressive values of historically dominant groups, the experience of suffering in the text is framed by the different ways of encountering the text available to the teacher which are likely to produce different degrees of emotional affect. Furthermore, and crucially, the effect of most tragedy—Greek, early modern and contemporary in particular—is to encourage reflection upon what has been encountered and not to be the passive victim of the work's emotional impact, as those who accuse tragedy of being harmful would assume. The intellect is engaged and knowledge and understanding can be elicited of those great matters of which the playwright Edward Bond says theatre must speak: 'the causes of human suffering and the sources of human strength' (Bond 2013: 109). That reflection is, typically, social and political but can also be philosophical. The teaching of tragic narratives must always provide just such opportunities for such reflection.

At the very beginning of the history of the genre, the Athenians developed an art form which, as Simon Goldhill puts it, 'leads to self-questioning through the pain of others' (Goldhill 2004: 229). 'Tragedy again and again takes the ideology of the city and explores its flaws and contradictions' (231). Jonathan Rauch's remark only echoes Aeschylus, the very first tragedian whose work survives. In the *Agamemnon* the Chorus make a statement which embodies the tragic experience: they sing that 'it was Zeus who set/men on the path to wisdom/when he decreed the fixed law that suffering alone shall be their teacher … by violence, it seems, grace comes' (Aeschylus 2011: 51) [176–178; 182–183]. Tragedy is educational. It is not an accident that the plays we have from ancient Greece survived because they were taught in schools in the succeeding centuries.

The rebirth of the performance and study of classical tragedy in the Romantic era went hand in hand with that power of social and political critique (see Hall and Macintosh 2005: 215ff., 283ff.). From Hegel onwards the critical learning about our social and political condition that comes from reading or watching tragedy has been an important part of how we understand the genre. Rather than tragedy offering some kind of mystified 'transcendence' of the historical circumstances in which we live, as some Brechtian critics have alleged, Terry Eagleton rather suggests that 'it is the lesson of a good deal of tragedy that only by an unutterably painful openness to our frailty and finitude—to the material limits of our conditions—can we have any hope of transcending it' (Eagleton 2008: 345). The teaching of tragedy, where it seeks to reflect upon what the text is making us think about the historical circumstances in which we live—as well as seeking to provoke an emotional response—can only provide that learning even more powerfully.

There are then good educational, moral and political reasons for believing what we gain from studying tragedy to outweigh any suffering or potential harm caused to students reading a text, if such harms exist. In writing this chapter I surveyed my own students who over a two-year course had studied a range of dramatic texts: *Othello*, *Antigone*, Lorca's *Blood Wedding*, Butterworth's *Jerusalem* as well as the novels *Tess of the D'Urbervilles* and Hamilton's *Hangover Square* in addition to poetry by Plath, Donne and Keats. There was no response from any of them to indicate that they had been distressed inappropriately by the depictions of murder, suicide, rape and mutilation to which they were subjected in lessons. Some took quite a dispassionate, technical approach to what they had learnt. One student wrote that 'I wasn't emotionally affected but I would say that it affected me intellectually. I understood and empathised with the characters, but I mainly was appreciating the craftsmanship of the writers (layering the aspects of tragedy so effectively).' When asked whether studying tragedy had affected his response to suffering in the real world, he replied,

> To some extent. Many of the tragedies that we studied were caused by miscommunication or reckless action… But in terms of reality, many horrible tragedies happen through no fault of the person but through the malice of the perpetrator (such as a member of ISIS committing a massacre, or a rapist attacking a woman). The nature of tragedy is versatile, and although I have gained a greater literary understanding of it, I do not think it has affected my understanding of real life tragedies. Having said that, it is now one of my favourite genres.

Another student, who was born in Somalia, found studying *Othello* and the significance of race in the play much more affecting:

> I think one would expect me to be uncomfortable with the racist scenes of *Othello*. But, on the contrary I wasn't. As a black woman, racism is something I have almost grown accustomed to, and the racist scenes in *Othello* did not faze me. What was interesting with *Othello* was that often I would look up and scan the room, some eyes would quickly dart away as they pretended not to be looking at me, and others who looked completely bewildered at what was written on the page, as if they have never experienced racism secondhand. As I'm writing this, I have come to realize that perhaps it was the white students in the class that were more uncomfortable with the racist scenes than I was. It was an enormous elephant in the room, heightened by my presence. And I think that this was a good thing. For those who most probably never experienced racism to feel uncomfortable and to be challenged.

She concluded that 'I believe I have learned a lot about myself and this world that we live in through reading tragedies in class, that concern issues that are not discussed enough in our education system.' As Raymond Williams puts it, 'the varieties of tragic experience are to be interpreted by reference to the changing conventions and institutions' (Williams 1979: 46). The emotional power of the tragedy of Othello brought about something valuable for her and, it seems, for her classmates.

There are also important philosophical reasons why it is right to teach tragedy. Tony Nuttall's exploration of the paradox of how we find pleasure in tragic suffering reaches an interesting conclusion. On the assumption that we all identify with the doomed protagonist (Nuttall 1996: 74), he argues that tragedy is a thought-experiment where we try out the hypothesis of our own death (or of our own grievous suffering), but it is the hypothesis itself that dies instead of us when the play ends. The pleasure we get is in our sense that, unlike the protagonist, we have cleverly avoided death and yet 'the spectator achieves a moment of recognition, faces a truth known to be necessary for all' (79). It is not necessary to agree that there is something timeless in human nature (75) in our response to tragedy to see what we might gain from this rehearsal of the worst in life:

> The human race has found a way, if not to abolish, then to defer and diminish the Darwinian treadmill of death. We send our hypotheses ahead, an expendable army, and watch them fall. It is easy to see how the human

> imagination might begin to exhibit a need, in art, for a death-game, a game in which the muscles of psychic response, fear and pity, are exercised and made ready, through a facing of the worst, which is not yet the real worst. (77)

Nuttall regards *catharsis* as an active, not a passive force, an 'exercise' of the emotions both in the sense of their use and in the sense of a trying out, a practice. In teaching the narratives of tragedy we are, perhaps uniquely in the curriculum, allowing our students to learn through 'play' about how to face the inevitability of death or suffering, but also, as Nuttall does not mention, to understand the reasons for suffering and how death can have a meaning and even a purpose in the lives of those who survive. Tragedy is also about those left alive on stage and about how they will respond to the consequences of the play's events in the future as much as it is about those who die. The death of those we love is usually harder to deal with than our own.

Tragedy as a literary genre has been the subject of extended philosophical treatment, attracting much more attention than comedy, for example. Aristotle, Hume, Hegel, Schopenhauer and Hegel have all been concerned with its nature and it remains an important matter for philosophers today. George W. Harris has gone so far as to declare 'the problem of tragedy' to be 'the most important philosophical problem facing the twenty-first century' (Harris 2006: 18). He defines this problem as

> coping with loss, both personally and culturally, where the losses are very deep and when it is no longer possible to ignore them or to be consoled by pernicious fantasies. Making sense of the bad, even horrible things in life and resolving how to feel, to think, and act in the clear knowledge of good and evil is the task. (19)

Harris sees humanity in the twenty-first century as aware that 'some day everything that has and will transpire here on Earth, including all that we cherish, will perish without a trace, leaving behind a universe indifferent to our history, our values, our sorrows' (23). What we learned in the twentieth century about humanity's capacity for self-annihilation and the dangers that we can see ahead inherent in our continuing destruction of the planet's biosphere have only focused our attentions more acutely on this fact. Harris argues that there is no 'moral law', no ultimate conception of the Good which will guide us through and make everything right if only we followed its precepts. Instead we live in a world where 'values are plural, conflicting and sometimes incomparable and nothing is of unqualified value' (29). The choices we face in the most difficult parts of life can be between fundamentally incomparable things, and in striving to do good we lose the things we value greatly. 'Loss', writes Harris, 'contrary to some forms of the pernicious fantasy, is an inevitable function of human valuing'. And sometimes

> where incomparability obtains between options of great importance that are in conflict but where choice must be made, there arises a new tragic thought: that what is lost, no matter what we do, cannot be compared to what is gained in any of the options. This is reason's grief, the outer limit to rational choice, the end of the consolation of reason for loss, and a distinctive source of tragic experience that pernicious fantasies work to conceal. (31)

Harris is writing as a moral philosopher who is developing an ethical theory for the twenty-first century, but the dilemma he describes could be the dramatic situation common to Orestes in Aeschylus' *Libation Bearers*, to Sophocles' Antigone, to Shakespeare's Hamlet, to Kleist's Prince of Homburg, to Lorca's Bride in *Blood Wedding*, to Bond's Shakespeare in *Bingo* or to Churchill's Joyce in *Top Girls*. If Harris is right, when we teach tragedy we are actually conducting an exploration into the nature of value itself in an open-eyed, honest way. For as Terry Eagleton puts it, 'there can be no tragedy without a sense of value, whether or not that value actually bears fruit'. Furthermore,

> if tragedy cuts deeper than pessimism, it is because horror is laced with an enriched sense of human worth. Perhaps we could pass beyond tragedy only by abandoning the view that there is anything to be cherished in the first place, in which case we might prefer to tarry with it. (Eagleton 2015: 115)

Given the essentially tragic nature of our ethical lives, *not* to teach tragedy would seem an abrogation of our moral duty as educators. (Unless we were to take the view that the moral education of our students is none of our business. But I would not like to my daughter or son to have to study in a school or college where that was the attitude of the teachers.)

Rather than being any kind of moral or psychological danger to students, a good case can be made for tragedy's unique moral and even psychological value as a genre for study. Tragedy's greatest impact will be created when we teach it such a way as to allow its emotional and aesthetic effect to be accompanied by its capacity to provoke profound reflection on the nature of human suffering and our own mortality. I would go so far to say that the teaching of tragedy should be an entitlement in any rational and humane system of education.

## Notes

1. The late plays of Euripides such as *Alcestis* or *Helen* are often referred to as tragedies, and have the usual generic structure, but have 'happy' endings. The same can be said of Kleist's *Prince of Homburg*.

## Works Cited

Aeschylus. 2011. Agamemnon. In *The Complete Aeschylus, Vol. 1: The Oresteia*, trans. and ed. Peter Burian and Alan Shapiro. New York: Oxford University Press.
Aristotle. 2013. *The Poetics*. Translated by Anthony Kenny. Oxford: Oxford University Press.
Bond, Edward. 2013. Notes to Young Writers. *The Activist Papers [1976], in: Plays: Four*. London: Methuen.
Brecht, Bertolt. 2015. *Brecht on Theatre*. Edited by Marc Silberman, Steve Giles, and Tom Kuhn, 3rd ed. London: Bloomsbury.
Bromwich, David. 2016. What Are We Allowed to Say? *London Review of Books* 38 (18): 3–10. September 22, 2016. http://www.lrb.co.uk/v38/n18/david-bromwich/what-are-we-allowed-to-say
Eagleton, Terry. 2008. Commentary. In *Rethinking Tragedy*, ed. Rita Felski. Baltimore: John Hopkins University Press.
———. 2015. *Hope Without Optimism*. Charlottesville: University of Virginia Press.
Felski, Rita. 2008. *Rethinking Tragedy*. Baltimore: John Hopkins University Press.
Furedi, Frank. 2014. *First World War: Still No End in Sight*. London: Bloomsbury.
Goldhill, Simon. 2004. *Love, Sex and Tragedy: Why Classics Matters*. London: John Murray.
Gritzner, Karoline. 2015. *Adorno and Modern Theatre: The Drama of the Damaged Self in Bond, Rudkin, Barker and Kane*. Basingstoke: Palgrave Macmillan.
Hall, Edith, and Fiona Macintosh. 2005. *Greek Tragedy and the British Theatre, 1660–1914*. Oxford: Oxford University Press.
Harris, George W. 2006. *Reason's Grief: An Essay on Tragedy and Value*. New York: Cambridge University Press.
McEvoy, Sean. 2017. *Tragedy: The Basics*. London: Routledge.
Nuttall, Anthony. 1996. *Why Does Tragedy Give Pleasure?* Oxford: Clarendon Press.

Plato. 1974. *The Republic*. Translated by Desmond Lee, 2nd ed. Harmondsworth: Penguin Books.
Rauch, Jonathan. 2014. *Kindly Inquisitors: The New Attacks on Free Thought*. Chicago: Chicago University Press.
Wallace, Jennifer. 2007. *The Cambridge Introduction to Tragedy*. Cambridge: Cambridge University Press.
Williams, Joanna. 2016. *Academic Freedom in an Age of Conformity: Confronting the Fear of Knowledge*. Basingstoke: Palgrave Macmillan.
Williams, Raymond. 1979. *Modern Tragedy*. Rev. ed. London: Verso.
Woodruff, Paul. 2008. *The Necessity of Theater*. New York: Oxford University Press.

CHAPTER 5

# Teaching Comic Narratives

*Rachel Trousdale*

Comic narratives present special challenges for students, especially students at the beginning of their college careers. But the very obstacles to understanding such narratives—a category I take to include fiction, drama and narrative poetry—also make them extremely rewarding to teach. Comic narratives offer especially productive ways to train students in nuanced approaches to literary analysis; precision in their placement of the literary text in its historical context; and sensitivity to the cross-currents and tensions that underlie literature's discursive flexibility. And, of course, comic narratives are fun to read. To access all these benefits, however, students often need clearly articulated, structured support as they learn to treat amusement as a starting point for interpretation rather than as an end in itself.

One of the most common difficulties students face in reading comic texts has been created for them by their educations. We have taught them that 'literature' is serious. Many students enter college having taken literature classes that were described to them as a kind of educational and moral corrective; they have been told that reading fiction is a way to witness the struggles of the past, to find role models, or perhaps to improve their own prose writing. These are all good reasons to read, and as we defend our discipline's place in the curriculum, the value of literature as moral and

R. Trousdale (✉)
Framingham State University, Framingham, MA, USA

stylistic education deserves a major place in our argument. But this account of the value of reading leaves out one of the most important reasons that people read: for fun. Students know that there is such a thing as pleasure reading, but their experiences have taught them that the books they read for pleasure will never be assigned at school, because those books do not contain the moral or aesthetic lessons that their teachers want them to learn. Besides, if students can be counted on to read fun books on their own, there is (the logic goes) no reason to assign them in class.

This expectation of seriousness can make it difficult for students to recognize that an assigned text is funny. For example: a student taking my British literature survey, presented with a nanny named Miss Prism who accidentally puts the manuscript of her three-volume novel in a perambulator while she puts the baby in her handbag—and is delighted to be reunited, twenty-eight years later, with the handbag, but shows no concern about the whereabouts of the baby—recently objected, 'That makes no sense! Who *does* something like that?'[1] More encouragingly, a first-year student, halfway through reading *The Tempest* in a literature course for non-majors, observed, 'I just don't see how he's going to kill them all off. I mean, it's Shakespeare, so everyone has to end up dead, but right now, if I didn't know better, I'd think this play was supposed to be funny.' Both of these students' responses to their texts grow out of experiences of English courses that treat realism as the norm and Shakespeare as the literary equivalent of eating one's spinach. They also show that context plays a large, but not determinative, role in our ability to perceive humor.

It is not surprising that we do not train students to recognize and analyze comic texts. The omission reflects a larger tendency among critics to bypass analysis of humor. Scholars writing about texts that contain humor often refrain from commenting on the nature of that humor, or do so only in passing before moving on to 'serious' analytic points. Some even seem to apologize for mostly serious texts' comic components.[2] There is a pervasive critical attitude that things that make us laugh are trivial or, in some cases, even immoral.

This idea that comedy is intellectually light-weight and often ethically flawed is a very old one. Since the Greeks, comedy has been the 'low' dramatic genre—not just in its perceived value but in its frequent focus on people of lower classes or lower morals. The language of comedy is often the language of the everyday. Comic writing uses slang and obscenity, as opposed to the elevated diction of tragedy. But such disapproval extends well beyond the boundaries of literature: laughter itself is suspect. Plato says that the Guardians of the Republic should not laugh, as they will set a bad example for others. Aristotle acknowledges that laughter is not necessarily immoral, but warns that it can too easily lead us away from the wisest path, that of moderation. Thomas Hobbes, whose view of humanity is rarely sunny, exemplifies the grimmest view of humor: Hobbes argues that we laugh when we experience the 'sudden glory' of considering ourselves better than someone else (Hobbes 1985: 124). Hobbes suggests that laughter is a sign of weakness, because only people who are unsure of their power or position require such reassurance. This old and well-established belief that humor necessarily involves unkindness, weakness and self-centeredness (as well as triviality) seems to lie behind much of the critical suspicion surrounding laughter.

The laughter Hobbes describes, the laugh of *Schadenfreude*, is a common form of comedy. But even if we agree that such laughter is a moral failure, it is still worthy of study: examining who believes themselves to be better than whom, and why, can be a fruitful line of discussion. More importantly, however, as anyone who examines their own experience of laughter can confirm, this is only one of the many kinds of laughter human beings engage in. Our responses to the comic are as varied and as complex as our responses to the aesthetic. To help students approach comic texts, we must give them an appropriately flexible range of theoretical tools with which to engage in the remarkably slippery work of reading comic narratives.

## Theoretical Contexts

I prefer to run my classes as seminars, but I have found it useful to give students a brief lecture outlining relevant theories of humor before we discuss a comic text. An important first step in talking about a comic narrative is simply to let students know before they start reading that the text is supposed to be funny—this actually makes a significant difference in their reactions on the first day of discussions. Because students have rarely engaged in formal study of humor, however, it is essential to equip them with conceptual categories for analyzing the texts we discuss.[3] It is particularly important to let them know that theorists disagree about the nature and causes of laughter, and to lay out a preliminary vocabulary of terms for discussing the comic. I generally give a ten- or fifteen-minute lecture on humor theory during the first class we spend on a comic text. During this lecture, I find it useful to ask students to provide examples of each kind of humor I discuss. In addition to keeping them engaged and verifying that they are understanding the subject matter, this interaction also raises the likelihood that they will find the examples of humor I discuss funny—and thus more convincing. While most students have not thought about humor from a theoretical standpoint, they catch on quickly to theories of humor, even those that are comparatively subtle, because their own experiences provide them with a vast body of examples.

The precise content of this lecture varies depending on the text we are reading, but some of the ideas I have found most consistently helpful to mention are:

1. *Superiority theory.* Hobbes' notion that we laugh when we feel we are better than someone else. Essential to superiority theory, and the moral judgment of laughter superiority theorists often make, is the idea that we do not feel sympathy with the objects of our laughter. Slapstick can often be explained in terms of superiority humor; Mel Brooks articulates the basics of superiority theory in *The 2000 Year Old Man* when he says, 'To me, tragedy is if I'll cut my finger. That's tragedy!… And to me, comedy is if you walk into an open sewer and die' (Reiner and Brooks 1967). While Freud is not, strictly speaking, a superiority theorist, his term 'tendentious' humor—humor that contains a veiled (or not-so-veiled) attack on its object—is useful here (Freud 2003: 84). Superiority-based humor can be instrumental in forging bonds between laughers, who share their pleasure in their common superiority over the object of laugher, and can be an easy way to delineate in-groups and outsiders. I tend to start the lecture with this theory for several reasons: it is the oldest articulated theory of humor; it is still a dominant theory in the field; it is easy to grasp; and it is easy to demonstrate the theory's limitations. For example, we may feel that superiority theory does not adequately explain why we laugh at a pun or a clever rhyme; or that a straightforward superior–inferior relationship may not satisfactorily explain underdog humor, such as the way that Jewish humor frequently pokes fun at all parties involved (see Wisse 2013).

2. Freud's theory of laughter as *release from repression* (Freud 2003: 115). Freud writes extensively on humor, so it is impossible to do justice to his work on the subject in a brief lecture, but his discussion of comic release from repression is a particularly useful counterbalance to superiority theory. In *The Joke and its Relation to the Unconscious,*

Freud suggests that we laugh when the energy we are using to maintain our civilized selves—the effort by which we repress our unacceptable desires and thoughts, or to stay in the realm of sense rather than nonsense—is suddenly rendered unnecessary. When someone makes a fart joke, for example, we laugh because we suddenly do not need the energy we were using to pretend that there is no such thing as a fart; when someone makes a pun, we laugh because the energy we were putting into maintaining our understanding of language as a coherent system of meaning suddenly loses its purpose.

This theory, too, has its drawbacks—most importantly, it rests on a nineteenth-century model of neurology that recent science has shown to be incorrect (Martin 2007: 42). But while Freud's account of laughter's physiological underpinnings appears to be inaccurate, his discussion of laughter as relief and release offers an entirely different account from the superiority theorists', and one which seems to explain a very different affective experience. Hobbes' laughter is inherently oppositional: his laughers are an 'us' and the objects of laughter are 'them'. In Freud's model of repression and release, laughers and objects of laughter are revealed to share fundamental repressed needs and desires. But while Freud's model can provide a satisfying alternative to superiority theory in explaining why we laugh at bathroom humor, his suggestion that this notion of relief can explain why we laugh at wordplay may be less convincing. Freud's release theory is more complex than superiority theory, but students generally do not have difficulty understanding it (especially if you use the example of fart jokes).

3. *Incongruity theory.* This may be the most flexible and broadly applicable single theory of humor, which is why I introduce it last in my lecture: it resolves some (though not all) of the problems raised by the first two approaches. While elements of incongruity theory can be found in Aristotle, it is not worked out as a separate theory until much later. Major incongruity theorists include Kant, Schopenhauer and Kierkegaard (for these and other key texts, see Morreall 1987). Incongruity theorists argue that we laugh when we have formed an expectation which is then overturned. This theory seems to be best supported by recent psychological and neurological studies, but such research is still in the early stages, and preliminary results may still do better at identifying which areas of the brain are involved in laughter than at identifying precisely what kinds of incongruity make us laugh (see Leys 2011).

Puns are excellent examples of incongruous humor: our amusement at a pun is generated by the fact that context has led us to expect Meaning A, and the punch line delivers Meaning B: 'Two guys walk into a bar. Which is funny, because you'd think at least the second guy would have noticed it.' *Monty Python's Flying Circus* is a non-stop series of examples—'And now for something completely different!'—but they also make frequent use of superiority and release from repression, and demonstrate how difficult and reductive it can be to argue that a single theory best describes a particular comic moment.

These are the three most important theories of humor. While each has more complexities than I have described above, quick explanations like those given here can help students identify productive questions to ask about comic aspects of a text.

It is also helpful to point out that some rhetorical strategies and affective responses which students have already discussed in literature classes are particularly relevant to the discussion of comic texts. While the precise terms I discuss naturally vary depending on the text we are studying, a brief discussion of satire, irony and—perhaps surprisingly, in this context—sympathy can often help students bring their existing analytical skills to bear on comic texts.

1. *Satire*. Students tend to be very familiar with satire; almost all of them have watched *Saturday Night Live* or read *The Onion*. Humor that makes an argumentative attack on its object is a genre they understand intuitively. Satire can be used as an example of Hobbesian superiority theory, although it is important to make it clear that not all Hobbesian laughter is satirical (one can be mean-spirited without being argumentative). It is an efficient way to show how the texts we discuss participate in a long-standing comic tradition, and to remind students that writers do not always mean precisely what they say.
2. *Irony*. It is helpful to discuss irony during a lecture on humor theory in part because students have encountered the term elsewhere. Attention to comic irony can help students understand how their existing analytical skills can be brought to bear on comic material: as in any close reading, the study of humor frequently entails identifying the different, competing, apparently contradictory meanings inherent in the text. Discussing irony can also help illustrate the ways we might use different theories of humor to examine a single

comic moment. In Tom Stoppard's *Arcadia*, for example, the poet Ezra Chater inscribes a copy of his book to Septimus Hodge, in thanks for Septimus' promise of a good review, writing, 'To my dear friend Septimus Hodge, who stood up and gave his best on behalf of the Author.' The moment is funny for several simultaneous reasons. First, it contains a dirty joke (an example of Freudian release theory): 'stood up and gave his best' reminds us, although apparently not Chater, that Septimus has recently had sex with Mrs. Chater (Stoppard 1993: 9). It is an example of comic irony: Chater speaks the truth without intending to. It is an example of comic incongruity: we can see that Chater intends one meaning while accidentally conveying another. It is also an example of superiority humor: we laugh at Chater's foolishness, while admiring Septimus' superior wit (he has just talked Chater out of challenging him to a duel). Identifying such moments of irony can help students begin to unpack—and to analyze—the layered and sometimes contradictory comic elements within a text.

3. The complex relationship between laughter and *sympathy* is the final concept I address. As we have seen in the discussion of superiority theory, many theorists of humor believe that we laugh only when we feel no sympathy with the object of our laughter. Henri Bergson, for example, argues that we laugh at other people when we see them as only partly human, and suggests that laughter is a corrective which reminds us to conform to the rules of humanity (Bergson 1956: 63–64). Bergson's discussion of sympathy can help explain why dramatic irony is not funny: we feel sympathy with Oedipus, for example, so the irony of his vow to punish whoever is responsible for the curse upon Thebes is not funny but tragic, since we know (as he does not) that he has vowed vengeance upon himself. Once again, students will be able to think of many examples of this sort of humor, but they will also be able to suggest counterexamples, moments when laughter comes from a moment of fellow-feeling or mutual recognition. This discussion of sympathy helps establish humor as a site of productive conflict and debate, both within a text and within a broader theoretical conversation.

Three theories, two rhetorical terms, and one emotional state are far from an exhaustive overview of the history of comedy, but I have found that briefly presenting these concepts to students at the beginning of a section on comic texts serves several related and essential functions. This brief and partial discussion gives students a vocabulary for analyzing humor. It helps them see that a text's comic moments are not just jokes to 'get' or 'not get', but points at which conflicting ideas are brought into dialogue. It establishes the idea that humor almost by definition does more than one thing, that comedy can be a form of substantive, polyvocal discourse. My goal when explaining these terms is not to teach students a particular theoretical apparatus, but to give them the basis from which to consider humor a starting point for analysis, an intellectual endeavor which can have several simultaneous valences and which brings different ideas and linguistic registers into productive tension.

## Informational Contexts

If the first problem students encounter when reading comic narratives comes from their academic contexts, the second problem they most frequently encounter is the highly contextual and referential nature of humor itself. As the theories of humor I have discussed imply, much of humor is situational, requiring specific knowledge and established expectations to get the joke. This is one reason why humor is notoriously hard to translate; many jokes depend not only on their own immediate linguistic content but on detailed knowledge of a cultural context.

Some contexts are easier to understand than others. Jane Austen is highly accessible, because much of her humor depends on phenomena that have changed very little since 1813. The precise social markers with which she identifies the class snobbery, hypocrisy, and selfishness that she satirizes have changed, but most students have no difficulty understanding the humor of *Pride and Prejudice*, because the fundamental story she tells (girl meets boy, boy is obnoxious, girl's family is embarrassing, girl nonetheless marries boy) deals with values and problems with which they are familiar.

Other comic texts are far more difficult. Alexander Pope's satires depend on detailed knowledge not just of the social conventions of the British upper classes in the early 18th century, but of the particular reputations and behavior of dozens of real, long-dead people. This information can be provided in footnotes, but while a critical apparatus can provide the basic data to explain Pope's jokes, it cannot provoke a strong affective response—it is a rare student who laughs at a footnote. To get the humor of a text—that is, to feel amusement rather than merely acknowledging that someone may have once found a joke funny—students must already know something about the underpinnings of the text's jokes. So how can we help students recognize the comic elements of difficult texts—both because we want them to have the pleasure of laughing, and because we want them to engage in the substantive analysis laughter can prompt?

Depending on the text at hand, there are several useful ways to frame comic narratives so that students can recognize, enjoy and most importantly analyze the humor they encounter. One of the most efficient ways to do this is by assigning students to educate each other about the necessary material. This can be done via in-class presentations, but I have found it particularly effective to assign students to prepare handouts. Each student signs up for a handout topic, and is responsible for distributing the handout electronically at least 24 hours prior to the class meeting, so the rest of the class has time to read it. Handouts have two distinct advantages over presentations: first, since they are distributed ahead of time, they give students a chance to assimilate the information they contain; and second, I can ask students to show me a draft ahead of time, so that I can verify they are covering the necessary material.

For comic texts, it can be particularly effective to assign a handout on a topic explaining some of the dominant comic materials in the text—not just spelling out the jokes, but giving the in-depth background material that provides the jokes' underpinnings. For example, in a class on Vladimir Nabokov's *Pale Fire*, I might assign a handout on the roots of Zemblan, a language invented by the character Charles Kinbote. The student writing the handout would be responsible for identifying (with the help of some scholarly sources) the roots of Nabokov's puns, double entendres and deliberate mistranslations, and then providing discussion questions to help students find thematic continuities among Kinbote's insertions of Zemblan into the novel's English text. While reading a fellow student's handout does not provide a belly laugh any more than reading a footnote does, asking students to consider how the comic continuities and disjunctions within the text are flagged by Kinbote's made-up words helps them discuss the text at a far higher level of fluency and sophistication than joke-by-joke explanations could. Writing and reading these handouts helps students gain the necessary expertise to return to the text with fresh eyes, becoming speakers of Zemblan themselves—or of whatever other comic discourse a text deploys. Ideally, students gain a deep enough knowledge of the subject that on rereading, the text that has initially been confusing becomes actually funny, and tracing what has changed in their own reaction to the text helps them identify the text's substantive concerns.

Another way to provide the necessary context for a comic narrative is through its placement on the syllabus. Students find Virginia Woolf's *Orlando*, for example, a difficult text to understand for a variety of reasons. They may be confused by the novel's treatment of time (Orlando ages approximately twenty years over the course of 300 years of history), or its treatment of gender (Orlando begins the novel as a boy, but at the age of thirty abruptly and without obvious cause becomes a woman). But while these plot points are surprising, the novel contains the necessary material to discuss them, as Orlando's biographer engages in long meditations on the difference between clock time and experiential time or the constructed nature of gender. More challenging are the passages in which Woolf describes the Elizabethan, eighteenth-century, Romantic and Victorian eras in terms parodically distilled from each period's literary texts. These passages can be hilarious to readers who recognize the parodies, but can be baffling to anyone else. For example, Woolf's treatment of the Victorian era's prescriptive gender roles, long sentences, decorative excess and sentimentality—all of which Woolf describes as 'damp'—is delightfully merciless:

> The puce and flamingo clouds made her think with a pleasurable anguish, which proves that she was insensibly afflicted with the damp already, of dolphins dying in Ionian seas. But what was her surprise when, as it struck the earth, the sunbeam seemed to call forth, or to light up, a pyramid, hecatomb, or trophy (for it had something of a banquet-table air)—a conglomeration at any rate of the most heterogeneous and ill-assorted objects, piled higgledy-piggledy in a vast mound where the statue of Queen Victoria now stands! Draped about a vast cross of fretted and floriated gold were widow's weeds and bridal veils; hooked on to other excrescences were crystal palaces, bassinettes, military helmets, memorial wreaths, trousers, whiskers, wedding cakes, cannon, Christmas trees, telescopes, extinct monsters, globes, maps, elephants and mathematical-instruments—the whole supported like a gigantic coat of arms on the right side by a female figure clothed in flowing white; on the left, by a portly gentleman wearing a frock-coat and sponge-bag trousers. (Woolf 2006: 169–170)

While any reader will see that this pyramid of miscellaneous objects is nonsensical, its parodic nature will be illegible to students unfamiliar with Woolf's subject matter. This is a loss not only because the parody is fun, but because Woolf's examination of periodicity and literary genre in *Orlando* is intimately linked to her more readily recognizable examination of gender and consciousness. The novel's experiments with fluid gender are allied with its discussion of genre and period; literary and gender categories are revealed throughout the text as similarly and interdependently constructed-yet-determinative. *Orlando*'s critique of binary gender is also a critique of literary history. Understanding the novel's comedy, then, is essential for understanding its complexity.

The difficulty of understanding the text without some familiarity with British literature, however, makes *Orlando* an exciting novel to teach toward the end of a survey course. The preposterous pile of Victorian stuff becomes far more legible—and amusing—if students have just read, for example, *Hard Times* and an excerpt from 'In Memoriam'. The novel's parodies provide a starting point from which to ask students to consider the boundaries of period and genre within the materials already covered by the class, and the conceptions of literary periods on display within other texts. Designing a syllabus to end on *Orlando* turns out to be an excellent way to spur students to consider the nature of the survey itself, with its perpetual juggling act between treating texts on their own terms and treating them as representatives of an era. The novel's oddness and tomfoolery invite students to examine and reimagine how we receive literary history. The comic narrative's dependence on context, then, turns out to be a pedagogical tool as well as a pedagogical challenge, since such texts force students to examine the competing cross-currents in the literary and social histories that comedy holds in tension.

## Internal Contexts

Comic texts can be particularly effective tools for teaching the importance of rereading. Students returning to a comic text after an initial reading may find that jokes which did not initially amuse them have become funnier on the second pass, after they have learned the text's concerns and techniques. This is potentially true of 'footnote jokes' (Shakespeare's dirty jokes are funnier once you've had a chance to learn some Elizabethan slang), but even more so for comic elements that are closely tied to the text's main ideas. Orlando's boyhood romances are funnier once we know to read them as the beginning of an education in gender fluidity. Kinbote's description of his imaginary Zembla is funnier when we know that he is not describing an intradiegetically real country but the product of his own absurd, hybridizing imagination. Comic elements we were initially able to recognize as funny also gain resonances on rereading:

Kinbote's madness is far more moving when we return to the text. The chaos of Joseph Heller's *Catch-22*, which may initially appear to be pure slapstick, is revealed as poignant once we understand that the text's absurdity is motivated by trauma. While an explained joke is not funny, a revisited comic text shows us when a narrative's humor is not decorative but structurally significant. Rereading for comedy can thus provide an intensive training in the tools of textual analysis, as we are better prepared to catch overtones, identify emerging patterns and synthesize competing readings.

## Uncomfortable Humor

Comic texts dealing with charged topics present an additional set of challenges both to students individually and to group discussions. While some uncomfortable topics are comparatively easy to address—texts dealing with sex, sexuality and sexual orientation may produce an initial silence, but, depending on who is in the room, this discomfort often dissipates after a few minutes of conversation. Texts dealing with questions of race and racism, on the other hand, often require additional framing in the classroom. The opening to Sterling Brown's narrative poem 'Slim in Atlanta' may be difficult for many students to discuss in a seminar:

> Down in Atlanta,
>     De whitefolks got laws
> For to keep all de niggers
>     From laughin' outdoors.
>
>     Hope to Gawd I may die
>         If I ain't speakin' truth
>     Make de niggers do deir laughin
>         In a telefoam booth. (Brown 1996: 81)

The problems with discussing this text are clear: its use of the word 'nigger' and its transcription of dialect render it uncomfortable for students of any race to read, and especially to read out loud. Further complicating the difficulty is the question of whether we are allowed to laugh: students may feel that the Jim Crow South is not a joking matter. And as ever, the problem of contextual knowledge remains: students may wonder if there *were* laws against people of color laughing in public. (There were not, but the traditional tall tale of the 'laughing barrel', which Brown adapts for this poem, speaks to the very real danger attending black people who expressed disruptive emotions in public (Carmody 2010: 827; Ellison 1986: 187).)

The challenges that comic texts like 'Slim in Atlanta' pose, however, constitute part of their importance and their value in the classroom. Brown's parodies of legally codified racism offer students an unexpectedly nuanced view of black life under Jim Crow, suggesting both the bitterness of the experience and the creative resilience with which black people fought back against it. Once again, the humor of this comic narrative demands an analysis of how the text interacts with context: not just because students will need explanations of real-world laws, but because the poem's self-awareness raises the question of humor's role in combatting injustice. Acknowledging students' discomfort with the opening to 'Slim in Atlanta' can lead directly to a substantive discussion of humor's power to unsettle us, which in turn casts light both on Brown's choice of light verse for his critique of segregation and on the complexity of the experiences he describes.

Analysis of discomfiting texts can benefit from attention to the differences among superiority humor, comic release from repression and the many kinds of sympathy formed by shared laughter. These terms may help students articulate why a racist term which is deeply offensive when spoken by someone who is not a member of the group being described can be understood as empowering or reclamatory when spoken by a member of that group. More importantly, discussing the interplay of superiority, repression and sympathy in Brown's mockery of segregation helps students understand Brown's critique of racism as fundamentally absurd.

The uncomfortable aspects of comic texts can challenge students to reconsider what topics are worth taking seriously. Stoppard's *Arcadia* suggests a philosophy of sexual attraction which grounds a complex argument about the possibility of intellectual immortality in the ephemeral lightheartedness of the bedroom farce. Students often love *Arcadia*; in addition to appreciating its wit, they find the process of tracing its fractal patterning rewarding. But on the way to building a satisfying reading of the relationships Stoppard sees between past and present, many students encounter difficulty with the text's dirty jokes. Students have asked what it means that Mrs. Chater's 'chief renown is for a readiness that keeps her in a state of tropical humidity as would grow orchids in her drawers in January'; been utterly baffled by what Valentine means when he says 'Lending one's bicycle is a form of safe sex, possibly the safest there is'; and been merely offended by the playwright's 'dirty mind' (Stoppard 1993: 7, 51).

The origins of this incomprehension vary. The line about Mrs. Chater may be obscure because a student is unfamiliar with the term 'drawers' for underclothes, with the biology of female sexual arousal, with the possibility that one might actually *discuss* female arousal, or all three. More interesting and potentially important is the incomprehension of the bicycle joke, which also casts light on the 'dirty mind' comment. While sex is not an entirely taboo topic—students will often laugh at jokes about sex, though such laughs may be expressions of discomfort—its semi-taboo nature means that it is often discussed in highly determined and formulaic terms. Valentine's description of lending a bicycle as a form of safe sex suggests a very different definition of 'safe sex' than the one with which students are familiar. 'Safe sex' denotes a whole health class full of embarrassing, morally fraught instructions, and appropriating the term for an activity that involves none of the familiar accouterments (bodily contact, condoms) can seem to strip the words of their meaning rather than simply playing with them.

Once again, these points of difficulty help point us toward a central concern of the text: the philosophical import of sex's absurdity. 'It is a defect of God's humor that he directs our hearts everywhere but to those who have a right to them', says Lady Croom (Stoppard 1993: 71); while her use of the word 'humor' here may imply more 'nature' or 'constitution' than 'sense of humor', the line points us to the play's serious consideration of the relationship between unruly, sometimes laughable sexual desire on the one hand and questions of fate and free will on the other.

Comic narratives provide an opportunity to help students at any level to become not just more adept close readers but far more sophisticated theoretical thinkers. The process of unpacking a joke or explaining the absurdity of a character's behavior can provide an unusually dense microcosm of our work as literary critics. Studying comic narratives requires us to pay attention to language, to investigate a text's sometimes conflicting values, to consider a broad array of historical and literary references, and to repeatedly reexamine our own critical perspectives. How convenient, then, that it is also enormously fun.

## Notes

1. As Sos Eltis notes, such reactions to Wilde's absurdity are not uncommon (Eltis 2008: 101).

2. See, for example, Stan Smith's discussion of how critics like F. R. Leavis and Donald Davie disapprovingly link W. H. Auden's humor to his homosexuality (Smith 2004: 96).
3. I prefer to focus on this theoretical background rather than, for example, a history of comic genre, because the theories' contradictory and sometimes unsatisfying accounts of why we laugh provoke students to engage in complex analysis of the texts at hand, whereas a history of comedy lends itself more towards simple classification (this text is a comedy of manners, this one is a political satire, etc.).

## WORKS CITED

Bergson, Henri. 1956. Laughter. In *Comedy*, ed. W. Sypher, 1st ed., 61–191. Baltimore: The Johns Hopkins University Press.

Brown, Sterling A. 1996. *Collected Poems of Sterling A. Brown*. Chicago: Northwestern University Press.

Carmody, Todd. 2010. Sterling Brown and the Dialect of New Deal Optimism. *Callaloo* 33 (3): 820–840.

Ellison, Ralph. 1986. *Going to the Territory*. New York: Random House.

Eltis, Sos. 2008. An Introductory Approach to Teaching Wilde's Comedies. In *Approaches to Teaching the Works of Oscar Wilde*, ed. Philip E. Smith, 1st ed., 100–107. New York: MLA.

Freud, Sigmund. 2003. *The Joke and Its Relation to the Unconscious*. New York: Penguin.

Hobbes, Thomas. 1985. *Leviathan*. New York: Penguin.

Leys, Ruth. 2011. The Turn to Affect: A Critique. *Critical Inquiry* 37 (3): 434–472.

Martin, Rod A. 2007. *The Psychology of Humor: An Integrative Approach*. Boston: Elsevier Academic Press.

Morreall, John. 1987. *The Philosophy of Laughter and Humor*. Albany: SUNY Press.

Reiner, Carl, and Brooks Mel. 1967. *The 2000 Year Old Man*. Accessed August 3, 2016. https://www.youtube.com/watch?v=EQWDxrKS1Z4

Smith, Stan. 2004. Auden's Light and Serio-Comic Verse. In *The Cambridge Companion to W. H. Auden*, ed. Stan Smith, 1st ed., 96–109. Cambridge: Cambridge University Press.

Stoppard, Tom. 1993. *Arcadia*. London: Faber and Faber.

Wisse, Ruth R. 2013. *No Joke: Making Jewish Humor*. Princeton: Princeton University Press.

Woolf, Virginia. 2006. *Orlando: A Biography*. New York: Harcourt.

CHAPTER 6

# Teaching Crime Narratives: Historicizing Genre and the Politics of Form

## Will Norman

Among the many challenges of teaching and researching a modern mass genre like crime fiction, perhaps the greatest is the demand to be both a formalist and a historicist. On the one hand, we must build for ourselves some kind of typological archive which might serve to orientate us in our field of study. We need to be able to distinguish between the various generic subsets we find there, and to develop a formal protocol for organizing the archive, in which narratology will necessarily play a considerable part. This process of archive building is involved and painstaking if compressed into a semester, a period of study leave or a summer break. If, as sometimes happens, one is already a fan with a long period of familiarity with various examples of the genre, then, by contrast, one will already have an instinctive facility that requires little effort to convert into a protocol. Either way, whodunits and noir thrillers, police procedurals and hardboiled tales can eventually be identified by their structural features and filed away. On the other hand, however, we will need to tell our own critical and historical narrative about the evolution of crime fiction, into which the contents of the archive can be arranged diachronically. This task does not simply involve placing the establishment of detective fiction by Edgar Allan Poe in the 1840s, hardboiled stories in the 1920s and

W. Norman (✉)
University of Kent, Canterbury, UK

police procedurals in the post-war period. Rather than simply re-arranging our archive using a different protocol, the process of creating a convincing narrative requires that we go further by accounting for *how* and *why* certain subgenres became dominant at certain historical moments. In order to do this we might need to know something about shifting class and labour formations, about evolving technologies of publishing or ideological conflicts over the construction of gender and race. Suddenly, it seems like we are having to perform several types of work at once, and indeed we are.

This chapter, then, is about the difficulty and necessity of undertaking and even saying several things at once when we are studying mass genres. It is guided in part by my experience of teaching an undergraduate module on American crime fiction, but it also derives from my efforts at researching and writing about the topic for publication. I will begin by offering some reflections on critical method, using essays by Tzvetan Todorov and Franco Moretti, before going on to explore how those reflections might help us to address concrete instances of authors and texts in their historical moments, looking first at the emergence and heyday of hardboiled fiction, and then at more recent crime novels published in the late twentieth and early twenty-first centuries.

## TODOROV, MORETTI AND THE NARRATIVE FORM OF THE WHODUNIT

Tzvetan Todorov's 1966 essay, 'The Typology of Detective Fiction', is a canonical piece of criticism in the study of crime fiction, and for good reason. It sets out clearly and accessibly the formal, narratological structure underpinning the classic detective tale, or whodunit, which gradually developed in the second half of the nineteenth century and enjoyed its period of dominance in the 'Golden Age' of detective fiction during the interwar period, when authors such as Dorothy L. Sayers, Agatha Christie and Ellery Queen were operating at the heights of their powers.[1] 'At the base of the whodunit', he explains, 'we find a duality, and it is this duality which will guide our description. This novel contains not one but two stories: the story of the crime and the story of the investigation' (Todorov 1977: 44). The whodunit, it transpires, provides an ideal occasion upon which to demonstrate the practical implications of the old Russian Formalist distinction between *fabula* (crudely, what happened in life) and *sjuzhet* (plot, or the way the author presents it to us).² A novel such as Christie's *Murder on the Orient Express* (1934), for example, evokes quite separately the crime and the investigation, keeping the two fastidiously separate. Almost the entire plot is taken up with the investigation of the crime, until the novel's conclusion, when the reader, along with the various characters clustered around Hercule Poirot, are finally able to determine what happened on the day of the murder in chronological and causal sequence. In doing so, they are at last given access to what the plot had withheld from them, the *fabula*. Todorov's mapping of formalist narratology onto the structure of the whodunit illustrates the way in which classic detective fiction is constitutively reflexive in its concern with narrative emplotment, telling the story of its own construction, and becoming, as Peter Brooks was later to call it, a 'narrative of narratives' (Brooks 1984: 25).

Having established the foundational narratological concepts of *fabula* and *sjuzhet* in their application to the whodunit, Todorov then moves on to the real strength of his essay, which is his demonstration of how the shifting relationship between the two terms can also be used to make sense of later developments in crime fiction. In particular, Todorov is interested in what happens when the taboo on conflating *fabula* and *sjuzhet* is no longer observed, and various forms of interference are thus permitted. There are crime novels, for example, in which 'we are no longer told of a crime anterior to the moment of the narrative; the narrative coincides with the action' (Todorov 1977: 47). The effect of such a collapse of the conventional distinction is to necessitate a different generic appellation, 'the thriller', in which category we might find works such as Chester Himes' *For the Love of Imabelle* (1957), or James Hadley Chase's *The Fast Buck* (1952). The attention of the reader in these cases is driven forwards to anticipation of what is to come, rather than backwards, to determining what has already happened. In addition, Todorov also describes a subgenre that lies between the whodunit and the thriller, that of the suspense novel, in which properties of the other two are combined. In works by Dashiell Hammett and Raymond Chandler, he explains, we find the mystery element of the whodunit combined with the attention to action in the present associated with the thriller, so that *fabula* and *sjuzhet*, rather than collapsing into one another, or being held separate, are instead held in conflicting tension. In the case of the suspense novel, the two can even be said to compete with one another for the reader's attention, leading to a sense of narrative entanglement.

In pedagogical terms, one value of Todorov's essay lies in offering students a simple protocol that they can use in organizing both their own archive of crime fiction and that presented by the module itself, which runs from Edgar Allen Poe to the contemporary. However, the essay is more valuable in demonstrating the limits of formalist thinking about genre evolution. Todorov's analysis is dogged by the same problem that was faced by Russian Formalists such as Boris Eichenbaum and Yuri Tynianov earlier in the twentieth century, of how to account for the extra-literary factors that might play a role in determining the evolution of generic forms.[3] The strain of his account can be discerned in the strange phrasing of his concluding remarks, where he suggests, 'we might say that at a certain point detective fiction experiences as an unjustified burden the constraints of this or that genre and gets rid of them in order to constitute a new code' (52). In seminars I discuss with my students the problems with a statement of this sort, which imputes to an abstract notion of genre some kind of anthropomorphic agency of its own, existing independently from its social and historical climate. Genres, according to this way of thinking, are in some sense programmed to seek out formal novelty and innovation. Deploring constraints and burdens, they move inherently towards freedom, but in this sense are always self-abolishing, wishing to break out of their own rules and to constitute themselves as autonomous literary works, thereby transcending the question of genre altogether. Todorov's essay is radically ahistorical, and offers a hermetic account of genre that is exclusively concerned with itself. Despite the conceptual possibilities that are opened up by the *fabula–sjuzhet* distinction in its various combinations, we find ourselves nevertheless in an intellectual impasse that will not allow us to think historically about crime fiction, or even to speculate on how and why it evolved into different forms at different times. In the context demanded by our module on American crime fiction, we might legitimately ask how such an account will help us to understand how Hammett and Chandler succeeded Poe's Dupin tales and Anna Katharine Green's *The Leavenworth Case*.

The limits we identified in Todorov's formalist work on crime fiction send us in the direction of Franco Moretti's 1978 essay, 'Clues'. Moretti's densely argued and bristling essay combines a number of approaches deriving from the structuralist tradition as well as that of Marxist ideology critique in building a sociological account of classic detective fiction that undertakes simultaneously a formalist and a historicist analysis of Conan Doyle's Sherlock Holmes stories. It is a corrective to Todorov in the sense that the establishment of detective fiction as a mass genre, with its own distinctive narratological form, is rendered inseparable from the ideological function that it fulfilled for Victorian bourgeois society. The historical anaemia we noted in Todorov's work is remedied through attention to the changing class structures of Victorian Britain, where a new bourgeois class legitimated and consolidated its dominant social position by promoting ideologies that concealed its interests and its agency, while moralizing to the consumers of detective stories in mass print culture.

What makes this work so applicable to our situation, despite the focus on Britain rather than the United States, is the way it so directly takes up the terms of Todorov's analysis—*fabula* and *sjuzhet*—and demonstrates the profoundly social and historical implications of their interrelation in Doyle's tales. Moretti's chief hypothesis in this regard is that the work of covering up the deep historical causes of social conflict is performed in detective fiction by the privileging of the solution over the plot: 'its syntax consists in combining the same elements in two different ways so that the combination enacted in the *fabula* (that is, the solution) detracts all value from the combination proposed by the *sjuzhet*: in this way, detective fiction abandons the narrative form of the novel in favour of that of the short story' (Moretti 2005: 134). The detective story accordingly emerges as a conservative *anti-bildung*, in which the solution creates a social erasure or amnesia concerning plot, which comforts the reader and functions to 'dispel the doubt that guilt might be impersonal, and therefore collective and social' (135). Here is not the place not rehearse in detail the many turns and combinations that make up Moretti's argument, but with my students we tend to concentrate on those moments that foreground what he calls the 'syntax' of the stories, their narrative codes. The Holmes stories, like the Dupin stories by Poe that we study on the module, are structured by the 'syntactic regression (from *sjuzhet* to *fabula*, from crime to prelude)', the aim of which is always 'to *return to the beginning*...to reinstate a preceding situation' (137).

In the context of Poe's work (itself hugely influential on Doyle), this idea of the 'return to the beginning' provides a fertile ground upon which students can generate and experiment with readings of the tales that think about narrative form in political terms. What does it mean to read 'The Murders in the Rue Morgue' as a narrative not about solving a murder mystery but about the process of restoring private property (even an orangutan!) to its owner? Are 'The Mystery of Marie Rogêt' and 'The Purloined Letter' more interested in *suppressing* the public circulation of scandalous stories than in telling them? And what of that strange anti-detective story, 'The Man of the Crowd', in which the syntax of the tale unravels, the return to the beginning is never accomplished, and the *fabula* is promised but never given? In Moretti's terms, my aim in provoking such questions is to engage both structural *and* functional analyses. That is to say, we need to combine a thoroughgoing analysis of the internal narrative structure of the fiction with an analysis of its function within a wider social system. We need to look inwardly and outwardly at the same time, and as a way of reading this can feel alien and arduous.

The good news is that many advanced undergraduate students are to some extent already accustomed to the discomfort of such a diplopic perspective, even if they have not identified it explicitly. Indeed, it seems sometimes that self-conscious reflection on method, rather than the critical practice itself, is the cause of intellectual anxiety and doubt. After all, the structural and functional analyses of literary texts are in a sense the very foundation of undergraduate English, though they tend sometimes to be addressed in isolation from one another, a problem reflected in the curricula at many institutions, where practices of 'close reading' and 'reading in context' are addressed early in the programme but in separate places. The importance of Moretti's intervention in this regard is more than the insistence that one is meaningless without the other. It is also that they must be undertaken simultaneously and dialectically, each testing the other. To do otherwise, he declares, is to render our work entirely futile: 'At this point, it would be more logical and more honest to take up another profession' (131).

In practice, this kind of critical work makes considerable demands on the time and attention of both scholar and student. To answer satisfactorily a question about the function of Poe's tales there must be some rudimentary knowledge about the periodical print culture of the antebellum United States, as well as some awareness of the ideological currents of the time, as they intersected with questions of class, gender and race. Some students will arrive with knowledge of this sort gained from other parts of their programme, and some orientation can be provided through lectures and directed reading. The reward for strenuous research, however, is worth the effort if history is saved from its status as 'background' to literary texts, and becomes instead a dynamic component of our method as readers. Then we can at last ask not only what genre fiction means, but also what kind of function its common narratological structures perform in the social world of its circulation.

## Hardboiled Entanglement

Moretti's analysis of the ideological functioning of classic detective fiction can be intimidating for undergraduate students in its polemical force and density, while more experienced scholars might find it somewhat bombastic in its full-throated denunciation of mass culture as the monolithic culture of amnesia. Students wonder what more there can be left to say about a form that seems so inherently conservative. The rest of my module, however, responds to the complex after-history of classic detective stories in the twentieth and twenty-first centuries, when it was taken up, inverted, subverted, assimilated, broken down, travestied and parodied by a range of subgenres of what we now call crime fiction. On turning to the hardboiled fiction of the 1920s, 1930s and 1940s, it is immediately apparent that our analysis of the structure and function of crime stories requires revision in ways that Moretti's conclusions cannot necessarily help us with, though his methodology can.

A well-known anecdote about Raymond Chandler serves as a route into our concerns here. Chandler's first novel, *The Big Sleep* (1939), was adapted into a feature film directed by Howard Hawks and released in 1946. During the process of adaptation, Hawks and his screenwriter, William Faulkner, became confused about the novel's plot. Who, they wondered, was responsible for the second of the many mysterious deaths in the novel, that of Owen Taylor, the Sternwoods' chauffeur? Their confusion was understandable. *The Big Sleep*'s labyrinthine plot is a long way from the cut-and-dried cases of Dupin or Holmes. Six killings take place in the course of Marlowe's quest to find the missing person, Rusty Reagan, and each is committed by a different character. In four of those cases, the killer is also dead by the end of the book. To cap it off, Marlowe's discovery at the conclusion is that Reagan isn't just missing—he is dead too, murdered before the events of the investigation even began. Hawks and Faulkner wired Chandler for clarification on the murder of Owen Taylor. Chandler replied to say that he had given the matter much thought, but that he had no idea who killed the chauffeur.[4]

Many students find this story not only amusing, but also rather shocking. With some effort, it is in fact possible to determine the likely killer of Owen Taylor using the internal evidence provided by the novel (the probable culprit—a faceless grifter named Joe Brody). Nevertheless, can it be possible that an author of Chandler's stature, credited along with Hammett with having reinvented crime fiction, had so little understanding of his own narrative? Isn't the revelation of the *fabula* at the end of the story supposed to be compulsory, providing the reader with assurance of the social world's ultimate transparency? This anecdote serves to prise open new approaches to crime fiction, with the realization that at certain stages in its evolution, the formal arrangement of narrative became unruly or ungovernable, unamenable to the kind of authority exerted by Dupin or Holmes in their efforts to reinstate order and 'return to the beginning'.

The chauffeur problem in *The Big Sleep* is symptomatic of that disorientating sense of *entanglement* that pervades classic hardboiled fiction and finds its apotheosis in Chandler's work. While for Holmes and Dupin, the process of mastering the mystery requires a disciplined, even fastidious maintenance of distance and therefore objectivity from the case, Chandler's Marlowe is beaten, drugged and seduced en route to the novel's ending. He is forever waking up in strange places, and blundering into crime scenes either too late or too early. In Poe's 'The Purloined Letter', Dupin discourses on a game in which players must find a word selected by their opponent on a chart. 'The most adept', he claims, 'select such words as stretch, in large characters, across the length of the chart' (Poe 1986: 345). Marlowe, correspondingly, is always in such close proximity to the mystery as it unfolds that he is never able to see it whole. The tracing of such claustrophobic entanglements during teaching is a productive activity that can lead in a number of different directions. Some students find the experience of disorientation within Chandler's work an important component in producing certain distinctive kinds of narrative pleasure, that renounce or bracket the desire for stability and order to be restored. We sometimes discuss *why* it is that Chandler produced narrative in this shape, and consider his own alcoholism in parallel to Marlowe's drinking, which punctuates the course of the fiction to the extent that it sometimes forms the most consistently reliable marker of its temporality. Alternatively, we might think about entanglement as one effect of Chandler's tendency in writing novels to recycle and stitch together narrative parts lifted from his earlier pulp stories, a process he described as 'cannibalizing' his work, and which leads on to material questions about the economics of cultural labour.[5] In this regard, Erin Smith's excellent study, *Hardboiled: Working Class Readers and Pulp Magazines*, makes some provocative claims about the disjointed and fragmentary nature of much hardboiled fiction, for instance arguing that its narrative structure rehearses the Taylorized work patterns of its blue collar readers (Smith 2000: 81–84). Whatever the merits of this argument, which can be evaluated in seminars, my goal here is once again to encourage students to think structurally and functionally at the same time, by posing narrative questions within a historical frame.

Eventually, *The Big Sleep* does stage its own return to the beginning. Rusty Reagan, the missing person whom Marlowe was hired to find, was dead all along, killed before the private eye had ever even appeared on the scene. Carmen Sternwood had shot him at the site of her family's wealth—an oilfield further down the hill from their mansion—where his body decayed in the sump. It takes Marlowe to confront her at this same place, and for her to attempt to kill him like she did Reagan, for him to be able to straighten out this narrative thread. Chandler's choice of the oil sump as primal source for his narrative, the place from which the Sternwoods gain their fortune as well as where they bury their victims, plunges us into the historical imaginary of Los Angeles itself, as surely as it directs culpability for the wrongdoings of the novel away from the appropriation of natural resources towards female sexual caprice. Oil, before the movie industry and before aeronautical manufacture, was Los Angeles' first big business, and it is where Chandler was employed before becoming a pulp writer in the 1930s. The return to the beginning, then, is not to some stable grounds for social power, as in Moretti's formulation, but rather to the violent, unstable and fluid territory of primitive accumulation in the United States, a stinking swamp that contains dead bodies as well as future capital. Despite the symbolic freight carried by the oil wells, however, it is in Carmen's jealous and predatory sexuality that Marlowe recognizes the generator for the novel's sequence of evil, claiming that Carmen kills in retribution for men's refusal of her advances. The ambivalence of *The Big Sleep*'s conclusion, which gestures symbolically to a narrative of the development of class and capitalism in Los Angeles only to turn to a misogynist stereotype for the plot's engine, reveals something of the tensions evident in Chandler's own ideology as it takes narrative form in the crime fiction genre. These tensions are productive areas for discussion. How can a narrative be simultaneously so sophisticated and yet so reductively crass? Satisfactory answers to this question can only be proposed in the context of the novel's relationship to the history of the hardboiled genre, with its tradition of the *femme fatale* sitting alongside its appeal to working-class male readers at a time of economic crisis.

If the social order in *The Big Sleep* is restored, we must recognize that it is already rotten, like Reagan's body, and structured by gross inequalities. Carmen goes unpunished, as does the gangster boss, Eddie Mars. In his closing address to the dead Reagan, Marlowe laments, 'you just slept the big sleep, not caring about the nastiness of how you died or where you fell. Me, I was part of the nastiness now' (Chandler 1995: 764). With this bald statement, he articulates a conflicted and compromised position far from the aloof, aristocratic detective of the classic whodunit, but also at a distance from the working-class readers who bought *The Black Mask* magazine in the Depression-era, where he published his first stories. Marlowe has made his accommodations with power, folding his critique of contemporary Los Angeles into an admission of hopeless complicity with it.

## POSITIVE ENTANGLEMENT IN CONTEMPORARY CRIME NARRATIVES

Having passed through the era of classic hardboiled fiction with the work of Hammett and Chandler, in the latter part of the module we turn to post-war authors who have in various ways rewritten the genre against its ideological grain, challenging the construction of that white, masculine subjectivity we have already observed in *The Big Sleep*. Two novels in particular, Sara Paretsky's *Blood Shot* (1988, published in the UK as *Toxic Shock*) and Attica Locke's *Black Water Rising* (2008) offer direct responses to the narratological challenges laid down by Marlowe's admission of despairing complicity. Both novels evoke the problem of hardboiled entanglement, but attempt to transform it into a positive structure that might serve as a foundation for social change in the future. They have much in common, for example their settings in large industrial US cities in the 1980s (Houston and Chicago respectively), their focus on corporate corruption and its responsibility for social inequalities, and the use of environmental pollution as a synecdochic figure for wider social harms. For our purposes here, however, the most important ground they share is a rejection of classic hardboiled fiction's insistence on the violent autonomy of the white male protagonist. Rather, their female (Paretsky) and black (Locke) protagonists are shown to be deeply embedded in their respective communities, and indeed find in those communities reserves upon which they draw in order to fight corporate criminality.

The reversal of the conventional valence for hardboiled entanglement is best introduced by Paretsky's memoir, *Writing in an Age of Silence*, in which she explicitly addresses the ways in which she conceives the politics of inheriting the genre. She places it within a much longer cultural history in North America, whereby the lone figure of rugged individualism is valorized in his rejection of society and pursuit of private illumination and self-sufficiency. It is a cultural myth, she explains, that began with Roger Williams' departure from the Massachusetts Bay Colony for Rhode Island, and is perpetuated in classic US fiction such as James Fenimore Cooper's Leatherstocking trilogy. Eventually, *Black Mask*'s advent in the 1920s 'started a formal vehicle for the bringing of this loner hero to the American people' (Paretsky 2007: 92) in ways exemplified by the work of Hammett and Race Williams. The evolution of the hardboiled detective hero from the dual sources of the frontier myth and the British gentleman sleuth is a familiar enough critical orthodoxy, but in a contemporary neoliberal context Paretsky sees the ideology of self-reliance function more perniciously in the fetishization of private property and private space by the wealthy, who have 'retreated into their own isolation, a place where they try to use money and power as a shield between themselves and the rest of the world' (99). Paretsky appropriates the conventions of the hardboiled genre in order to represent the negativity of such isolation, and thus reconfigures entanglement as necessary social truth:

> The powerful believe their position insulates them from everything but fulfilling their own desires. It is part of the function of the detective novel to show that no one is isolated—murder occurs and forces a confrontation with the rest of society.
>
> In a sense, the villains of the private eye novel are the Roger Williamses of the corporate world—what they want counts far more with them than what the good of the community as a whole demands. And in a funny way, the private eye, or at least *my* private eye, has moved out of the loner Natty Bumpo tradition and into the community. (100)

With that term 'function' we are returned to Moretti's distinction between the structural and functional analysis of classic detective fiction, but now it is the author herself who is addressing the politics of form. With Paretsky we enter a new era of detective fiction as explicitly and consciously political, espousing a social-democratic perspective on the need for social justice, and exposing the harms created by unrestrained corporate capitalism.

In a pedagogical context, Paretsky's radical reappropriation and inversion of generic codes create an occasion upon which to re-evaluate what genre really is. The weakest conceptualizations of genre tend to be those that see it as a static and reified set of conventions, but in reading Paretsky students are obliged to consider how a variation in the *angle* of entry into a genre can loosen it from its previous frame and allow an author to change its function.[6] The most visible reversal, and the one students are most likely to seize upon, is the change of gender from male to female detective. The easy labelling of Paretsky's work as feminist fiction on this basis, however, threatens to obscure the broader extent of her genre ambitions. In *Toxic Shock*, V. I. Warshawski is embedded in her community in a way that crosses race and class lines too. She commences the narrative, for example, at a college basketball team reunion, the multiracial team formed 'when race fights were a daily disruption in hall and locker room' (Paretsky 1990: 14). Discussion in seminars can quickly uncover the other senses in which the novel binds its protagonist to various social networks, detailing her warm relationships with old friends, her place in the Polish community of Chicago's south side, and her romantic liaisons. A more difficult question to pose, however, is about how such revisions sit alongside those narrative conventions that Paretsky has chosen to retain from the genre's past—the missing person case that turns into a murder case, the implication of respectable society with the criminal underworld and so on. How are we to describe the jarring effect of such juxtapositions of convention and novelty? Does Paretsky stage some kind of resolution between the two?

In my own view, the closest Paretsky comes to resolving the tension between her socially integrated, community-minded private eye and the alienating effects of corporate capitalism is through her deployment of environmental pollution and urban decay as major tropes. In *Toxic Shock*, Humbolt Chemical is revealed to have poisoned its employees through chemical by-products and conspired to smother compensation claims. In a more nebulous and unspecified sense, however, the company is implicated with the neglect of Chicago's South Side and the creation of a polluted marsh, Dead Stick Pond, where one body is discovered and V. I. Warshawski nearly meets her own end. The pond is a gothic, post-industrial space, which 'used to be a great feeding area for migrating birds. Now the water was a dull black, with stark tree stumps poking surreal fingers through its surface. Fish having been returning to the Calumet River and its tributaries since the introduction of the Clean Water Act, but the ones that make their way into the pond show up with massive tumors and rotted fins' (103–104). This location serves as the double of the Sternwood's oil sump in the *Big Sleep*, but in this case the space is a public one, and its metaphorical freight as a toxic wasteland at the topographical heart of the South Side takes the effects of crime into the realm of public health. In this way, by dragging the traditionally private crimes of the hardboiled novel into the public and making them visible, Paretsky is able to channel the impulses of social-democratic protest into the genre.

As *Writing in an Age of Silence* makes very clear, Paretsky's participation in the protest movements of the late 1960s had a lasting influence on her approach to crime fiction, and her conviction that 'fiction mustn't stay too far from the issues of voice, power, and lives of people who lack both' (Paretsky 2007: 47). In a comparable way, Locke's *Black Water Rising* also looks back to the protests of that period from the vantage point of the 1980s, the moment at which it is set. The novel's protagonist, Jay Porter, is a small-time lawyer who was involved with the Black Panther Party. As a young man he had been narrowly acquitted from a charge of conspiring to commit the murder of an agent of the federal government, a paid FBI informant who had infiltrated the party under the COINTELPRO programme. In the present of the novel, as Jay has entered into a respectable if precarious black middle class, he fears being dragged back into entanglement with a racist police force, and therefore decides not to report a possible murder and sexual assault after pulling a woman from the bayou one evening. In this sense, a 'return to the beginning…to reinstate some previous situation' is the thing that Jay fears the most, representing as it does the possibility of being jailed again, of losing his hard-won middle-class status, and even of risking the achievements of the Civil Rights movement. Like Paretsky, however, Locke seems to understand the alienation and isolation of American middle-class individuals under Reaganite neoliberalism in the 1980s as precisely the problem to be overcome by her protagonist, through a return to the spirit of social solidarity forged by the protest movement a generation earlier. Jay's victory at the end of *Black Water Rising* is to accept his entanglement with the black community in Houston, and to assume a visible, audible position in that society as a champion of the underprivileged in their cases against powerful corporations. Like Warshawski in *Toxic Shock*, Jay concludes the novel with a resolution to begin the work of launching legal action against unaccountable corporate power, in this case a major oil company. In both cases there appears little assurance of success, but it is the process of *re-engagement* between individual, community and corporation in the public sphere that is emphasized. 'What are you trying to prove here, Jay?' asks one character in the final pages, 'I mean, think about who you're taking on. This thing is much bigger than you.' He replies, 'it doesn't matter, not really. It only matters that I remember to speak up' (Locke 2009: 424).

As in *Toxic Shock*, much of the work done in suggesting a resolution to the tensions between the public and the private that were set up in rewriting the genre against the grain, is undertaken not at the level of narrative, which fails after all to bring its corporate criminals to justice, but rather at the level of metaphor, allegory and the representation of environmental degradation. The 'black water' of the title refers on one hand to the oil secretly stockpiled in an old salt mine underneath a deserted town in Texas, concealed in order to drive up its price. This oil now rises up through the ground, 'coming up around the foundation of the house, black, like raw sewage' (316), causing the area's community to collapse. On the other hand it alludes to the repressed histories of racism and black struggle from which trouble re-emerges into the present, allegorized by the white woman that Jay hauls from the dark waters of the bayou in the first chapter of the narrative. The relationship between these two allegorical registers presents an interesting conundrum for students to reflect on, asking them as it does to search for connections between race, oil and capital in the United States. We read alongside the novel Ta Nehisi Coates' essay 'Letter to my Son' (2015), which uses a similar metaphorical confluence. Coates traces the deep history of racist policing in the United States back to the institution of slavery, arguing that the enslaved 'were not bricks in your road, and their lives were not chapters in your redemptive history. They were people turned to fuel for the American machine' (Coates 2015). In *Black Water Rising*, once Jay has touched the oil he finds it to be 'loose, but thick, like melted gelatin. It slips and slides between his fingertips...coats his skin completely, covering his pores, clinging like a parasite that has found an unsuspecting host' (Locke 2009: 318). For Locke, race and capital are fluid, unwelcome entities that can be made visible but remain ungraspable. They are external to the human but colour it. They remind us of the repressed stories we have been trying to forget, but which remain untellable.

It is with some surprise, then, that students choosing an option to study American crime fiction discover that they are immersed in a narrative genre they encountered elsewhere in their literary studies, the Gothic, with its distinctive tropes of buried secrets, deserted ruined spaces and the surfacing of unwelcome visitors. It is not so difficult, once generic lenses have been readjusted, to discern in the Gothic return of the repressed something like the return to the beginning that Moretti observed in classic whodunits. For him, the arrangement of *fabula* and *sjuzhet* facilitated a form of historical amnesia, by which the fictional world was autonomous and capable of correcting itself when unbalanced by crime. 'Because the crime is presented in the form of a mystery, society is absolved from the start: the solution of the mystery proves its innocence' (Moretti 2005: 145). In the Gothic crime narratives of Paretsky and Locke, by contrast, haunted spaces and repressed stories are actively conjured, wounds reopened, precisely so that they may not be forgotten. Indeed, Locke makes this objective explicit enough in the 'personal note' she appended to the paperback edition of the novel, claiming that 'in the early Reagan era, the whole country was caught up in a collective fit of amnesia over the wounds and hurt feelings of the 1960s and 70s' (Locke n.d.). In order to comprehend the way that the changing narrative structures of contemporary crime fiction relate to their changing function, students need to think about what happened in that early Reagan era to have brought about a collective fit of amnesia, and what might have been forgotten. They need to think, in other words, about the era of neoliberal economics heralded by the assent of Reagan in the USA and Thatcher in the UK, and about the promise that a free market could satisfy the demands of citizens in ways that state intervention couldn't. Why might it be in the interests of government and corporations for us to forget about the forms of collectivity, community and solidarity that structured the protests of the late 1960s and early 1970s in the United States? The demand to historicize their own contemporary moment is one of the most difficult things I ask of my students, but it is also the most necessary.

## Notes

1. On Golden Age detective fiction, see Symons (1972: 101–131).
2. This distinction between *fabula* and *sjuzhet* is commonly traced back to Viktor Shklovsky's essay on *Tristram Shandy* in *O teorii proza* (*The Theory of Prose*, 1925), and Boris Tomashevsky's essay 'Tematika' (Thematics) in *Teoriya literatury* (*Theory of Literature*, 1925). For English translations, see Shklovsky (1991: 147–170), Tomashevsky (1965). On Russian Formalist use of the *fabula–sjuzhet* distinction more generally, see Victor Erlich's classic account of the movement, Erlich (1965: 240–242).
3. For an overview of Russian Formalist writing on literary evolution, see Streidter (1989: 11–82).
4. Chandler refers to this event in his letter to Jamie Hamilton on 21 March 1949. Chandler (2000: 105).
5. On Chandler's practice of 'cannibalizing' his stories for his novels, see Hiney (1997: 103–104).
6. I am adapting this idea of 'angle of entry' from Sara Ahmed's theorization of happiness. Ahmed (2007–2008: 125).

## Works Cited

Ahmed, Sarah. 2008. Multiculturalism and the Promise of Happiness. *New Formations* 63 (Winter 2007–2008): 121–137.
Brooks, Peter. 1984. *Reading for the Plot: Design and Intention in Narrative.* Oxford: Oxford University Press.
Chandler, Raymond. 1995. *Stories and Early Novels.* Edited by F. MacShane. New York: Library of America.
———. 2000. *The Raymond Chandler Papers: Selected Letters and Non-Fiction 1909–1959.* Edited by T. Hiney and F. MacShane. London: Hamish Hamilton.
Coates, Ta Nehisi. 2015. Letter to My Son. *The Atlantic.* Accessed December 19, 2016. http://www.theatlantic.com/politics/archive/2015/07/tanehisi-coates-between-the-world-and-me/397619/
Erlich, Victor. 1965. *Russian Formalism: History—Doctrine.* 2nd Rev. ed. London: Mouton.
Hiney, Tom. 1997. *Raymond Chandler: A Biography.* London: Chatto.
Locke, Attica. 2009. *Black Water Rising.* London: Serpent.
———. n.d. A Personal Note. Accessed December 19, 2016. http://www.atticalocke.com/news/personalnote.html
Moretti, Franco. 2005. *Signs Taken for Wonders: On the Sociology of Literary Forms.* London: Verso.
Paretsky, Sara. 1990. *Toxic Shock.* Harmondsworth: Penguin.
———. 2007. *Writing in an Age of Silence.* London: Verso.
Poe, Edgar A. 1986. *The Fall of the House of Usher and Other Writings.* Edited by David Galloway. Harmondsworth: Penguin.
Shklovsky, Viktor. 1991. *Theory of Prose.* Translated by Benjamin Sher. Elmwood Park, IL: Dalkey Archive.
Smith, Erin A. 2000. *Hard-Boiled: Working Class Readers and Pulp Magazines.* Philadelphia: Temple University Press.
Streidter, Jurij. 1989. *Literary Structure, Evolution and Value: Russian Formalism and Czech Structuralism Reconsidered.* Cambridge, MA: Harvard University Press.
Symons, Julian. 1972. *Bloody Murder: From the Detective Story to the Crime Novel.* London: Faber.
Todorov, Tzvetan. 1977. *The Poetics of Prose.* Translated by Richard Howard. Ithaca: Cornell University Press.
Tomashevsky, Boris. 1965. Thematics. In *Russian Formalist Criticism*, ed. L.T. Lemon and M.J. Reis, 66–78. Lincoln: University of Nebraska Press.

CHAPTER 7

# Teaching Historical Fiction: Hilary Mantel and the Protestant Reformation

*Mark Eaton*

> *Beneath every history, another history.*
> —Hilary Mantel, Wolf Hall (2009: 55)

In a famous essay, 'The Hedgehog and the Fox', Isaiah Berlin writes that Leo Tolstoy was troubled by the difficulties that confront all historical novelists: 'he could not justify to himself the apparently arbitrary selection of material, and the no less arbitrary distribution of emphasis, to which all historical writing seemed to be doomed' (Berlin 2000: 447). Historians typically select one aspect of the material, say the political or the economic, 'and represent it as primary, as the efficient cause of social change', while neglecting other causes of social change, which leads Berlin to ask a pointed question: 'but then, what of religion, what of "spiritual" factors, and the many other aspects—a literally countless multiplicity—with which all events are endowed?' (447). By restricting themselves to the political or economic factors of social change, historians provide at best an incomplete picture of any given period, and at worst, as Tolstoy himself claimed, 'perhaps only 0.001 per cent of the elements which actually constitute the real

---

M. Eaton (✉)
Azusa Pacific University, Azusa, CA, USA

© The Author(s) 2018
R. Jacobs (ed.), *Teaching Narrative*, Teaching the New English,
https://doi.org/10.1007/978-3-319-71829-3_7

history of peoples' (447). Notwithstanding such hyperbole, Berlin grants Tolstoy his main point:

> History, as it is normally written, usually represents 'political'—public—events as the most important, while spiritual—'inner'—events are largely forgotten; yet prima facie it is they—the 'inner' events—that are the most real, the most immediate experience of human beings; they, and only they, are what life, in the last analysis, is made of. (447)

According to Berlin, no one has ever surpassed the Russian novelist in capturing what we might call the inner life of history, which Berlin elegantly describes as 'the inner and outer texture and "feel" of a look, a thought, a pang of sentiment, no less than of a specific situation, of an entire period, of the lives of individuals, families, communities, entire nations' (466).

One contemporary writer who arguably comes close to Tolstoy in capturing this texture of history is Hilary Mantel. In the first two novels of a projected trilogy about Henry VIII, *Wolf Hall* (2009) and *Bring Up the Bodies* (2012), Mantel attends to the well-known events of Tudor history by focalizing her narrative through the perspective of a compelling protagonist, Thomas Cromwell, King Henry VIII's privy counselor. Using a narrative technique that Henry James, an undisputed Master of third-person limited-omniscient narration, called 'central consciousness', Mantel draws readers into the lived experience of history through Cromwell's canny perspective on events. In her hands, Thomas Cromwell comes across as a slightly different historical figure than the man we thought we knew from previous portrayals of him.[1] Indeed, Cromwell emerges as nothing less than an unabashed pragmatist who negotiates Henry VIII's imperious manner and impetuous decision-making with considerable political acumen: 'He never spares himself in the king's service; he knows his worth and merits and makes sure of his reward: offices, perquisites and title deeds, manor houses and farms. He has a way of getting his way' (Mantel 2012: 6).

The greatest challenge for the historical novelist is to create suspense even when readers already know the outcome in advance. Mantel intuits that the best way to do this is to transport her readers directly into the action as it unfolds—experiencing, feeling and wondering along with her characters how things will turn out in the end. 'When she is writing historical fiction', writes Larissa MacFarquhar in a profile of Hilary Mantel in

*The New Yorker*, 'she knows what will happen and can do nothing about it, but she must try to imagine the events as if the outcome were not yet fixed, from the perspective of the characters, who are moving forward in ignorance. This is not just an emotional business of entering the characters' point of view; it is also a matter of remembering that at every point things could have been different' (MacFarquhar 2012). By installing Cromwell as the narrative's central consciousness, Mantel meets the basic challenge of creating suspense with aplomb, for in serving a mercurial king, or in outmaneuvering his rivals, Cromwell knows full well that every day could be his last: 'Every day Master Secretary deals with grandees who, if they could, would destroy him with one vindictive swipe, as if he were a fly' (Mantel 2012: 6). With Cromwell, readers can only wonder what's coming down the pike:

> His inner voice mocks him now: you thought you were going to get a holiday at Wolf Hall. You thought there would be nothing to do here except the usual business, war and peace, famine, traitorous connivance; a failing harvest, a stubborn populace; plague ravishing London, and the king losing his shirt at cards. You were prepared for that.
> At the edge of his inner vision, behind his closed eyes, he senses something in the act of becoming. It will arrive with morning light; something shifting and breathing, its form disguised in a copse or grove. (26)

War and peace: surely Mantel pays homage here to a celebrated predecessor in the genre. What is remarkable about this passage, though, is the way the narrator turns inward to represent not just the outer, but also the inner texture of history that Tolstoy tried to capture in his fiction, too.

This chapter proposes to analyze Hilary Mantel's Wolf Hall Trilogy as a case study for what historical fiction can contribute to our understanding of history. In particular, I will attend to what her novels reveal about the complex processes of historical and religious change that occurred during the Protestant Reformation, which marked its 500th anniversary in late 2017. Guided by my experience teaching Mantel's fiction in courses on contemporary British fiction and historical fiction at a large regional university in the USA, I want to examine the ways that literature offers a unique perspective on major historical developments in religion and theology, especially by giving readers an opportunity to encounter, and indeed inhabit, religious interiority. By showing how new religious ideas and sensibilities develop, how they come into conflict with older viewpoints, and how they are by turns absorbed, adopted, challenged, resisted or rejected, Mantel discloses how religion is subject to the same historical contingencies as anything else. Far from being timeless and unchanging, it is contextual and more often than not syncretistic.

These novels also offer students one example of how a writer can take even a period as thoroughly documented as the Tudor dynasty, or a movement as widely studied as the Protestant Reformation, and somehow defamiliarize them, make them seem fresh, or new. She does this in part by rendering central episodes in early modern history from a more intimate point of view. Like Tolstoy, Mantel is less interested in the politics of the period than in what it felt like to live through it. As such, history becomes more than simply the 'background' to historical fiction; rather, it becomes part of the very method of historical fiction. In turn, students are invited to reflect on their own methods of reading and interpreting literature. Reading historical fiction necessarily involves us in multiple temporalities: the time period when the work is set, when it was written and when we are reading it. Students may be led to reconsider their own beliefs, whether or not they are religious, in light of an earlier period of momentous historical change.

## How to Do Things with Historical Documents

What better way to begin a course on historical fiction than by defining the genre and tracing its genealogy? In a highly successful massive online open course (MOOC) available through Coursera called 'Plagues, Witches, and War: The Worlds of Historical Fiction', the literary scholar Bruce Holsinger, a historical novelist himself, defines the genre this way: 'Historical fiction is a genre of imaginative narratives set in the past, whose authors make a deliberate effort to convey chronologically remote settings, cultures and personages with accuracy, plausibility, and depth' (Holsinger 2013). Borrowing Holsinger's working definition, I lead students in a discussion of how this definition distinguishes historical fiction from history. The important thing for students to remember is that historical fiction is a hybrid genre, poised somewhere between the presumed fidelity to facts of historical writing and the imaginative license given to literary fiction. Writers of nonfiction use their imaginations, of course, but they typically do not invent conversations, personages or events that are not part of the historical record. Writers of historical fiction, on the other hand, often embellish, flesh out and fill in elements of the distant past that may not be fully known or documented in the extant historical archives. Of course, writers are not free to do whatever they want with their historical materials. While they may self-consciously fictionalize historical events, they are still under a contract of sorts with readers to convey those events accurately. For readers bring their own expectations to the genre, as MacFarquhar points out, and while some readers grant the writers of historical fiction considerable freedom, other readers are more scrupulous about fidelity to known facts: 'To some, if it is fiction, anything is permitted. To others, wanton invention when facts are to be found, or, worse, contradiction of well-known facts is a horror: a violation of an implicit contract with the reader, and a betrayal of the people written about. Ironically, it is when those stricter standards of truth are applied that historical fiction looks most like lying' (MacFarquhar 2012). Situated as it is in the liminal space between fiction and nonfiction, the genre of historical fiction depends upon the very distinction that it refuses—or even violates. From the outset of the course, students have already grasped this paradox simply by discussing Holsinger's helpful definition.

To fully appreciate how fiction at once depends upon and blurs the distinction between fiction and nonfiction, students must see this paradox at work in Mantel's fiction. To that end, I ask them to consider what Mantel does with the events surrounding Anne Boleyn's execution on May 19, 1536 in *Bring Up the Bodies*, the second volume in the trilogy. The day before she was to be executed, William Kingston, the Constable of the Tower where the queen was being held, wrote the following in a letter to Thomas Cromwell:

> This morning she sent for me, that I might be with her at such time as she received the good Lord, to the intent I should hear her speak as touching her innocency [*sic*] alway[s] to be clear. And in the writing of this she sent for me, and at my coming she said, 'Mr. Kingston, I hear I shall not die afore noon, and I am very sorry therefore, for I thought to be dead by this time and past my pain.' I told her it should be no pain, it was so little. And then she said, 'I heard say the executioner was very good, and I have a little neck', and then put her hands about it, laughing heartily. I have seen many men and also women executed, and that they have been in great sorrow, and to my knowledge this lady has much joy in death. Sir, her almoner is continually with her, and had been since two o'clock after midnight. (Burnet 1865: 328)

Mantel does not reproduce the letter verbatim in *Bring Up the Bodies*; rather, she reworks details from this letter into two separate scenes. In the first scene, Thomas Cromwell pays a visit to Anne Boleyn in prison. There is a sense of foreboding about the encounter: 'He feels himself on the edge of something unwelcome: superfluous knowledge, useless information' (Mantel 2009: 345). What Cromwell wants is some kind of confession. 'She is not innocent', he declares, 'she can only mimic innocence' (345). The interrogator presumes guilt even without the confession he seeks, and she herself reads the hopelessness of her cause in his face: 'She has seen his face change. She steps back, puts her hand around her throat. Like a strangler she closes them around her own flesh. "I have only a little neck", she says. "It will be the work of the moment"' (345).

Alert students will observe that Mantel has made several changes to the archival source. Whereas the original source was a letter from the constable to Cromwell, Mantel puts Cromwell himself in the Tower when Anne Boleyn delivers her lines, lending the scene greater immediacy. Of course, even if had she represented the scene more accurately, with the constable William Kingston being summoned to the Tower and then witnessing the Queen's surprising gesture, Mantel would still have to recreate a scene that had only been reported secondhand in the source. Yet Mantel's reworking of the source goes beyond replacing the constable with her protagonist, Cromwell, as the witness to Anne Boleyn's gesture. For the author also covers herself from the charge of historical inaccuracy by showing that the constable had witnessed the queen saying more or less the same thing to him previously: 'Kingston hurries out to meet him. He wants to talk. "She keeps doing that, her hands around her neck and laughing." His honest jailer's face is dismayed. "I cannot see that is any occasion for laughter"' (Mantel 2009: 345). Mantel invents this encounter between Boleyn and Cromwell, yet she relies on Kingston's account of an actual encounter with Anne Boleyn in the Tower, and we know that Cromwell also visited the Queen in prison, where he may well have heard a similar remark. By pointing out Mantel's subtle changes to the archival source, and by engaging students in a wide-ranging discussion of the implications of those changes, I help them understand how difficult the job of the historical novelist can be. Fidelity to the historical record seems more straightforward than it really is in practice, I think. Relying on Kingston's letter for the details surrounding this scene, Mantel nonetheless changes certain aspects of her astonishingly evocative historical source for even greater dramatic effect. Students will better appreciate both the possibilities and the potential pitfalls of this process if they have an opportunity to compare Mantel's fictional representation with her archival source.

The second scene also borrows details from Kingston's letter. In this scene, again related to us from Cromwell's perspective through a third-person limited-omniscient narrator, Cromwell laments that Anne Boleyn has got the date of her execution mixed up:

> Anne, he is sorry to learn, has mistaken the day of her death, rising at 2 a.m. to pray on the morning of May 18, sending for her almoner and for Cranmer to come to her at dawn so she can purge herself of her sins. No one seems to have told her that Kingston comes without fail at dawn on the morning of an execution, to warn the dying person to be ready. She is not familiar with the protocol, and why should she be? (Mantel 2009: 392)

Taking as her starting point Boleyn's confusion about the date of her execution—in fact she was executed the following day, May 19—Mantel includes the details related in Kingston's letter that her almoner was summoned to the Tower at 2:00 a.m. the morning she supposed she would die. Mantel describes the understandable guilt that a jailor might well have felt from such a mistake:

> Still, the constable is sorry for her misapprehension; especially since her mistake ran on, late into the morning. The situation is a great strain on both himself and his wife. Instead of being glad of another dawn, he reports, Anne had cried, and she said she was sorry not to die that day; she wishes she were past her pain. She knew about the friend executioner and, 'I told her', Kingston says, 'it shall be no pain, it is so subtle.' But once again, Kingston says, she closed her fingers around her throat. She had taken the Eucharist, declaring on the body of God her innocence. (392)

Again, Boleyn professes her innocence of the charges against her: adultery, incest and treason. As if unable to resist adding her own little narrative flourish to the scene, however, Mantel has the constable speculate that Anne Boleyn surely would not have insisted on her innocence, much less partaken of the elements in the Eucharist, if she were actually guilty of the alleged crimes:

> Which surely she would not do, Kingston says, if she were guilty?
> She laments the men who are gone.
> She makes jokes, saying that she will be known hereafter as Anne the Headless, Anne sans Tete. (392)

Perhaps Mantel discovered Anne Boleyn's remark that she would henceforth be known as headless Anne elsewhere; more likely, this is an embellishment attesting to her incongruous sense of humor while facing almost certain death. 'If I were to distort something just to make it more convenient or dramatic', Mantel once declared, 'I would feel I'd failed as a writer. If you understand what you're talking about, you should be drawing the drama out of real life, not putting it there, like icing on a cake' (MacFarquhar 2012). Mantel draws the drama out of real life, while also adding layers of psychological complexity, not least to the victim. The queen's morbid sense of humor is part of the historical record, to be sure, but it is likewise icing on a cake. The author manages to find dark comedy in the execution of a queen, no less, even as she foregrounds the fraught experiences of doubt and fear, guilt and innocence for all those involved. By discussing the play of emotions in these scenes, while also parsing the subtle shifts in point of view and character interactions that Mantel has brought to her otherwise faithful representation of Anne Boleyn's execution, my students not only come to see how a skillful historical novelist such as Hilary Mantel can have her cake and eat it too; they also develop their interpretive skills by practicing what we might call historical formalism, which is formalist and contextual at once. Historical fiction lends itself particularly well to a method of close reading that attends to minute details in the literary text, while also considering what that text is doing with historical contexts.

In his important work on the genre, *The Historical Novel* (1937), first published in English in 1962, Georg Lukács wrote that 'historical faithfulness' was best achieved not by scrupulously following every last detail of the historical record but by remaining true 'to the authenticity of the historical psychology of his characters, the genuine *hic et nunc* (here and now) of their inner lives and behavior' (Lukács 1983: 59–60). For Lukács, not Tolstoy but Sir Walter Scott is the unsurpassed exemplar of historical fiction. While acknowledging that Scott's fiction can be melodramatic at times, Lukács argues that it shows how individuals can act passionately, against their own self-interest or even 'against their individual psychology', thus revealing 'the historical necessity of a concrete situation', which 'has its roots in the real social and economic basis of popular life' (59–60). Historical necessity is obviously an important concept for Lukács. It appears to mean something like historical contingency, the way in which history depends on a number of interrelated social and individual forces. While individuals are free to make choices and exercise human agency, their actions are constrained by, or at least contingent upon, the historical necessity of a concrete situation. 'Measured against this authentic reproduction of the real components of historical necessity', Lukács concludes, 'it matters little whether individual details, individual facts are historically correct or not' (59–60). Following Lukács, the literary critic Franco Moretti likewise credits Scott with a key innovation in the history of the realist novel: 'Scott manages to *slow down* the narrative, multiplying its moments of pause. And within these pauses, he finds, literally, the "time" to develop a new analytical-impersonal style—which makes possible in its turn a new type of description, where the world is observed with more precision' (Moretti 2006: 376). Taking liberties with documentary sources, then, does not necessarily jeopardize historical faithfulness. If anything, it allows writers to get a little closer to how individuals actually experience history.

## THE EUCHARIST AND THE ENGLISH BIBLE

Another dimension of Mantel's historical fiction that is important for my purposes, especially considering Isaiah Berlin's claim about the significance of religion in shaping history, is her remarkably astute and persuasive account of the Protestant Reformation in *Wolf Hall* and *Bring Up the Bodies*. This religious dimension prompts students to consider what advantages literary fiction might bring to the study of religion, compared to other discourses. Scholars have applied various methodologies and theoretical approaches to the study of religion, ranging from sociology to history, cognitive science to 'lived religion', and so on, yet historical fiction might yield dividends by way of demonstrating, or 'knowing', that religiosity as such pertains not just to our intellects but also to our aspirations, to our deepest emotions and fears. While the sorts of phenomena we call religious exist in the here and now, they nonetheless transport us, inevitably pointing beyond the material world to some notional realm of transcendence. In Mantel's fiction, she imagines religious interiority and situates competing ideas and understandings dialogically, thereby giving her readers a glimpse into the processes of religious change, even as she gestures towards what makes religion so powerfully numinous, if also divisive, and often dangerous.

Students often have limited exposure to religious history, much less to liturgy and theology. Some background information about the Protestant Reformation may be required. Depending on their own experiences and upbringings, they typically bring different assumptions about religion to the classroom, both positive and negative. One salutary result of studying religion through fiction is that it has a way of disarming whatever presumptions students may have about the subject. Studying religion historically I find has a similarly depersonalizing effect. At the least, students are hardly surprised to learn that people have always fought over religion. Yet I like to think that discussing doctrinal debates or other matters pertaining to religious history not only makes us more informed but also puts religious pluralism in practice, as it were, by enacting the very civility and tolerance that is all too often missing from our highly polarized public spheres.

One major source of disagreement among reformers and traditionalists alike during the Protestant Reformation was the sacrament of the Eucharist. Christians had always wondered exactly what Jesus meant by the so-called words of institution, 'But in the sixteenth century, as the divisions within Western Christendom deepened, conflict over what Jesus meant by "take and eat" erupted with visceral force' (Orsi 2016: 17). In short, the Eucharist was a lightning rod.

At the center of the controversy was the doctrine of transubstantiation, the so-called 'real presence' of Christ's body and blood in the consecrated Host. Early in *Wolf Hall*, the narrator is describing Cardinal Thomas Wolsey's dissolution of some thirty decaying monasteries, diverting the funds to found a grammar school in Ipswich and a college at Oxford called Cardinal College (later renamed King Henry VIII's College after Wolsey lost favor with the king, it is now Christ Church College). Mantel tells us that Cardinal Wolsey 'is learned in the law but does not like its delays: he cannot quite accept that real property cannot be changed into money with the same speed and ease with which he changes a wafer into the body of Christ' (Mantel 2009: 17). At this point, the doctrine of transubstantiation is not yet being contested, but soon enough, it will be. In his book *The Reformation: A History* (2003), Diarmaid MacCulloch traces the 'subtle shift in theological stance' towards the Eucharist during Henry VIII's reign (MacCulloch 2003: 248). Broadly Lutheran in their sympathies, most evangelical leaders continued to affirm the real presence in the Eucharist, but doubts about transubstantiation were growing, despite the risk of severe punishment for running afoul of official church doctrine. In one passage from *Wolf Hall*, an orphaned boy named Dick Purser, who was adopted by the Lord Chancellor, Thomas More, lets it be known that 'he did not believe God was in the Communion host' (Mantel 2009: 285).

This is no minor disagreement over church doctrine, but a sticking point that instigates violence: 'More had him whipped before the whole household' (Mantel 2009: 285). Other dissenters suffered far worse fates.

In the turbulent final decades of Henry VIII's life, the king's 'complex religious views began moving crabwise in an evangelical direction', as MacCulloch puts it (MacCulloch 2003: 248). Indeed, Mantel employs the same metaphor in *Bring Up the Bodies* (or borrows it, as she has almost certainly read MacCulloch's synthetic history of the period): 'He knows the king is devout and afraid of change. He wants the church reformed, he wants it pristine; he also wants money. But as a native of the sign of Cancer, he proceeds crab-wise to his objective: a side-shuffle, a weaving motion' (Mantel 2012: 45). Yet Henry would remain committed to Christ's real presence in the Eucharist, and the last religious crisis of his reign was over the doctrine of transubstantiation. A royal proclamation in 1538 affirmed, 'the most blessed and holy sacrament of the altar is the very body and blood of our Lord Jesus Christ', and Henry's Act of Six Articles of 1539 made the real presence a litmus test of religious allegiance (Malson-Huddle 2010: 4).[2] Of course, this further exacerbated an already volatile theological dispute. 'The Eucharistic presence was the most explosive doctrinal issue in 1540s England', historian Alec Ryrie attests. 'If there was a single fault line dividing English evangelicalism, this was it' (Ryrie 2003: 138).[3] Six Articles mushroomed to Forty-Two Articles by 1552, then to Thirty-Nine Articles in 1563. Thomas Cranmer codified the Church of England's stance on transubstantiation in the *Book of Common Prayer* (1549, 1552), which accommodated a range of sacramental theology. 'I do as plainly speak as I can', Cranmer wrote in 1551, 'that Christ's body and blood be given to us in deed, yet not corporally and carnally, but spiritually and effectually' (MacCulloch 1996: 616).

Another source of contention during the Reformation was the Bible itself, or rather the Bible in English, which Henry VIII had long banned yet eventually he would come to endorse. Prior to Henry's change of heart, however, English Bibles were contraband. Cromwell obtains a copy of a pirated edition of William Tyndale's English translation of the Bible in the novel, and what he finds therein up-ends much of what he thought he knew, or what the Church had taught. 'Surreptitiously read and discussed during the 1520s and 1530s', MacCulloch writes, 'it worked on the imaginations' of anyone who could get their hands on a copy of 'the first English printed New Testament' (MacCulloch 2003: 197). Mantel accounts for both the surreptitious aspect of reading a banned book and the way it worked on the imaginations of men and women who had long regarded Church teachings as incontrovertible. 'As the word of God spreads', the narrator remarks, 'the people's eyes are opened to new truths' (Mantel 2009: 422). By some estimates, literacy rates were as low as two percent in England, yet Tyndale's Bible sold as many as 30,000 copies before 1539 (Whipps 2007). Clearly, there was popular demand for a vernacular Bible. 'They must have a Bible, sir, in their own tongue', a minor character named John ap Rice tells Cromwell, who reassures him that he's working on it: 'It is his daily, covert crusade: for Henry to sponsor a great Bible, put it in every church. He is very close now and he thinks he can win Henry to it' (Mantel 2012: 70). In fact, Cromwell does win him over; Henry VIII will direct Cromwell to oversee an authorized Bible in English to call his own, the Great Bible of 1539.[4]

In *Wolf Hall*, Mantel portrays this burning desire to read the Bible as one of the engines of the Protestant Reformation. As Cromwell explains to his nephew Richard, 'They have seen their religion painted on the walls of churches, or carved in stone, but now God's pen is poised, and he is ready to write his words in the books of their hearts' (Mantel 2009: 422). A common trope of much Protestant writing, such as the devotional poetry of George Herbert, for instance, the metaphor of God writing on one's heart conveys both the intense introspection of evangelical sensibilities and a newfound insistence on the Bible as the highest authority, or *sola scriptura*. 'You read it', Cromwell confides to his wife Lizzie, 'you'll be surprised what's not in it' (32).

Not everyone was hospitable to new ideas, of course. Musing about Sir Thomas Moore's dogmatism and intransigence, Cromwell asks himself in one passage,

> Why does everything you know, and everything you've learned, confirm you in what you believed before? Whereas in my case, what I grew up with, and what I thought I believed, is chipped away a little and a little, a fragment then a piece and then a piece more. With every month that passes, the corners are knocked off the certainties of this world: and the next world too. Show me where it says, in the Bible, 'Purgatory.' Show me where it says 'relics, monks, nuns.' Show me where it says 'Pope.' (Mantel 2009: 32)

In this passage, Mantel shows Cromwell pondering unquestioned religious verities of his time, which have suddenly been thrown into question through his reading of Tyndale's English Bible. Elizabeth Malson-Huddle writes, 'Even Cromwell worried that lay people would begin to read and interpret the Bible in English and that these interpretations could weaken Church authority' (Malson-Huddle 2010: 5). Mantel portrays his worry in a more positive light as Cromwell's openness to new ideas; as such, this passage reads as a very subtle portrayal of a mind in motion. A similar passage has Cromwell fretting about giving up the comforting doctrine of Purgatory:

> Imagine the silence now, in that place which is no-place, that anteroom to God where each hour is ten thousand years long. Once you imagined the souls held in a great net, a web spun by God, held safe till their release into his radiance. But if the net is cut and the web broken, do they spill into freezing space, each year falling further into silence, until there is no trace of them at all? (Mantel 2012: 118–119)

Both passages show Cromwell thinking through some of the issues that led reformers to dissent from Church teachings, to the point of being exiled, or worse, executed, as when he reflects on Thomas More's relentless prosecution of heretics: 'He would chain you up, for a mistranslation. He would, for a difference in your Greek, kill you' (Mantel 2009: 125). Sir Thomas More was particularly vigilant about persecuting Lollards, originally followers of John Wycliffe who not only smuggled Bibles into England but also contended that the consecrated Host is merely 'a piece of bread', not Christ's body, and thus denying the doctrine of transubstantiation (289).

The number of characters included in Mantel's novels is so vast that she includes a Cast of Characters, yet the author brings many personalities to life through their actions, blunders, conversations, emotions, gestures or jokes. The character Hans Holbein the Younger, for instance, based on the great painter of the Tudor court, expresses his exasperation at the way theological disputes about the metaphysics of bread and wine, about whether priests must remain celibate, about the sacraments, and about graven images wreak so much havoc across Europe:

> Hans grunts, downs his cup of wine and talks about what he's left behind: talk about Basle, about the Swiss cantons and cities. Riots and pitched battles. Images, not images. Statues, not statues. It is the body of God, it is not the body of God, it is sort of the body of God. Priests may marry, they may not. There are seven sacraments, there are three. The crucifix we creep

to on our knees and reverence with our lips, or the crucifix we chop it up and burn it in the public square. (Mantel 2009: 303)

Enumerating the recurring points of disagreement, Holbein gives voice to the vertiginous quality of the time, when momentous changes to official doctrine could easily be reversed with a change in power, or simply a change of heart by the monarch. Mantel portrays Holbein as a pragmatist much like Cromwell: 'All I ask is to do some good work and be paid for it. And I prefer not to have my efforts wiped out by some secretary with a pail of whitewash' (303). While this last comment refers to the vehement iconoclasm of English evangelicals, perhaps the most important reversal in official policy was Henry VIII's decision to authorize an English Bible. Ironically, it was Holbein who later created an astonishing woodcut depicting Henry VIII as the supreme head of the Church for the frontispiece of Miles Coverdale's 1535 English translation of the Bible.[5]

Holbein's portraits are an extraordinary record of important figures in the Tudor court, including several portraits of Henry VIII in all his regal power and splendor. These paintings can certainly help students visualize the immense Cast of Characters in Mantel's Wolf Hall trilogy. My PowerPoint presentation contains no fewer than four Holbein portraits of characters named Thomas (Sir Thomas More, Thomas Howard, Thomas Boleyn, Thomas Cromwell). By virtue of being painted from life, Holbein's portraits do give us a more accurate visual reference than the TV miniseries of *Wolf Hall* (2015), a very fine adaptation first broadcast on BBC Two in 2015 and starring the brilliant actor Mark Rylance as Cromwell. Yet Holbein's portraits also give us something more than visual information. When I show reproductions of these paintings in class, I try to elicit responses from students about what we can glean from them about Holbein's sitters. Do not portraits offer a glimpse, however fleeting and partial, into the inner lives of the sitters? Like Mantel but in a different medium, Holbein captures some of the idiosyncratic qualities of his subjects through facial expressions—a twinkle in the eye suggesting a sense of humor, say—convincing us that we know them better. Students often marvel at how life-like the portraits are. Holbein's portraits enhance our sense of knowing who these characters are, even as they give us an opportunity to deepen our consideration of art and fiction alike as historical representations. In a joke seemingly at painting's expense, as if to say, look at what fiction can do, Mantel in fact points to their complimentary powers of discernment when she registers Cromwell's complaint about

Holbein's portrait of him, done in profile: 'When he saw the portrait finished he had said, "Christ, I look like a murderer"; and his son Gregory said, didn't you know?' (Mantel 2012: 7). Cromwell's fixed, impenetrable gaze in the Holbein portrait does indeed look rather sinister, yet Gregory's cheeky (and very funny) takedown of his father reminds us of the actual ruthlessness behind the man's form of *realpolitik*, which comes across as mostly positive in Mantel's fiction.

'Where much historical fiction gets entangled in the simulation of historical authenticity', writes James Wood in a characteristically insightful review essay, 'Mantel bypasses those knots of concoction, and proceeds as if authenticity were magic rather than a science. She knows that what gives fiction its vitality is not the accurate detail but the animate one, and that novelists are creators, not coroners, of the human case' (Wood 2012).[6] Above all, Mantel's fiction provides us extraordinary access into the inner lives of her characters, and hence the 'inner life' of history. At one point in *Wolf Hall*, the narrator offers a comment about historiography that strikes me as roughly similar to Leo Tolstoy's perspective, as paraphrased by Isaiah Berlin at the outset of this chapter. Remarking on a behind-closed-doors meeting of minds between Thomas Cromwell, her protagonist and Bishop Eustace Chapuys, the Spanish Ambassador to England, Mantel writes,

> The fate of peoples is made like this, two men in small rooms. Forget the coronations, the conclaves of cardinals, the pomp and processions. This is how the world changes: a counter pushed across a table, a pen stroke that alters the force of a phrase, a woman's sigh as she passes and leaves on the air a trail of orange flower or rose water; her hand pulling close the bed curtain, the discreet sigh of flesh against flesh. (Mantel 2009: 499)

It is difficult to imagine a more eloquent statement of Mantel's method. From passages like this, students come to understand historical fiction as a way of going behind closed doors to peer into clandestine meetings between two diplomats, or pulling back the bed curtains to witness an illicit encounter. Among the many pleasures of historical fiction is voyeurism. Because readers usually know the outcome of the characters in advance, we get to enjoy how the author brings it about. But I think historical fiction can be an invaluable resource for urging students to reflect on how we come to know history in the first place, which involves them in questions about epistemology and representation: What counts as history? Whose history? What is the best way to represent it?

Similarly, Hilary Mantel may potentially prompt students to rethink what they thought they knew about the Protestant Reformation, or religion for that matter. Scholars have found it surprisingly difficult to escape the binary logic of a secularization thesis that pits the secular against religion, rather than viewing them in a dialectical relationship. As Peter Coviello and Jared Hickman have argued, 'the things we kill off tend not to disappear. They have a mysterious tenacity, afterlives not easily reckoned with. Just so, it is our sense that, here in the aftermath of the demise of the secularization thesis, we are only now beginning to grasp how deeply we remain in it: how shaped our conceptual frameworks are, down to their most elemental premises, by secularization' (Coviello and Hickman 2014: 646).[7] In the classroom, historical fiction can become a means for exploring what it means, if anything, to say that we are post-secular. My pedagogy is meant to trouble the presumption that we are indeed post-secular, urging students to move beyond familiar binaries to explore religion in the fine-grained specificity of its contexts.

Historical fiction offers new avenues for thinking about religious and secular positions as something like what Raymond Williams called structures of feeling. He chose the word 'feeling' carefully to 'emphasize a distinction from more formal concepts of "world-view" or "ideology"' (Williams 1977: 132). He demonstrates how 'formal or systematic beliefs' often coexist with 'pre-emergent' beliefs and ideas that are 'not yet fully articulated' (126). Williams continues:

> We are talking about characteristic elements of impulse, restraint, and tone; specifically affective elements of consciousness and relationships: not feeling against thought, but thought as felt and feeling as thought: practical consciousness of a present kind, in a living and interrelating community... Yet we are also defining a social experience which is still *in process*, often indeed not yet recognized. (132)

Among the highest ambitions of Mantel's historical fiction is to investigate how religious ideas and practices change. By attending to 'meanings and values as they are actively lived and felt', to borrow Williams' phrase, Mantel tries to parse the differences between emergent and residual beliefs during the Protestant Reformation (132). She teases out the theological implications of evolving views about the Eucharist, for instance, and provides a plausible account of how the English Bible accelerated religious innovation. But Mantel's novels do more than this: they also probe into human affects—anguish, desire, ecstasy, joy, love, suffering and the like—and these are the things that give fiction a quasi-religious capacity to speak to the deepest part of our being.

There is a beautiful passage at the end of *Bring Up the Bodies* that speaks to fiction's capacity not only to preserve history from oblivion but also to contribute, in its own inimitable way, to human flourishing. By now, readers will have become familiar with the narrative voice, the way it freely enters into Cromwell's head:

> He thinks, strive as I might, one day I will be gone and as this world goes it may not be long: what though I am a man of firmness and vigour, fortune is mutable and either my enemies will do for me or my friends. When the time comes I may vanish before the ink is dry. I will leave behind me a great mountain of paper, and those who come after me … they will sift through what remains and remark, here is an old deed, an old draft, an old letter from Thomas Cromwell's time: they will turn the page over, and write on me. (Mantel 2012: 407)

Fortunately, Mantel is not done with Thomas Cromwell just yet. She has promised a third and final volume, reportedly titled *The Mirror and the Light*, which will cover the last four years of Cromwell's life. Sometime in the near future, then, she will again transport us back into the past.

## Notes

1. For instance, the unsympathetic portrayal of Thomas Cromwell as Henry VIII's enforcer in Robert Bolt's play *A Man for All Seasons* (1960), and its film adaptation of the same name (1966), in contrast to Bolt's portrayal of Thomas More as a conscientious objector to tyranny. Mantel more or less reverses the roles.
2. Among those burned at the stake for denying the real presence was the layperson Anne Askew. See Elizabeth Malson-Huddle (2010). In his monumental work *The Stripping of the Altars: Traditional Religion in England c. 1400–c. 1580*, Eamon Duffy calls the Act of Six Articles 'a decisive turning-point for the progress of radical Protestantism under Henry' (Duffy 2005: 424). On Archbishop Thomas Cranmer's shift towards a more symbolic understanding of the Eucharist, conveniently after Henry VIII's death in January 1547, see MacCulloch (2003, 248).
3. See also Ryrie (2013: 336–351).
4. For a lively account of the origins and history of the Bible in English, see Simpson (2007).

5. See John N. King (2002), for a discussion of Holbein's woodcut for the Coverdale Bible.
6. Titled 'Invitation to a Beheading', Woods' review essay for *The New Yorker* is accompanied by Marco Ventura's wonderful illustration of Mantel in a style that is unmistakably 'after Holbein'.
7. For the most influential account of secularization as a 'subtraction story', see Taylor (2007).

## Works Cited

Berlin, Isaiah. 2000. *The Proper Study of Mankind: An Anthology of Essays.* New York: Farrar, Straus and Giroux.

Burnet, Gilbert. 1865. *The History of the Reformation of the Church of England, Part 1.* Oxford: Clarendon Press.

Coviello, Peter, and Jared Hickman. 2014. Introduction: After the Postsecular. *American Literature* 86 (4): 645–654.

Duffy, Eamon. 2005. *The Stripping of the Altars: Traditional Religion in England c. 1400-c. 1580.* 2nd ed. New Haven: Yale UP.

Holsinger, Bruce. 2013. *Plagues, Witches, and War: The Worlds of Historical Fiction.* Coursera. Accessed February 1, 2017. https://www.coursera.org/learn/historical-fiction

King, John R. 2002. The Royal Image, 1535–1603. In *Tudor Political Culture*, ed. Dale Hoak, 104–132. Cambridge: Cambridge UP.

Lukács, Georg. 1983. *The Historical Novel.* Lincoln: U of Nebraska P.

MacCulloch, Diarmaid. 1996. *Thomas Cranmer.* New Haven: Yale UP.

———. 2003. *The Reformation: A History.* New York: Viking.

MacFarquhar, Larissa. 2012. The Dead Are Real: Hilary Mantel's Imagination. *The New Yorker*, October 15. Accessed January 30, 2017. http://www.newyorker.com/magazine/2012/10/15/ the-dead-are-real

Malson-Huddle, Elisabeth. 2010. Anne Askew and the Controversy Over the Real Presence. *Studies in English Literature, 1500–1900* 50 (1, Winter): 1–16.

Mantel, Hilary. 2009. *Wolf Hall.* New York: Henry Holt.

———. 2012. *Bring Up the Bodies.* New York: Henry Holt.

Moretti, Franco. 2006. Serious Century. In *The Novel, Volume 1: History, Geography, and Culture*, 364–400. Princeton: Princeton UP.

Orsi, Robert A. 2016. *History and Presence.* Cambridge: The Belknap Press of Harvard UP.

Ryrie, Alec. 2003. *The Gospel and Henry VIII: Evangelicals in the Early English Reformation.* Cambridge: Cambridge UP.

———. 2013. *Being Protestant in Reformation Britain.* Oxford: Oxford UP.

Simpson, James. 2007. *Burning to Read: English Fundamentalism and Its Reformation Opponents.* Cambridge: The Belknap Press/Harvard UP.

Taylor, Charles. 2007. *A Secular Age*. Cambridge: The Belknap Press/Harvard UP.
Whipps, Heather. 2007. Historian: First English Bible Fueled First Fundamentalists. *Live Science*, December 11. Accessed February 2, 2017. http://www.livescience.com/2107-historian-english-bible-fueled-fundamentalists.html
Williams, Raymond. 1977. *Marxism and Literature*. Oxford: Oxford UP.
Wood, James. 2012. Invitation to a Beheading. *The New Yorker*, May 7. Accessed March 24, 2017. http://www.newyorker.com/magazine/2012/05/07/invitation-to-a-beheading

CHAPTER 8

# Text and Context: Using Wikis to Teach Victorian Novels

*Ellen Rosenman*

I am lucky enough to teach in a department that requires all English majors to take a course entitled Text and Context. Instructors choose a single text and place it in a larger field such as subject matter, literary history or genre. My context of choice reflects my scholarly commitment to cultural studies: I ask students to research primary sources in the period to explore the themes, issues or questions raised by a Victorian novel. Having fallen victim to the romance of the archive myself, I love introducing students to the rich, sprawling body of extent Victorian texts. I don't see how they can truly understand the novels without contextual knowledge or appreciate the novel's status as a respected form of social discourse (a role that, sadly, it no longer plays). When students handle an issue of Charles Dickens's journal *Household Words* knowing nineteenth-century readers turned the same pages, or stumble upon the virtual image of a Victorian marriage license and imagine the real people who signed it, the 'time travel' aspect of archival research can spark a more intense imaginative investment in the period (Michie and Warhol 2010: 415). They can be equally enthralled by real research: driven by genuine questions;

E. Rosenman (✉)
University of Kentucky, Lexington, KY, USA

involving wild goose chases, dead ends and serendipity; shaped by the critical assessment of sources rather than the algorithm-generated results of a Google search.

Unfortunately, the traditional research assignments I devised tended to produce somewhat canned results. Asked to explore the role of governesses in Victorian society, students might summarize several sources but have difficulty relating them to one another or using them to think through Jane's position in *Jane Eyre*. They tend to look for one-to-one correspondences or state that the novel reflects the general plight of the governess.

In two recent classes, however, I have turned to wikis, which have improved students' ability to relate contextual material to novels in visible, dynamic ways. Working through George Eliot's *Middlemarch* and Anthony Trollope's *The Way We Live Now*, two massive tomes chock full of references and allusions that engage some of the most pressing, contested issues of their time, we created digital editions of the novels linked to essays designed to help future undergraduate readers make sense of their complex engagements with the Victorian world: 'The Middlemarch Magnifying Glass' and 'Understanding the Way They Lived Then'.

## Cultural Studies and Its Discontents

One of many approaches in opposition to New Criticism, cultural studies insists that literary texts are enmeshed in the values, assumptions and mystifications of their surrounding culture, broadly defined. The label 'text', now commonplace, signals the descent of literature from an aesthetic pedestal into the hurly burly of social issues, along with its shared space with other kinds of writing, now also called texts. Rather than seeing novels as static, self-contained formal objects, we routinely study them as public narratives—stories told from a specific cultural location to a specific readership, explicitly or implicitly in conversation with other narratives. In some fields, like my own, this contextual approach has been practiced for some time: before cultural studies, there was Victorian studies and *Victorian Studies*, the premier journal in the field, founded in the 1950s; *American Studies* was founded in 1960. As cultural studies gained scholarly traction, other fields swapped out 'literature' for 'studies' to signal their interdisciplinary intentions. ('Contextual', 'interdisciplinary' and 'cultural studies' are not exact matches, but a Venn diagram of the three categories would include a significant overlap.) The scholarly practice of reading literature this way is so ubiquitous that it has made its way into the classroom. Fredric Jameson's edict 'Always historicize!' has become a pedagogical as well as a critical mantra.

With the explosion of digitized materials, it is now much easier to introduce students to documents in social, political and economic history. For-profit companies such as Cengage and Adam Matthew make primary sources available in quantity, though their business model is controversial: professors do the work and the company sells the results back to university libraries for huge sums. But if your library is fortunate enough to have funds to buy them (as my chronically underfunded public southern university does, somehow), students have access to a mass of sources, sometimes curated and introduced by scholars in the field. Most valuably, many are searchable by subject. Open sources such as hathitrust.com (paying members have access to more data, but the free titles are extensive), Google Books, Project Gutenberg and archive.org are easily available. The internet is now a treasure trove of Victorian documents—often uploaded for no apparent reason. There lies the other side of accessibility: undergraduates cannot possibly do enough research to map and weigh the significance of their sources. Which texts are representative? Which are deliberately oppositional? Which are *sui generis* or just plain weird? The extent of these resources means that students' choices are likely to be somewhat random. Although instructors can help students identify reliable sources and steer them to responsible websites and databases, the problems of discrimination and information overload remain. However, though students need to know that questions about representativeness are important, it is unrealistic to expect them to do enough research to answer them. Whatever the limitations of online primary sources, there is no doubt that they give students an enormous window onto distant historical worlds.

As pedagogy has embraced cultural studies, however, scholars have increasingly criticized its theoretical assumptions and practical results. These critiques have raised arguments that teachers should be aware of, because, if in some ways they are intrinsic to the method, they can be mitigated with conscious effort and thoughtful assignments. While counter-approaches advance a variety of other methods—the New Formalism, surface reading, phenomenology, critical presentism, post-critical interpretation—they discern similar problems. Essentially, critics argue that cultural studies and its Marxist sibling New Historicism assume a simplistic understanding of literature and its relationship to context. These approaches read *through* literature to context; whatever questions a novel poses, context is the answer. Thus, literature becomes 'a branch of cultural history' (Cohen 2009: 52), reducing 'every text to its ideological or historical context' (Rooney 2000: 26). Literature becomes a mystified and mystifying genre that either cannot or will not cop to its bad ideological investments. Performing 'symptomatic readings' and exercising 'the hermeneutics of suspicion', critics ferret out the ideological complicities buried beneath a novel's surface. In a related problem, such approaches reduce context to a single, monolithic truth. In spite of the insistence of theorists and historians from Michel Foucault to Hayden White to Antoinette Barton that historical documents are also narratives that are neither transparent nor true—that the most apparently objective historical document is 'a narrative, a practice, a site of desire' (Burton 2003: 4)—the V21 Collective in my own field equates cultural studies with 'positivist historicism', the delusion that research can reconstruct the past '*wie es eigentlich gewesen*' (as it actually was) (Manifesto). Finally, critics claim that, after decades of ascendency, cultural studies has ossified, recirculating a 'stable repertoire' of 'prior insights' that are 'all too familiar' (Felski 2015: 7).

Are these objections relevant to classroom practice? In some ways, yes. Students can be quick to reduce a novel's complex, ambivalent engagement with context to a simple reflection or repudiation. Especially when dealing with representations of gender and femininity, they quickly default to stereotypes of 'the Victorians', a benighted people trapped in their outmoded beliefs (which, of course, we have happily transcended in modern times). Seizing on a single source, usually a prescriptive one such as a conduct book, they assume it gives an accurate account of what people uncritically believed and how they lived.

Though I am mindful of these pitfalls, I still believe that studying cultural context can genuinely enhance students' understanding of literature—in fact, primary research can mitigate these problems. To some extent, scholarly objections caricature cultural studies scholarship, much of which insists that the relationship between a literary text and its contexts is nuanced, multifaceted and unpredictable. The thoughtful practice of cultural studies can open up a range of genres and viewpoints, enhancing students' understanding of the ways in which different narratives and different *kinds* of narrative engage with each other. Rather than take primary sources as repositories of facts about the period, students became more sensitive to the specific intentions and characteristics of historical documents, while multiple sources unveil debates rather than a cultural party line. Bringing together a conduct book, a memoir and a feminist periodical, students could no longer claim that Victorians believed only one thing about femininity against which to measure the novel; instead, they became aware of women's roles as a live issue of the period. In fact, students came to see that certain genres, such as conduct books, attempted to stabilize social meanings while novels more often opened up areas of ambiguity or change.

## Fictional Narration and Cultural Contestation

By definition, fictional narratives insist on complexity, heterogeneity and ambiguity, lending fiction its distinctive ability to explore ideas 'on the ground' through plot, character and narration. This does not mean that other kinds of narratives are necessarily simplistic, as the historians mentioned earlier insist. But novels are designed to put different points of view, experiences and meanings in motion.

One dimension that accomplishes this end is narrative temporality. As novels move through diegetic time, they open up multiple possibilities and facets of an issue even as they drive toward resolution—or at least toward an ending. Reflecting on narrative temporality, Paul Ricoeur identifies a dynamic relationship between succession, the series of events and interactions that develops the novel's plot, and configuration, the organization of this heterogeneity into a meaningful whole (Valdés 1991: 427). Proliferating possibilities, succession is reinforced and played out among characters who voice different opinions, experience different emotions and have different ethical commitments depending on their personalities, age, social positions and vested interests. What Bakhtin calls the polyphonic or dialogic nature of the novel is a constitutive generic feature, built from different voices and points of view. Through dialogue, narration, interior monologue and free indirect discourse, rhetorical heterogeneity multiplies meaning, in spite of novels' teleological structure. As students in my classes worked through their reading and research, they came to appreciate the narrative features that make novels especially complex and challenging. Though critics of cultural studies fear that it ignores the literariness of literature, students sharped their understanding of the novel as a distinctive genre.

Moreover, though scholars dismiss 'positivist historicism' and the accumulation of facts, students are not part of the same interpretive community as scholars. Our 'prior insights' are often news to them. Novice readers lack basic facts that set the parameters for persuasive interpretations, or that simply help them understand what the novel is talking about. What was the Anatomy Act of 1832? Why does Eliot make her character Lydgate a surgeon rather than a physician? As Mike Sanders says in his response to the V21 anti-historicist manifesto, 'For the empiricist [historical-positivist], the idea is the opposable thumb which transforms the hammer of fact into the chisel of analysis. For the idealist, the matter of fact (or fact of matter) is the steadying hand which guides the chisel.' In other words, without empirical knowledge, readers can draw misguided conclusions or be unable to draw any conclusions at all. Armed with this knowledge, readers can trace the intricate interconnections of a novel's design: the issues of inclusion and exclusion, innovation and tradition, power and submission that play out in every aspect of the novel, from medical reform to political change to kinship relations to marriage. Students can discover the general shape of these issues from the text itself or read long explanatory footnotes, but thinking through the implications of primary sources gives them a deeper, more detailed understanding of them and a greater investment in their significance.

## ANNOTATIONS, ALLUSIONS AND INTERTEXTUALITY: A CASE FOR POSITIVIST HISTORY

Epigraphs, mythological references and literary allusions add layers of meaning, a kind of semiotic harmonics that resonates through the text. In *Middlemarch*, when Rosamund is compared to the tragic Ariadne, students can measure the intense irony with which Eliot represents her self-serving marital ambitions, an effect that is intensified when they compare a graceful classical statue to fashion plates that Rosamund takes as her model. Our understanding of Edward Casaubon in *Middlemarch* was enriched by one student's research. When a character imagines him as looking like John Locke, students wondered, 'Is that a good thing?' The scrupulously factual footnote in the Oxford World Classic edition is no help; we are told only that 'there are two famous portraits of the philosopher John Locke (1632–1704) by Sir Godfrey Kneller'. One student tracked down the portraits, which displayed an elderly, unimpressive physical specimen (so, not a good thing). Further, she discovered an allusion to a now-obscure sixteenth-century theologian named Isaac Casaubon. Though the two Casaubons share a self-destructive obsession with their work, this resemblance only emphasizes the ironic contract between them: although his namesake is a prolific and innovative writer, Eliot's character is a fussy, ineffectual scholar out of touch with his field. (Kendra Sanders, http://middlemarchuk.pbworks.com/w/page/65601128/Edward%20Casaubon's%20 vita, http://middlemarchuk.pbworks.com/w/page/65601235/Isaac%20 Casaubon's%20vita). An epigraph from *Don Quixote* underlines his deluded ambition. Of course, we could not track down every allusion. But as students gained an appreciation of Eliot's superhuman erudition, they also recognized the novel as 'a story that is *told*...that is, it is converted into *signs*', to borrow Mieke Bal's rather mechanical way of putting this way of making meaning (Bal 2009: 9). Decoding allusions reminded them that everything had been constructed and chosen to evoke a particular meaning or connotation; nothing was 'just there'.

## Text Vs. Text

Through another form of intertextuality, which H. Porter Abbott calls 'narrative contestation', both *Middlemarch* and *The Way We Live Now* claimed authority in relation to other texts (Abbott 2002: 138). Abbott asserts, 'battling narratives are everywhere' (152), stressing the ways in which narratives actively engage and disagree with one another, jockeying for cultural authority. Reading financial periodicals clarifies Trollope's satire in *The Way We Live Now*, which can seem broad and obvious to modern students. But contextual reading reveals that these publications do not simply provide objective information but also aim to stir up excitement about the fast-paced, modern economy of investment capitalism. As a student-scholar wrote, 'There was a thrill involved with investing and participating in this new society that revolved around money. By participating in the stock exchange, people were able to show the expendable income, and status that they had in society.' Investment, then, was a social as well as financial act. Lists of investment opportunities and expert-sounding advice normalize investment capitalism, suggesting that it is a rational system that can be mastered. Trollope's novel counters this normalization, using the motif of gambling to re-contextualize investing as irrational, unpredictable and even immoral. At the same time, the periodicals' columns of advice reflect the novelty of the stock exchange, an insight that makes the novel's biting satire less broad and more telling. Uploading the first page of a periodical, the student-scholar continues, 'As you can see from the image, what to invest your money into caused a lot of commotion in everyone's life. The image lists multiple venues of investment starting from railways and ending with mining. The image demonstrates how much the public relied on the media to provide accurate information about the stock exchange' since lay people had no way to decide on their own (Ellen Gaines, 'After all, what was wanted ...', http://thewaywelivenow.pbworks.com/w/page/88507526/After%20all%2C%20what%20was%20wanted%20from%20Mr%20Melmotte%20was%20little%20more%20than%20his%20name%2C).

The naiveté of Trollope's wealthy young lay-abouts may be exaggerated, but it is not entirely unrealistic. Similarly, *Middlemarch* explicitly intervenes in the discursive field that shapes young women's development with references to *Lallah Rookh*, a popular and romantic Orientalist poem, and the *Keepsake*, a richly bound annual collection of middlebrow art and wisdom, the coffee table book of its day. While these texts promote a static, superficial ideal of femininity, *Middlemarch* tracks the psychological and ethical challenges of multiple characters over time. Subsuming other texts within their narratives, authors implicitly establish the novel as a superior source of insight.

Reading novels in relation to other sources often reveals a heterogeneous field of possible attitudes, breaking down the binary categories with which students sometimes approach familiar topics. Was Trollope progressive or conservative in his representation of women? Faced with a range of commentary, the answer becomes difficult to pin down. On the one hand, the novel cannot imagine a happy ending for respectable women outside of marriage, cheerfully shipping off two single women, both bold foreigners, to America. While students might assume that any other fate was literally unthinkable, *The English Woman's Journal* and Mary Taylor's *The First Duty of Women*, two sources discovered by a student, envision employment as a satisfactory alternative. On the other hand, Trollope registered the power imbalance of marriage in multiple subplots of domestic violence. Indeed, unlike most of his contemporaries, Trollope represented marital abuse at all social levels, aligning himself with feminist Frances Power Cobbe, one of the few writers to blame the structure of marriage rather than the pathology of the working classes. How radical, then, is Trollope's representation of marriage and women's life stories? Confronting the difficulty of situating *The Way We Live Now* in this complex discursive landscape, students realized that even a single novel cannot be categorized as 'conservative' or 'progressive', even or especially in an arena such as women and marriage, one that they initially expected to involve a set of simple precepts.

As students traced the divergences of these battling texts, the Victorian novel emerged as a distinctive, complex kind of narrative. In contrast to conduct books and financial journalism, which were more limited in scope and more tightly contained ideologically, students were better able to gauge the ambitions of these 'loose baggy monsters', as Henry James called them. Multiple plots with their own rising and falling actions, a diverse cast of characters, shifts in time and place, metaphorical and structural repetitions—even their daunting length—enabled them to make sweeping critiques of a society in transition. As an added bonus, this recognition helped students move beyond character identification. This reorientation was especially important for *The Way We Live Now*, which initially frustrated students because they could not find a likeable or complex enough character with which to identify (one of them dubbed Paul Montague 'the token human' in the novel, a label the whole class immediately adopted to signal their lack of empathy for other characters). Certainly character identification is one of the pleasures of reading, but students are sometimes at a loss when they lack a fictional double whose life they can enter vicariously. Focusing on larger issues, they came to see characters not or not only as proxies for real people but also as markers on a social map and nodes in a structure of ideas—that is, as part of the novel's symbolic design.

## Narrative Negotiation

The novel's polyphony and movement through time also enable what Abbott calls 'narrative negotiation' (Abbott 2002: 156). 'Narratives', he writes, 'are structures made up of contests, the claims of which they may or may not negotiate successfully' (156). Abbott classifies this characteristic as internal and constitutive, but novels are hospitable environments for playing out social disputes through different plots and characters. With knowledge of cultural context, students can 'map' the contests in more meaningful ways, understanding what the different claims would have meant to the novel's original audience. When one student noticed that 'the word gentleman appears frequently in *Middlemarch* (almost 90 times), and its meaning, often vague, is applied to many characters in the novel', she decided to investigate the social meanings in circulation at the time. She was able to attribute these diverse uses to characters' social status, their vested interests and a cultural context in which land, money, family, manners and ethics competed for priority (Anita Iyer, The 19th-

Century English Gentleman, http://middlemarchuk.pbworks.com/w/page/71487675/The%2019th%20century%20English%20Gentleman).

As with the subject of women and marriage, students struggled to understand the ambiguous portrayal of Jewish characters in *The Way We Live Now*. A spoiled young woman contemplates marrying a Jew as she begins to age out of the marriage market, pointing to examples of other respectable women who have done so: 'People don't think about that as they used to, papa. He has a very fine income, and I should always have a house in—' (Ch. LXXVII). Her father explodes with anti-Semitism: 'A Jew! A dirty Jew!' he repeats over and over again. The Jew in question is middle aged and overweight, not especially appealing, but he behaves honorably to his callow lover. One student-scholar explored the history of Jews in England and contemporary Victorian essays and 'gathered a better historical context that explained the tension between the Jewish community and the rest of society'. She notes, '*The Way We Live Now* was written when the rights of Jews were being debated' and attributes the conflict in part to generational difference: 'The Longestaffe family is seen as old fashioned, which means that they would hold a more traditional—or negative—view towards Jews' (Venecia Procter, 'The man was an absolute jew', http://thewaywelivenow.pbworks.com/w/page/88507178/The%20man%20was%20absolutely%20a%20Jew). Rather than debate whether or not Trollope was anti-Semitic, an either/or question that tends to be unproductive, she saw the ways in which the ambiguity of Jewishness was useful representationally, registering the conundrum of the elite as they attempted to capitalize (literally) on economic opportunities while clinging to social boundaries. Puzzling patterns of inclusion and exclusion, acceptance and rejection, appeared as rather arbitrary, on-the-fly, debatable judgments rather than the effect of clearly defined rules of etiquette. This understanding also revealed the novel's dialogue as truly heteroglossic in the classic Bakhinian sense. The father's formulaic 'dirty Jew' signified an established public opinion as well as his individual prejudice, one that needed no elaboration, while his daughter's wordier, indirect response reflected the lack of a prevailing narrative that could be reduced to a slogan as well as her personal ambivalence.

## Critical Presentism

Although anti-historicist critics such as the 21V Collective emphasize the dangers of a historical approach as 'bland antiquarianism', an informed understanding of another period can illuminate our own, just as generic differences become more obvious when different kinds of texts stand side by side. As students analyzed the ways in which Trollope's swindler conned the social elite, they also sought out reports of contemporary investment scams, which appeared on a regular basis throughout the semester. Again, Trollope's satire became more relevant and less outdated when students recognized parallels between the victims—mostly young, privileged men unaccustomed to managing their own money. Athletes and actors are the baronets of our time, they concluded, seduced by flattery, displays of wealth, the promise of insider status and technical-sounding mumbo jumbo. Viewing *Enron: The Smartest Guys in the Room* consolidated these parallels. In addition to emphasizing the credibility of Trollope's satire, contemporary accounts provided some lessons in capitalism: in spite of the historical distance between the novel and modern life, capitalism has not developed safeguards against fraud, nor do its participants always make decisions based on an objective assessment of financial self-interest. Charismatic hucksters with expensive clothes, gaudy mansions and a facile command of financial jargon continue to exploit individuals' greed and insecurity. Far from being a historical set piece, then, *The Way We Live Now* seems ahead of its time, critiquing the *homo economicus* theory of the rational economic actor and the master-narrative of capitalism as a self-regulating system that has overcome its chaotic beginnings.

## BUILDING THE WIKIS: ADVICE AND REFLECTIONS

If I have sold you on the rewards of this approach, let me describe my classroom practice and assess its successes and failures, for my examples so far have emphasized the most insightful essays. We certainly encountered problems, and not all the results were positive. To begin with, though, let me assure you that the process of creating the wikis was easy, even for a technologically challenged person like me. In both classes, we used PBWorks to create our wikis, a platform that is free, easy to use and can support texts, images and videos. Since both *Middlemarch* and *The Way We Live Now* are available from Project Gutenberg, we had free access to the novels themselves without violating copyright laws. In a class period, students familiarized themselves with the platform by uploading multiple chapters of the novel using their personal devices. Some browsers and some devices worked better than others (tablets vary, phones are a nightmare). Immediately, one side benefit of the project became apparent: students worked together spontaneously to solve technical problems. The atmosphere of festive chaos built a sense of community, while technologically savvy students took the role of expert, implicitly defining the wiki as the students' project as well as my assignment. For this reason, I encourage anyone building a wiki to spend multiple class periods on the process. By the end of the semester, class spirit was high, and students felt that they owned the wiki and the novel.

I broke down the research into multiple stages so they could practice finding and using sources. We discussed a short graduate-student essay linking a novel to primary texts in order to think through the intellectual aims of the approach. Then students chose a general issue germane to the novel, either from a list I provided or inspired by their own curiosity. After I created a page on the university library's website with links to online sources and databases, a research librarian came to class to explain why they were reliable, to stress the importance of properly citing sources (in particular, I limited their use of image databases to those in the public domain such as Wikimedia and Compfight), and to train them to do effective searches: how to use specific databases, how to vary search terms, how to assess the relevance of the source (British or American? Early or late nineteenth century?). Students wrote several smaller essays throughout the semester, beginning with a single source and receiving feedback from me, then including more sources and more explicit connections to the novel. At every stage, students reviewed copyright restrictions and practiced proper citation format. Many subjects were obvious: gender and marriage for both novels, medical reform for *Middlemarch*, the Stock Exchange for *The Way We Live Now*; others, such as Victorian popular novels, suicide, English views of American women and broken engagements, were less predictable. When I failed to fully solve the canned report problem in the *Middlemarch* class, I required *The Way We Live Now* students to frame their research explicitly in terms of questions rather than topics: what passages interested, puzzled or annoyed them? Their charge was not to provide some inert thing called 'context' but to help readers understand a problem or issue that the novel dealt with. Though I rather mindlessly chose the annotation format as a version of footnoting, it proved an important part of the assignment's success, since it forced students to deal with a specific moment in the text, explaining why it was problematic or complex.

At the end of the semester, in another period of festive chaos, they uploaded their essays and images, linked to a specific passage. Again, students helped each other, consolidating their ownership of the final product. They were extremely proud of their mastery of such a long, complex novel. Reflecting on the project, one student suggested cogent questions to guide the work of future authors: '(1) What aspects of *Middlemarch* are especially difficult to understand for a modern day reader? (2) Why did Eliot insert this particular literary, mythological, historical, or cultural reference? (3) How can I better understand the complexity and expansiveness of *Middlemarch* for myself?' (Anita Iyer, 'If you want to contribute', http://middlemarchuk.pbworks.com/w/page/65601840/If%20you%20want%20to%20contribute%3A%20wiki%20words%20of%20wisdom). Another student was more poetic in her assessment of the project: 'I didn't know the extent to which [Eliot] was making fun of Mr. Brooke until I understood the tenant and political references better. This means research. But really, research is awesome—like swimming around in a great...pool of new information and other people's insights. And then you, personally, get to put all that together in a condensed place for other people to swim around in! You are organizing knowledge. You are a historian and some kind of literary archaeologist. If that isn't intoxicating, I don't know what is' ('If you want to contribute', Anya Lorenzo, http://middlemarchuk.pbworks.com/w/page/65601840/If%20you%20want%20to%20contribute%3A%20wiki%20words%20of%20wisdom).

From the beginning, students knew that I was going to publish the wiki, announce it to my Victorian colleagues around the world through a scholarly listserv, and use it in future classes when I taught the novels. Ironically, the virtual nature of the project gave them a real audience. They took their writing seriously, instinctively crafting what Sheldon George calls a 'performed self' that melded their everyday selves with the role of expert (George 2012: 319). George calls attention to the gap between students' selves as they experience them in daily life, and the rhetorical and intellectual demands of college work, attributing some writing problems to the breakdown of a 'sense of effectiveness' (322). Fearing that 'the identities they already know how to perform are at odds with the expectations confronting them', students revert to comfortable colloquialisms or attempt to ventriloquize scholarly diction in stilted, awkward prose (322). As real players in a scholarly enterprise, however, addressing a student audience like themselves, most students gained access to a functional writing voice they could perform with some confidence, even with flair. Beginning her essay with an account of her frustration over the inconsistent behavior of a character, one imaginative scholar-student wrote,

Dear Reader,
    While reading Anthony Trollope's *The Way We Live Now*, I found myself unable to understand the greediness, the selfishness, and the money-hungry attitudes of the majority of Trollope's characters. As I read, I began to identify with Mr. Paul Montague, finding him to be an honest breath of fresh air within a novel of suffocating lies and secret agendas. Mr. Montague was a man of integrity, a man of honor; a man who completely changed when Mrs. Hurtle came to London. I was shocked and appalled as I learned Paul led on Mrs. Hurtle, visiting her almost daily, taking her to the theater, and kissing her goodbye! I thought to myself 'Why, Paul? You ended this engagement! I am on Team Hetta!' My love for this fictional character turned sour as his actions left me confused and upset. I did not understand why he could not tell Mrs. Hurtle to leave him alone. Dear Readers, I am here to tell you that Mr. Montague was not a confused man with conflicting emotions, unable to be honest with Mrs. Hurtle, but rather a victim of his era—an era that had numerous rules for entering and ending an engagement. (Tiana Sheehan, 'Broken Engagements', http://thewaywelivenow.pbworks.com/w/page/88507547/Broken%20Engagements%20in%20Victorian%20England)

Overall, student writing was smoother, more vivid and more purposeful than in the reports I assigned in the past.

Students also sought creative ways to frame their knowledge. Our Casaubon expert presented her research in the form of résumés for both men, including the unflattering portrait of John Locke and the more impressive image of Isaac Casaubon, making the contrast visually explicit. Intrigued by the connection, the student delved into the fictional scholar's accomplishments, not only listing all of his work but also learning which edition of which work Eliot was likely to have read. Moreover, with a scholarly audience metaphorically looking over their shoulders, students took citation seriously, scrupulously identifying websites and databases, and revising their citation formats until they were (nearly) perfect. When I published the wiki to colleagues, I was able to pass on their praise to the class. Students were thrilled that a professor at another institution voluntarily read and liked their work. When a colleague singled out the Casaubon pages for special praise, the student (a former science-type who had just switched majors to English, with much angst) was over the moon. The next *The Way We Live Now* class was impressed with the work of their peers, appreciating its accessibility and usefulness. Several students from the *Middlemarch* class continued the wiki as an independent study, adding annotations as well as more broadly focused essays. An unexpected opportunity arose when they received information about the National Undergraduate Research Conference. This prestigious showcase privileges science majors accustomed to group projects and poster presentations, but since the Middlemarchers had something to display, they were able to share their work with another audience. Needless to say, they were excited to be part of a national conference, gaining experience and a valuable credential that is often unavailable to humanities majors.

In short, the assignment placed students in a position to do real research: they were active producers of knowledge, with a real purpose and a real audience. Having a tangible (virtual) object to send out in the world left them with a stronger feeling of satisfaction than turning in a paper to a teacher, a private transaction that often seems to exist strictly for the purpose of evaluation. In these ways, it was a great success. As a teacher, I found I had a greater investment in their work as I followed their progress throughout the semester. I was genuinely eager to read the final results.

Of course, there were problems. The obvious issue is quality control. Some essays were outstanding; most were competent; a few were weak. Though the step-by-step process allowed me to catch some egregious errors, I still cringe over some of the dubious or simplistic interpretations. The author of the charming 'Broken Engagements' essay is not entirely right to absolve Paul of personal responsibility for leading Mrs. Hurtle on. If he is constrained by social pressures, he is also 'a confused man with conflicting emotions, unable to be honest with Mrs. Hurtle'. Perhaps this essay can be considered the bad kind of cultural studies that 'explains' a novel by invoking its context. But, as this student-scholar tells us, advice books provide genuine insight into Paul's predicament when they admonish young men, 'Should you ever be placed in such a situation, exercise the utmost tenderness and delicacy' (Tiana Sheehan, 'Broken Engagements, http://thewaywelivenow.pbworks.com/w/page/88507547/Broken%20Engagements%20in%20Victorian%20England). A comprehensive assessment would take into account both Paul's character and social mores. But this beginning scholar learned that characters do not behave in a cultural vacuum and that behavior that seems wrong to us might have different shades of meaning when placed in historical context. I considered making silent revisions, but in the end I respected the spirit of wikis and left the work as it was.

This brings me to my second disappointment. I began the wikis with the grandiose notion that they could become international resources as students in other classes used and revised them. Other readers could correct errors or offer alternative interpretations, leaving a record of student engagement as well as a repository of helpful essays. So far no one has taken me up on this offer. I invite readers of this essay to contact me if you'd like to fulfill this dream.

## Works Cited

Abbott, H. Porter. 2002. *The Cambridge Introduction to Narrative*. Cambridge: Cambridge University Press.

Bakhtin, Mikhail. 1981. *The Dialogic Imagination: Four Essays*. Edited by M. Holquist and translated by C. Emerson and M. Holquist. Austin, TX: University of Texas Press.

Bal, Mieke. 2009. *Narratology: Introduction to Narrative Theory*. Toronto: University of Toronto Press.

Burton, Antoinette. 2003. *Dwelling in the Archive: Women Writing House, Home, and History in Late Colonial India*. Oxford: Oxford University Press.

Cohen, Margaret. 2009. Narratology in the Archive of Literature. *Representations* 108 (1): 51–75.

Felski, Rita. 2015. *The Limits of Critique*. Chicago: University of Chicago Press.

George, Sheldon. 2012. The Performed Self in College Writing: From Personal Narratives to Analytical and Research Essays. *Pedagogy* 12 (2): 319–341.

Manifesto of the V21 Collective. n.d. *Ten Theses*. [online]. Accessed January 12, 2017. http://v21collective.org/manifesto-of-the-v21-collective-ten-theses/

Michie, Helena, and Robyn Warhol. 2010. Adventures in the Archives: Two Literary Critics in Pursuit of a Victorian Subject. *Victorian Studies* 52 (3): 413–441.

Middlemarch Magnifying Glass. 2012. [online]. Accessed January 12, 2017. http://middlemarchuk.pbworks.com/w/page/54359342/FrontPage

Rooney, Ellen. 2000. Form and Contentment. *Modern Language Quarterly* 61 (1): 17–40.

Sanders, Mike. 2016. Comment. Manifesto of the V21 Collective. n.d. *Ten Theses*. [online]. Accessed January 12, 2017. http://v21collective.org/manifesto-of-the-v21-collective-ten-theses/

Understanding The Way They Lived Then. 2015. [online]. Accessed January 12, 2017. http://thewaywelivenow.pbworks.com/w/page/84488110/Welcome%20to%20the%20wiki%21

Valdés, Mario J., trans. 1991. *A Ricoeur Reader: Reflection and Imagination*. Toronto: University of Toronto Press.

CHAPTER 9

# Digital Humanities in the Teaching of Narrative

*Suzanne Keen*

INTRODUCTION: VISUALIZING FICTIONAL WORLDS BY MAPPING

Rich resources supporting spatial visualization of novels and other narratives now exist online, making it possible to share the pleasures of tracing a character's steps through the kinds of fictional world that allude systematically to real places. One of the pleasures of reading novels set in cities that we know comes from mentally following along with peripatetic characters as they move through streets, parks, paths and neighborhoods. Digital Humanities projects such as Boston College's *Walking Ulysses: Joyce's Dublin Today* help guide the peregrinations of students fortunate enough to be studying abroad in Dublin as they read *Ulysses* (1922), while University of Victoria's *Dislocating Ulysses* provides a method for mapping the reading experience onto the modern city. As the authors remark, 'the project engages in the Joycean tradition of knowing through mapping by disrupting traditional mapping strategies... (1) suggesting that reading experiences can be mapped, visualized, and felt, and (2) suggesting that digital and physical models in fact, as Ruecker argues, make arguments in and of themselves' (Christie and Tanagawa). Asking students to

S. Keen (✉)
Washington and Lee University, Lexington, VA, USA

cross-reference their reading experiences of narratives with maps of real places is not a new pedagogical technique, but it has become easier to do because of the plethora of interactive maps, guides to walking tours and collections of visual images now available online. Engaging undergraduates in the creation of such resources (whether just for the class, or to be published on the web) amplifies their reading experiences, provides opportunities for writing that will be read by others beyond the professor and invites students into the process of discovery.

One of the premises of Digital Humanities work is that it employs data derived from and surrounding traditional objects of study in order to provoke fresh interpretations. For example, Emily Lethbridge's *Icelandic Saga Map* uses geo-referencing to annotate the map of Iceland with cross-references to the texts of the *Íslendingasögur*. Though such annotations might inform the discussions of archaeologists, the map was created to demonstrate that these medieval texts are still a living literature, albeit containing valued 'representations of historical Icelandic environments'. As Lethbridge and Hartman detail, the research questions and discoveries that arise from inscribing environmental memories from the sagas onto the map also reveal blends of historical memory and outright fictional imagining in the sagas: 'the descriptions of the past do not merely preserve memories; they also shape and transform them for use in the present and the future' (386). In short, a digital humanist still professes the humanities, frames humanistic research questions and privileges interpretation.

Employing the techniques of Digital Humanities analysis within a novel course need not require the sophistication and technical expertise of adepts in GIS in order to benefit students reading and analyzing narratives. This chapter suggests how one might go about integrating group work on a Digital Humanities mapping project within a novel course. It discusses the immediate pedagogical yield garnered from such an assignment, a yield that may make it worthwhile to swap out a traditional paper, or to redesign an essay assignment to link up to Digital Humanities exercises. I describe a modest mapping exercise in a course about London novels, with a frank account of the start-up effort required and the surprising cognitive gains realized by its incorporation into a traditional English novel syllabus. In a brief account of a pedagogically focused Digital Humanities Initiative at a small liberal arts college, I show how undergraduates can gain a digital skill set and more acute engagement with narrative texts by participating in TEI markup of a digital edition of a medieval epic poem. I refer to colleagues' Digital Humanities projects, for example involving undergraduate students in research that maps characters' movements in space, leading to new interpretations of canonical texts. To underscore the point that using Digital Humanities assignments in a novel course still participates in the core endeavor of humanities scholarship and criticism, I conclude with an example of a literary discovery that came about from such a collaborative project.

## LONDON NOVELS: MAPPING AND VISUALIZATION

Recently I designed an undergraduate course on modern and contemporary British fiction, in which a focus on London novels enabled me to think about students' knowledge (or lack thereof) of the city. They read Monica Ali's *Brick Lane* (2003), Elizabeth Bowen's *The Heat of the Day* (1948), Joseph Conrad's *The Secret Agent* (1907), Sebastian Faulks' *A Week in December* (2009), Penelope Fitzgerald's *Offshore* (1979), Ian McEwan's *Saturday* (2005), Hanif Kureishi's *Gabriel's Gift* (2001), Alan Moore's *From Hell* (1999), Zadie Smith's *NW* (2012), Sarah Waters' *The Night Watch* (2006), and Virginia Woolf's *Mrs. Dalloway* (1925). I anticipated that these college-aged English majors would have different levels of familiarity with London, some with travel experience, some with only secondhand knowledge of famous landmarks, and some with only readers' and movie-viewers' envisioning of the fictionalized city: they have all seen Harry Potter and his friends flying on broomsticks above the Thames. I was interested in attuning these students' reading process to develop the mental visualizing that they would bring to the imaginative fictional world-making that so vivifies novel-reading. When reading novels with real-world settings, that co-creative process vacillates back and forth between mental images of real places (informed by experience, by maps and by visual representations) and their description in narrative texts. The textual cues in the London novels we read that semester varied widely, with *Gabriel's Gift* the least specific about actual locations and *From Hell*, a graphic narrative that includes mapping of traumatic events onto Victorian London, the most precise though historically most distant. One of my aims was to prepare students for later visits to the real city, where I hoped that they would experience its geography with a consciousness of the fictional texts that lend it some of its significance.

Palimpsests of fictional habitation lend layers of significance to real places. On some occasions remarkable preservation of streetscape and landscape features strike the twenty-first-century reader with the frisson of the time-traveler, who can visit the rose garden in Regent's Park, think of the characters of Sarah Waters' *The Night Watch*, and imagine them bumping into Elizabeth Bowen's characters from *The Heat of the Day*. Though the cultivation of the historical imagination has long been a project of the novel, fiction writers (Neil Gaiman, China Miéville, J. K. Rowling) have as often imagined alternative Londons that never existed tethered to the real city by street names and tube and train stations. The thousands of visitors to Kings Cross Station's Platform 9¾ find a shop in the real world selling tickets for impossible trips on the Hogwarts Express. Acknowledging the presence of a fantasy world one layer away in the multiverse cultivates a kind of reading and looking at the world that acknowledges those possible layers of signification, seeing through the present-day and current conditions to imaginary worlds. A similar thing goes on when reading works set in the past. The imaginative *flâneur*, reading *Mrs. Dalloway* or visiting London today can recreate Clarissa Dalloway's walk wearing Virginia Woolf goggles without stumbling too often. Sometimes, of course, the neighborhood a character traverses has since been changed irrevocably—by aerial bombardment, fire or gentrification—so that we readers of a character's perceptions gain an image of a place *as it once was* to overlay our own more recent experience. I wanted my students to begin to build the literary familiarity that would make palimpsestic experiences like this possible, for I believe that the mental visualizing that enhances immersion in narrative worlds also improves empathy and even the disposition to act altruistically on behalf of others.[1] Some critics and teachers of literature believe that today's students lack the adeptness in mental visualizing that earlier generations of readers possessed.[2] To enhance my students' mental visualizing, I needed to train them to notice details of setting, sometimes mentioned only in passing by the writers we read.

I devised a simple Digital Humanities exercise, which enabled students to fill out a simple form in order to transcribe a brief literary allusion to a specific London location. Having located the street or park or reach of the Thames, a student submitting such a form would pin the location on a Google map of London. With the help of an academic technologist, we adapted the location-pinning function of Google maps so that a color code referred to the different novels we read. Though my preparation of the form involved a few hours of collaboration with the specialist, training the students required only the surrender of a single hour-long class session to practice (and immediate discussion of results) in a computer lab. We were fortunate to have a wall-sized display for the projection of our work-in-progress. Since this exercise relied on the participation of all students, I injected a competitive element by establishing that each literary allusion could be used only once. This attuned their reading to details of setting and inspired prompt attention to the homework, which could be performed online from any networked device. Realizing that timely work gave them the juiciest quotations, students quickly populated the map of London with pins all over Regents Park, the East End, Willesden and so forth. The contrasting pin colors allowed students to notice that the movements of characters in Ian McEwan's and Virginia Woolf's novels enjoy a great deal of proximity eighty years apart, while the characters in *Brick Lane* only once venture out of their ethnic enclave into tourist London. Students who had never set foot in London started to build an awareness of London neighborhoods today as well as in the past, in part aided by our reading of three novels set in the interwar or war years. I made historical maps available to supplement the contemporary Google map with which they worked.

Some of those maps had already been augmented by more sophisticated and well-funded Digital Humanities projects, whose glossiness and complexity might discourage an undergraduate teacher of narrative from undertaking a Digital Humanities project with students. These professionally produced sites are in themselves wonderful resources for novel teachers. For example, interactive Digital Humanities exhibits such as *Bomb Sight* assist in visualization of London streets before and after the World War II period, by mapping the bomb strikes of the Blitz and augmenting the pinpointed targets with images and witness testimony. *The Economist*'s map of 'The Great Inversion' (2013) shows how even a decade can make a difference in the socio-economic status of a neighborhood. The impulse to map economic status of their residents street by street originated earlier than web-enabled digital visualization and geo-referencing techniques. Charles Booth (1840–1916) is well known to scholars as the author of the magisterial seventeen-volume study, *Life and Labour of the People in London* (1889–1903), a comprehensive social and economic survey of poverty, industry and religion in London. Originally motivated as a study of census date to assist in allocation of poor relief, the study ran from 1886 to 1903. As the *Charles Booth Online Archive* explains,

> One of the most striking products of the inquiry were the maps of London coloured street by street to indicate the levels of poverty and wealth. The first of these series was produced based on the information gathered from

the School Board visitors representing the situation in 1889 and was widely circulated and commented upon. Ten years later, as the inquiry was still progressing, it was thought necessary to revisit the maps and a second series was produced, the *Maps Descriptive of London Poverty 1898–99*. These were based on the observations made by investigators accompanying policemen on their beats around London. (*Charles Booth Online*)

Working closely with beat policemen, whose notebooks have been digitized and made available online, the social investigators updated census records with

> the existing street-level information for the *Maps Descriptive of London Poverty 1898–1899*. The policemen were able to supply local knowledge of the area and inhabitants as well as probably providing protection. The reports of the walks record vivid descriptions of the streets of London, inhabitants and often a description of the policemen. The report of each walk is accompanied by a sketch map of the area covered in the walk. (*Charles Booth Online*)

The *Charles Booth Online Archive* makes accessible at http://booth.lse.ac.uk/ the most famous visualization of Booth's economic data, known colloquially as the 'poverty maps': http://booth.lse.ac.uk/cgi-bin/do.pl?sub=view_booth_and_barth&args=531000,180400,6,large,5. Booth's maps of London indicate the poorest neighborhoods with streets colored black, indicating 'Lowest class. Vicious, semi-criminal'. Only slightly better off are the people living on dark blue streets: 'Very poor, casual. Chronic want'.

My students used Booth's later nineteenth-century color-coded maps, supplemented by glimpses of twenty-first-century streetscapes in Google Street View, to understand what kind of neighborhoods they were pinning with literary allusions in their annotated London map. Juxtaposing Booth's map with Bomb Sight while they read *From Hell* helped them better understand the East End, for example, a neighborhood they were unlikely to know unless they had gone on a Jack the Ripper tour. Overall, this exercise in investigating neighborhoods, making inferences about how they might have changed in the intervening century, and pinning literary allusions to the map certainly heightened my students' awareness of writers' London as a literary construction. A pair of students travelled to London the following summer and took our maps with them, and others sought out pleasure reading with London settings. Some of the gains of employing a Digital Humanities exercises throughout my course were unexpected. I had anticipated and planned for greater attunement to literary motifs involved in setting. I had hoped for improvement in students' perceptions of movement through liminal spaces and across cultural as well as literal boundaries. I had not realized the degree to which students left to their own devices usually skip or ignore all locational descriptions. Furthermore, I naively overestimated my students' basic map skills. I learned that a significant subset of young people, equipped as they are with phones that help them navigate through voice commands, have very little idea where in the world they are. Most of my students could not show me which way was east, south or west, despite the fact that the class was taught in a room with large windows looking east to the Blue Ridge Mountains, west to the Alleghenies and south towards the edge of campus and town. Paradoxically, the experience of immersing themselves in fictional worlds set in London, practicing mental visualizing and connecting the imagery in their minds to a map of London made their actual orientation in space, in the Shenandoah Valley of Virginia, more palpable.

## APPLICATIONS TO MEDIEVAL AND MODERN NARRATIVES

Heightening my sense of the significance of these intellectual gains were the parallel experiences of colleagues who were also experimenting with Digital Humanities pedagogy. Faculty participating in Washington and Lee University's Digital Humanities Initiative (https://digitalhumanities.wlu.edu/), which aims to integrate Digital Humanities into undergraduate teaching in order to equip students with new analytical techniques, also realized remarkable gains in student learning. We intended to adapt research-oriented digital practices into our teaching, to enhance our students' critical thinking skills. While my own pedagogical project was very simple, several more ambitious projects required the assistance of collaborators in the library and in information technology, who were involved in our Digital Humanities Initiative from the start.[3] We established a support group, the Digital Humanities Action Team (DHAT), comprised of expert librarians and technologists, upon whom faculty could call for assistance in planning and implementing Digital Humanities projects within courses. Encouraged by modest incentive grants funded at first by the dean and then by a grant from the Mellon Foundation, such courses proliferated across the humanities, arts and social sciences.

Several of the courses augmented study of narrative texts with ingenious Digital Humanities projects carried out by students. Professor of German Paul Youngman launched a project, 'Mapping the Literary Railway', that carried over from advanced German literature coursework to funded student summer research. The project began with the study of the canonical work of literary realism, Theodor Fontane's *Effi Briest* (2016), a novel that makes symbolic meaning out of fictional journeys on real railways.[4] Using Neatline, a digital storytelling tool (an Omeka plugin) developed by Scholars Lab at University of Virginia,[5] Youngman and his students charted the train journeys of characters on real and imagined railway lines. Like the *Icelandic Saga Map*, some of the mapping cleaves quite closely to recognizable and documentable correlates in the real world (which Youngman's students emphasize by scanning and integrating historical train timetables and images of stations), but other data reveal fictional routes added to the story world by Fontane. These discoveries empower students to interrogate the slippery relationship of a celebrated realistic text with historical reality by revealing the scaffolding of fictionality that undergirds Fontane's symbolic use of the railway. Youngman's students presented their work at undergraduate research conferences both on campus and at other universities, an experience that took the student research process out of the nearly private transactional space between professor and student and brought it into true conversation with critical interlocutors. Additionally, their handiwork is freely available on the web, so the audience for their research and interpretations reaches well beyond the usual limits of the classroom. Whether many or few external readers find their way to 'Mapping the Literary Railway' (a project that continues today as new groups of Youngman's students add additional nineteenth-century German texts), the students' attitude about their work is infused with consciousness of an audience. Any writing teacher will attest to the fact that student writing improves markedly when undergraduates write for one another and for an outside readership rather than 'just' for a professor.

Employing Digital Humanities projects that can be made accessible on the web harnesses this effect for student learning in courses on canonical works, especially when those works are out of copyright. Engaging advanced undergraduate students of the novel in conversation about fair use and fair dealing principles in quotation from primary texts is another useful side-effect of devising Digital Humanities assignments that link excerpts of texts to maps published on the web. Perhaps even more exciting, collaborative scholarly Digital Humanities projects can bring accessible translations of obscure narrative texts to a broad audience, allowing students to participate in the scholarship of recovery and editing. For example, Washington and Lee French Professor Stephen McCormick's *The Huon d'Auvergne Digital Edition* is an 'international, interinstitutional, interdisciplinary project that presents the Franco-Italian *Huon d'Auvergne* romance-epic to a general audience for the first time' (*Huon d'Auvergne*). Emboldened by early successes in integrating Digital Humanities assignments into the syllabi of traditional undergraduate courses, McCormick and his librarian colleague Mackenzie Brooks taught a course on the medieval epics in romance languages with a 1-credit Digital Humanities Studio co-requisite. In that course students learned the theory and practice of textual encoding,[6] and became adept enough at TEI markup actively to collaborate in the production of a digital edition. In addition to the rewards of participating in the team effort involved in producing a National Endowment for the Humanities-funded digital edition, students soon encountered the interpretive challenges involved, not only in using TEI markup, but in comparing multiple differing versions of narrative texts. The typically invisible editorial work that lies behind the standard school editions of medieval and early modern narratives students usually read suddenly became vivid to them. Helping to create an edition that acknowledges the differences of competing originals also productively destabilizes students' notions of textual authority. At its very best, Digital Humanities projects within courses on narratives can provide opportunities for undergraduates to contribute as active collaborators in scholarly work that their professors publish to a professional audience. Though *de rigueur* in science teaching and not at all unusual in the social sciences, co-publication with undergraduate co-authors is still very uncommon in the traditional humanities. Digital humanities projects can open the way to that experience, especially when co-inquiry and crowd-sourced labor leads to discoveries. In the final section of this chapter I describe one such discovery from my London novels course.

## Gold and Rust Streets of London in Conrad's *The Secret Agent*

An important consequence of Digital Humanities practice is the leveling effect that occurs when students and faculty collaborate on shared discovery. Though publications in traditional literary studies have been slow to recognize multiple authorship, scholarly work employing Digital Humanities methodologies more often involves the work of many hands than solo authorship. Thus I recognize here the students who were involved in the discussions I describe below: Katherine Ballou, Anna-Katherine Barnes, Laura Berry, Jaclyn Calicchio, Cory Church, Taylor McPherson, Maureen Nalepa, Amanda Newton, Ryan Scott, Sarah Shepherd, Scott Sugden, Madeline Thorpe, Margaret Tolmie, Katherine Toomb and Katherine Uhlir.

As part of the mapping exercise described above, my students noticed the movements of *The Secret Agent*'s protagonist (not yet revealed as an anarchist bomber) through the streets of London. The locations specified by Conrad made excerpting allusions to sites a relatively simple matter, and our Google Map of London novels soon identified his route. In Chap. 2 of *The Secret Agent*, Mr. Verloc walks westward towards Knightsbridge where he will meet with his handler Mr. Vladimir in the Embassy. On his way, he passes by Hyde Park Corner:

> The very pavement under Mr. Verloc's feet had an old-gold tinge in that diffused light, in which neither wall, nor tree, nor beast, nor man cast a shadow. Mr. Verloc was going westward through a town without shadows in an atmosphere of powdered old gold. There were red, coppery gleams on the roofs of houses, on the corners of walls, on the panels of carriages, on the very coats of the horses, and on the broad back of Mr. Verloc's overcoat, where they produced a dull effect of rustiness. But Mr. Verloc was not in the least conscious of having got rusty. He surveyed through the park railings the evidences of the town's opulence and luxury with an approving eye. All these people had to be protected. Protection is the first necessity of opulence and luxury. (Conrad 1907: 11–12)

Because my students had access to Google Street View, they took a look at recent images of this affluent neighborhood. They saw no red or gold, but the restrained grey and white of stone and stucco, and the black of iron railings. We discussed the possibility that in the time period of the novel the railings had become rusted, but contemporary images did not support that hunch. They recognized that the focalization through Verloc might color his perceptions as represented by Conrad. We asked, 'in a neighborhood of white, grey, and black, why does Verloc perceive the street scene in hues of old gold and rust?' Turning to the explanatory notes in the Oxford edition, they found the diffident editorial suggestion that old-gold tinge could be explained this way: 'perhaps glancing ironically as the commonplace that "the streets of London are paved with gold"' (Conrad 1907: 235n). This seemed plausible, and students usually accept editorial notes as authoritative. They did notice the editor's softening 'perhaps'. Were it not for the comparison of the contemporary Google Street View with Booth's Poverty Map, though, my students may not have arrived at a quite different explanation for Verloc's perception of the wealthy neighborhood he walks through on his way to the embassy.

The usual focus for our class discussions of the Booth Poverty map was the coding of poor neighborhoods as dark blue for 'chronic want' and black for the 'lowest class' of 'semi-criminal' residences (see Fig. 9.1). We had paused over some gold-coded 'wealthy' neighborhoods to notice the proximity of blue blocks, usually right behind the rich people, in mews. The students wondered, could Verloc have seen Booth's poverty map? Could he (or his real-world counterpart opportunists) have used the Booth map to identify targets of opportunity? Conrad might have represented Verloc as perceiving the wealthy neighborhood in rust and gold in an allusion to the Booth map (see Fig. 9.2). This raised the question of

**Fig. 9.1** Legend for color-coding streets by degrees of affluence or poverty. *Charles Booth Online Archive*, http://booth.lse.ac.uk/static/a/4.html

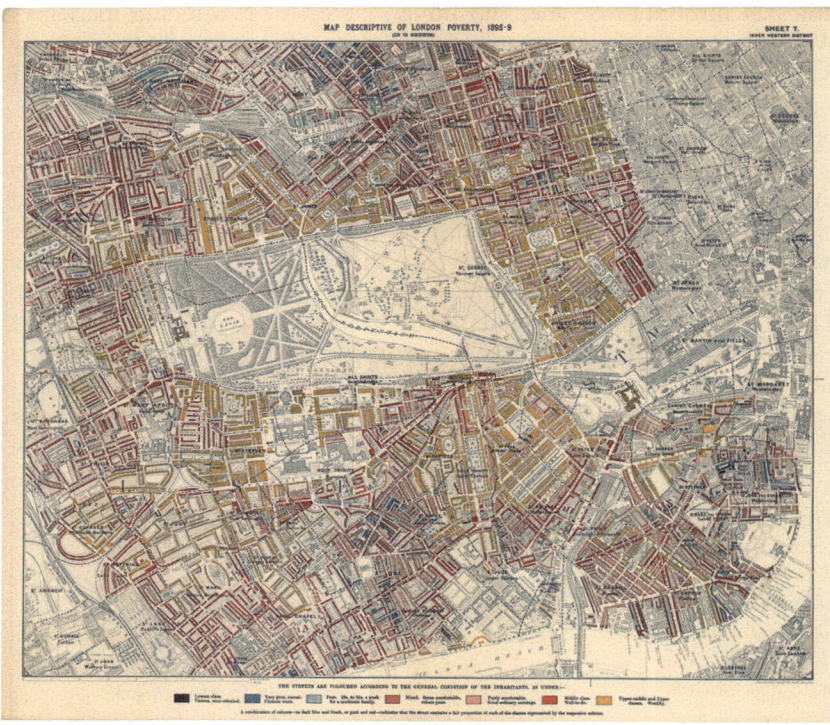

**Fig. 9.2** Hyde Park Corner, a wealthy neighborhood, from *Charles Booth Online Archive*. ('Printed Map Descriptive of London Poverty 1898–1899.' Sheet 7. Inner Western District. Covering: Pimlico, Westminster, Brompton, Chelsea, Mayfair, Marylebone, Paddington, Bayswater, Notting Hill, Kensington, Knightsbridge, Pimlico and Belgravia. LSE reference no. BOOTH/E/1/7.)

whether Joseph Conrad was aware of Charles Booth's map. The *Descriptive Map of London Poverty* was published in 1889 and updated and expanded in 1898–99. It was certainly possible that Booth had consulted the volumes. Since both men lived and worked in London at the same time, my students wondered if they knew each other personally.

The answer seems to be that Conrad knew of Booth, in more than one way. In a letter of 19 August 1908 to the painter William Rothenstein, who was painting a portrait of Charles Booth at the time, Conrad wrote,

> I am 'enormously' (as poor Flaubert would have said) pleased with what you tell me of Mr Booth. Of course his name has been familiar to me as the author of Life & Labour an undertaking whose very idea must have been prompted by a large human sympathy. As shipowner the name of his firm has been known to me much longer in the honourable reference of my fellow seamen. (Conrad 1983: v. 4, 105)

This remark in a letter establishes that Conrad knew Booth as the author of *The Life and Labour of the People*, which was published as a survey in 1889 and in nine volumes with maps in 1892–97, and in the full seventeen-volume version in 1902, just six years before this letter and five years before the publication of *The Secret Agent*. Conrad also knew of Charles Booth in his other identity, as the co-owner (with his older brother) of the steamship concern, Alfred Booth and Company (a Liverpool-based merchant-shipping company that operated between the UK and North and South America). To support this connection, I showed my students a letter from Charles Booth to Edward Garnett (an early editor of Conrad's outgoing correspondence). On 22 February 1896, Booth wrote to Garnett, who had evidently reached out to him seeking a favor on behalf of Conrad. Booth softens his rejection of Garnett's appeal with words of praise for Conrad the author: 'I am afraid I can do nothing to help Mr. Conrad. I wish I could. He certainly can write and it seems very hard if he cannot find present living with hope of future fame in his pen. He must be a very remarkable man' (Garnett 1928: 17). This compliment precedes a blunt assessment of the impracticality for Booth's large company of a scheme that Garnett had evidently proposed, by which a captain would own in part share his ship. Acknowledging that both the Norwegians and Welsh run such 'family' ships in businesses held by groups of relatives, Booth demurs, suggesting, 'there may be better chances of success in the South Seas with which Mr. Conrad is evidently acquainted' (Garnett 1928: 17). Blaming the economy but leaving open the possibility that Conrad lacks the necessary reputation to succeed, Booth remarks, 'I wish I had anything more encouraging to say—It is curious and rather melancholy that almost everyone has a discouraging word to say against the work with which he is most closely connected in these overcrowded days' (Garnett 1928: 17).

These remarks contribute to an ironic context for Conrad's oblique allusion to the wealthy gold and rust streets of London, marked out in those hues by the well-off social investigator Booth's economic maps.

Looking at the streets on the map opens up Conrad's imaginative characterization of the opportunistic Verloc, who traverses them apparently informed by Booth's analysis. Conrad sends Verloc to the foreign embassy (where he will receive his terrorist assignment, intended to stimulate class warfare) along a route already colored in the hues of wealth by Charles Booth. Looking approvingly at the wealthy as a class requiring protection, Verloc represents a menace to their security, and not only because he will be involved in a bomb plot (a plot that will actually injure only poor and pitiable characters close to him). Conrad suggests that Verloc uses well-intentioned tools of social analysis not to help the poor, but to identify the vulnerability of the affluent, leading to misplaced sympathies and harmful actions. Conrad suggests that Booth's project, which must have 'been prompted by a large human sympathy' (Conrad 1983: v. 4, 105), can point instead to whole neighborhoods of guarded riches. There may be a covert hint of opportunities in that situation for Verloc, but these are precisely not 'streets paved with gold', where anybody can make it rich, but roofs and edges colored in with powdery rust and gleaming gold, indicating precincts of entrenched wealth surrounded by barriers, as formally categorized by Charles Booth.

The preceding description suggests the kind of research question that can arise from applying spatial mapping techniques to texts commonly studied in an undergraduate novel course. The benefits of employing Digital Humanities pedagogy with undergraduate students are variable, diverse and sometimes unexpected, but they consistently include enhancement of students' purposeful writing for a real audience, of their opportunity to collaborate in the process of discovery (and sometimes, in co-authored presentations or publications), and of their familiarity with digital tools and techniques. As humanities graduates, our students are often called upon in their workplaces to demonstrate expertise in contemporary modes of analysis and communication. Experiences with Digital Humanities assignments help them build that skill set without abandoning the core intellectual purposes of their literary studies.

## NOTES

1. On the impact of mental visualizing, see Dan R. Johnson; on narrative empathy, see Keen, *Empathy and the Novel* (2007).
2. See for example, Alan Richardson, *The Neural Sublime* (2010: 54–55).

3. See Barry, Knudson, Sprenkle and Youngman, 'Launching the Digital Humanities Movement at Washington and Lee University: A Case Study' (2014).
4. Youngman and his student collaborators describe their project and its interpretive results in 'Visualizing the Railway Space in Fontane's *Effi Briest*' (2016).
5. On the open-source Neatline's development and uses, see Bethany Nowviskie, 'Neatline and Visualization as Interpretation' (2014).
6. Established in 1987 by a consortium (formalized as an international organization in 1999), TEI intended from the outset to develop standard methods for encoding humanities data electronically. It ensures both the longevity of digitally marked-up materials (for preservation purposes) and their accessibility as platforms change over time. See TEI: Text Encoding Initiative at http://www.tei-c.org/index.xml

## Works Cited

Barry, Jeff, Julie Knudson, Sara Sprenkle, and Paul Youngman. 2014. Launching the Digital Humanities Movement at Washington and Lee University: A Case Study. The Academic Commons for the Liberal Education Community, July 24, 2014. Accessed October 28, 2016. http://www.academiccommons.org/2014/07/24/launching-the-digital-humanities-movement-at-washington-and-lee-university-a-case-study/

*Bomb Sight: Mapping the WW2 Bomb Census*. Accessed November 9, 2014. www.bombsight.org, v. 1

Booth, Charles. (1902) 1903. *Life and Labour of the People in London*. 17 vols., 3rd ed. London: Macmillan.

Bowen, Elizabeth. 1948. *The Heat of the Day*. London: Knopf.

Charles Booth Online Archive. n.d. Booth Poverty Map & Modern Map. Accessed October 27, 2016. http://booth.lse.ac.uk/cgi-bin/do.pl?sub=view_booth_and_barth&args=531000,180400,6,large,5

Christie, Alex, and Katie Tanagawa. n.d. *Dislocating Ulysses*. Accessed September 19, 2016. http://web.uvic.ca/~achris/zaxis/index.html

Conrad, Joseph. 1983. *The Collected Letters of Joseph Conrad*. Edited by Frederick R. Karl and Laurence Davies, vol. 4. Cambridge and New York: Cambridge University Press.

———. (1907) 2008. *The Secret Agent*. Edited by John Lyon. Oxford and New York: Oxford University Press.

Garnett, Edward, ed. 1928. *Letters from Joseph Conrad: 1895–1924*. Indianapolis: Bobbs-Merrill.

'The Great Inversion'. 2013. *The Economist*, September 9. Accessed October 28, 2016. http://www.economist.com/blogs/blighty/2013/09/mapping-gentrification

Johnson, Dan R. 2012. Transportation into a Story Increases Empathy, Prosocial Behavior, and Perceptual Bias Toward Fearful Expressions. *Personality and Individual Differences* 52: 150–155.

Keen, Suzanne. 2007. *Empathy and the Novel*. Oxford and New York: Oxford University Press.

Lethbridge, Emily. *Icelandic Saga Map*. Accessed September 26, 2016. http://sagamap.hi.is

Lethbridge, Emily, and Steven Hartman. 2016. Inscribing Environmental Memory in the Icelandic Sagas and the *Icelandic Saga Map*. *PMLA* 131 (2): 381–391.

Nowviskie, Bethany. 2014. Neatline and Visualization as Interpretation. *Media Commons: A Digital Scholarly Network*, February 10. Accessed October 28, 2016. http://mediacommons.futureofthebook.org/question/how-can-we-better-use-data-andor-research-visualization-humanities/response/neatline-and-vi

Richardson, Alan. 2010. *The Neural Sublime: Cognitive Theories and Romantic Texts*. Baltimore: Johns Hopkins University Press.

Youngman, Paul, Gabrielle Tremo, Lenny Enkhbold, and Lizzy Stanton. 2016. Visualizing the Railway Space in Fontane's *Effi Briest*. *TRANSIT* 10 (2). Accessed October 28, 2016. http://transit.berkeley.edu/2016/youngman-et-al/

*Walking Ulysses: Joyce's Dublin Today*. 1922. Accessed October 28, 2016. http://ulysses.bc.edu/

Waters, Sarah. 2006. *The Night Watch*. London: Virago.

Woolf, Virginia. 1925. *Mrs. Dalloway*. London: Hogarth Press.

CHAPTER 10

# The Work of Narrative in the Age of Digital Interaction: Revolutions in Practice and Pedagogy

*Alec Charles*

> *All teaching is storytelling. 'Storytelling is the original form of teaching', notes Pedersen: 'There are still societies in which it is the only form of teaching'*
>
> (Pedersen 1995: 2)

At the one end of the scale there are the war stories and assorted anecdotes told by some of the grizzled old soldiers, reporters, writers, industrial chemists, small businesspeople and others who landed in the profession later in their careers. At the other end there is the fine and noble art of weaving tapestries of chronicles, vignettes, myths, metaphors and analogies to elaborate the grand narratives of history, culture, languages, sciences and mathematics.

Digital storytelling is simply the latest incarnation of this mode of pedagogic practice: 'For example', suggests Sadik, 'teachers can look at digital storytelling as a new way to humanize the teaching and learning of science and bring the beauty and power of mathematics to learners…digital storytelling [can] help teachers to make the connection between the subject

A. Charles (✉)
University of Winchester, Winchester, UK

© The Author(s) 2018
R. Jacobs (ed.), *Teaching Narrative*, Teaching the New English, https://doi.org/10.1007/978-3-319-71829-3_10

they teach and other subjects to provide a more meaningful context for learning' (Sadik 2008: 503). Digital narratives may involve the multimedia storytelling facilities of digital communication technologies; they may involve hypertextual multi-linearity (the use of links to generate a plethora of possible textual pathways), audience interactivity and instantaneous multiplatform distribution; but they are in essence still stories, ones whose modes of narration and reception have been facilitated by new media forms.

Let me therefore please, if I may, tell you a story.

## The Parable of the Two Sons

There once were two sons of a storyteller.

The first used traditional publishing platforms and modernist modes of literary discourse in order to create and disseminate his narratives. The second, younger son deployed digital media technologies in order to afford his reader semi-structured, non-linear journeys through his stories which involved a lot of clicking on underlined text in ways which reminded their father of the narrative choices which were afforded by those adventure game books which had been briefly popular during his youth.

The first son believed that his complex and finely crafted web of allusions, paradoxes and ambiguities promoted opportunities for interpretative choice which underpinned a collaborative, fluid and dynamic approach to the creation of meaning in radically re-envisioning the reader-(as)-writer relationship, and saw his texts as profoundly if problematically empowering to his readers.

The second son by contrast knew that his readers enjoyed the opportunity to click on things, and liked the sound and the moving pictures, and relished the idea that they could include their own comments, even though they knew that hardly anyone ever read those comments, and even fewer people valued them. And he knew that they even more adored the fact that they were encouraged to include photographic self-portraits of themselves in locations and situations pertinent (or vaguely pertinent) to his narratives, even though they secretly understood that all of his other readers ridiculed them for these images (just as they ridiculed those other readers for theirs).

And the second son became hugely rich and famous and popular and successful as a result of all this, because he knew that people prefer choice to quality, and that people prefer talking to listening, and shouting to talking, and just love the idea of power without responsibility.

But the first son sat back patiently and wrote his rather lovely stories, because he understood that wealth and fame and popularity and success built upon the whims and fashions of a fickle, narcissistic audience rarely last long.

And their father just worried what this might all mean for culture and civic society as a whole, especially as he would be retiring soon, and he was concerned for the value and security of his pension and the continuation of decent public healthcare services.

Yet his second son said to him, 'Father, my father, do not fret for I can offer you the most extraordinary array of navigational textual choices, so that you can really feel in control of your own destiny.'

Then his first son said to him, 'Father, dear father, do not fear, for I can offer you the most extraordinary array of interpretative textual choices, so that you can really feel in control of your own destiny.'

So the father looked from his first son to his second son, and from his second to his first, and from his first to his second again—and so on, and so on—and he recognized:

(a) that stories are incredibly important (because they define who we are) and that we need for all our sakes to get them right; or:
(b) that stories are incredibly important (because they elaborate our possibilities of being) but that, as there is no definitive narrative, what is important is to keep the conversation flowing for as long as we possibly can; or:
(c) that whichever way he turned, whichever mode of narrative he might choose, there was in the end very little difference between them.

So now it's up to you, then, isn't it? *You* choose.

## RISE OF THE CYBEROPTIMISTS

Papacharissi has suggested that new communication technologies tend to provoke 'narratives of emancipation' (Papacharissi 2010: 3). Curran et al. have observed that early advocates of the internet viewed that medium as 'a transformative technology' set to build 'a better world' (Curran et al. 2012: 34). Such cyberoptimists tended to suppose that these technologies offer a panacea for all of the ills of the world and thus herald an electronic utopia of democratic, economic and educational opportunities on a global scale, offering teachers, artists and writers the possibility of what Koskinen has called 'a New Alexandria' (Koskinen 2007: 117). As Tiffin and Rajasingham have suggested, in their envisioning of a 'global virtual university', the internet has been seen by some as 'a democratic virtual meeting place…a new Museion of Alexandria' (Tiffin and Rajasingham 2003: 26). Indeed, in the early days of mass internet use Tiffin and Rajasingham went further in their enthusiasm for the potential of this technology (Tiffin and Rajasingham 1995: 7):

> VR offers us the possibility of a class meeting in the Amazon Forest or on top of Mount Everest; it could allow us to expand our viewpoint to see the solar system operating like a game of marbles in front of us, or to shrink it so that we can walk through an atomic structure as though it was a sculpture in a park; we could enter a fictional virtual reality in the persona of a character in a play, or a non-fictional virtual reality to accompany a surgeon in an exploration at the micro-level of the human body.

One is tempted to recall in this context the avowed cyber-realist Andrew Keen's scepticism as to a 'mad utopian faith in our ability to conquer the physical world through virtual reality' (Keen 2008: xviii). While virtual reality continues to be used in the learning environment, its possibilities tend therein primarily to be exploited in response to the exigencies of distance learning, and, as Conrad et al. suggest, 'the adoption of a virtual self and immersion in a virtual environment' may offer its student-participants opportunities for journeys of self-exploration as much as for the acquisition of academic subject knowledge (Conrad et al. 2011: 272).

Despite this—or indeed because of this (insofar as we imagine education is as much about self-exploration as about knowledge acquisition)—there remains eager optimism in the beliefs of many teachers as to the potential of digital technologies to enhance the learning experience, and, in that teaching remains even in this digital age a mode of storytelling, as to the capacity of these technologies to promote educational techniques founded upon principles of narrative development. Signalling these capabilities of 'digital storytelling' Nilsson argues for the need for education to embrace 'the creative potential inherent in new media' (Nilsson 2010: 158)—while Tendero proposes that digital storytelling can enhance the practices of narrative education (Tendero 2006: 175).

Storytelling remains central to processes of both teaching and learning, not only as forms of instruction but also as mechanisms of integration, empowerment and the acquisition of cultural capital. The interactive potential of digital media may foster the development of dialogical spaces between teacher and learner which might blur those artificial boundaries between teaching and learning established by entrenched institutions of education, and which might transform learners from passive receivers of knowledge and wisdom into active elaborators and creators of their own experience and interpretations, and therefore into empowered, integrated and autonomous agents in cultural, political, professional, civic and epistemological praxis.

In their analysis of their own teacher-training programme in digital writing, Ching and Ching argue that the acquisition of narrative development skills affords learners opportunities 'to reflect on their histories and realign their identities and future trajectories' (Ching and Ching 2012: 217) insofar as, 'as humans we tell stories, not only to others but to ourselves, about ourselves, and these stories become real—more real, perhaps, than the phenomena being conveyed' (207). Bradbury also writes of her experience of 'using technology in the writing classroom' in order to support the development of digital narrative teachers: 'what students learned… was that the story we are being told by journalists, academics, cultural critics, and American popular culture is complex, inconsistent, at times polarizing' (Bradbury 2014: 64). Bradbury (64) adds that it is therefore crucial to 'teach twenty-first century literacy skills to students who not only daily engage in digital literacy practices that are changing the ways they learn, study, research, communicate, and think, but who also come to the classroom with their own set of assumptions about the role and power of technology in their lives'.

Bradbury's observations on the results of her own teaching practice demonstrate that digital storytelling offers opportunities for the development of a series of different literacies—verbal, technological, cultural, civic and media literacies—and also remind us that literacy involves not only the development of skills as a reader but also of those as a writer. There is clearly more to digital storytelling than the technology: the technology facilitates the scope, flow and flexibility of a process which allows students to write themselves into a socially situated mode of self-expression.

'It is not', write Underberg and Zorn, 'as some digital media students believe, just the software that needs to be learned' (Underberg and Zorn 2013: 8). They argue that there is a need in digital studies for learning 'how to understand a culture and how to communicate that information to non-members'. This learning is itself empowering: 'digital storytelling helps students become active participants rather than passive consumers in a society saturated with media' (Ohler 2006: 47).

Skouge and Rao propose that digital storytelling offers 'an approach that honours cultural diversity and empowers students to reflect on and share their experiences' (Skouge and Rao 2009: 54). Emert reports the value of digital narrative development in the empowerment of refugee children (both educationally and as an act of socialization): 'anchoring the literacy work in the narrative tradition allowed us to build on their interest in telling others about the transitions in their lives and, additionally, to use skills they already possessed to relate to us and to each other through storytelling' (Emert 2014: 37–38). In their study of the educational use of mobile telephone technology to develop narrative practices among young members of an immigrant community, Ranieri and Bruni conclude that 'storytelling seems to offer a favourable context for self-expression of marginalised groups. Digital media and online spaces seem to provide a fertile context for participatory culture and new engagement' (Ranieri and Bruni 2013: 233). Working in a similarly multicultural environment, Lotherington observes that her 'research to develop multiliteracies pedagogies through narrative learning' has revealed 'the overwhelming place of digital culture in children's…enculturation' (Lotherington 2011: 272).

Kajder similarly sees digital storytelling as a way to allow a 'culturally diverse, socioeconomically challenged' group of students to 'to tap into powerful communication tools to tell their story verbally, visually, and powerfully' (Kajder 2004: 64, 67–68). Flottemesch reports that digital storytelling can demonstrate impacts in bridging not only intercultural but also intergenerational divides as a process which may 'go beyond the classroom environment and translate to personal and meaningful intergenerational relationships' (Flottemesch 2013: 59).

Digital technologies and platforms have fostered attractive new modes of engagement in narrative practices. Anderson and Cook write of how digital narration can afford a process whereby children are 'empowered through the process of writing, narrating, illustrating, and ultimately assembling their own story' (Anderson and Cook 2015: 87). Couldry et al. note 'the possibilities for digital citizenship emerging through digitally supported processes of narrative exchange' supposing that 'digital media and digital infrastructures provide the means to recognise people in new ways as active narrators of their individual lives and the issues they share with others' and that 'such recognition matters within a view of democracy as social cooperation' (Couldry et al. 2014: 615). Fieldwork in a British sixth form college conducted by a related group of researchers observed that 'digital platforms and infrastructures, especially social media, offer heterogeneous preconditions for longer-term narrative exchange (what we have called "proto-agency") that potentially connects formal learning with wider society and social debate', but noted that in order to achieve this 'a shift had to be culturally negotiated from digital platforms focused on *delivery* to digital platforms and infrastructures facilitating *dialogue*, *exchange* and *collaborative participation* on scales far larger than the institution [the sixth form college] had, until now, negotiated' (Clark et al. 2015: 934–935).

Institutional needs have, however, often favoured the uses of digital storytelling development techniques for the purposes of vertical knowledge delivery and pedagogic instruction rather than to negotiate and promote the possibilities of such participatory collaboration and dialogical empowerment as Couldry and Clark imagine. Some more prescriptive educators emphasize the multimedia (but unidirectional) potentials of digital narrative pedagogy not in challenging authority-based notions of authorship but in underpinning more traditional modes of instruction: 'digital narratives are a multimedia authoring genre that can be used across a variety of school settings and for a variety of instructional purposes' (Fenty and Anderson 2016: 63). Alleyne (2015) also speaks extensively of the facilities of multimedia and hypertext in digital narrative composition; and it is evident that in this context the development of communication skills (including verbal communication skills) which are not exclusively dependent upon the written word permits a valid educational and epistemological shift beyond the precepts of an outmoded logocentrism (an emphasis of the word as the core of knowledge and culture). It may be noted that this process not only facilitates the development of such skills in students who may lack the advantages of traditional educational backgrounds; it also allows for the development of modes of intellectual understanding, interpretation and analysis which do not necessarily view the written word as the default medium of cultural communication—and thereby, for example, allows for the possibility that any particular medium might offer the best tool for the reflection and commentary upon artefacts within that medium (hence the rise, for example, of the photo-essay or the film-essay—an entirely photographic or cinematic construct—as the most appropriate vehicle for the analysis of photography or cinema).

There seems, however, something of an institutional conservatism in the perspectives of Fenty, Anderson and Alleyne: an underlying notion that the function of these technologies is to bolster extant institutional practices and structures (and therefore the *hierarchies* of teaching and learning) rather than to destabilize and deconstruct them. One might note in passing that academia has tended to express a comparable resistance to the development of Wikipedia (thus far, the world's most expansive manifestation of user-generated digital narrative) as a form of knowledge-authority independent of the institutional 'trappings and symbols of academic power' (Charles 2014: 165). Institutional structures are content to exploit those aspects of new technologies and platforms which maintain the academic status quo, but not to admit challenges to their epistemological hegemony.

Robin also emphasizes the multimedia aspects of digital storytelling rather than the more radical possibilities of interactive learning practices: 'at its core, digital storytelling allows computer users to become creative storytellers through the traditional processes of selecting a topic, conducting some research, writing a script, and developing an interesting story. This material is then combined with various types of multimedia, including computer-based graphics, recorded audio, computer-generated text, video clips, and music' (Robin 2008a: 222). Robin adds that 'digital stories usually contain some mixture of computer-based images, text, recorded audio narration, video clips, and/or music' (Robin 2008b: 429). Robin has in this way emphasized how digital storytelling in education may be employed to 'support instruction' (Robin 2006: 709)—but certainly not to deconstruct the primacy of pedagogic *instruction* itself.

In an essay on narrative pedagogy Gazarian depicts these digital texts as 'multidimensional stories conveyed through images, music, narration, text, and video clips' (Gazarian 2010: 287)—but also fails to emphasize the participatory and dialogical aspects of that multidimensionality. Seen this way, the 'instructional technology' of digital storytelling offers 'tremendous opportunities for teachers to engage and assess students' (Dreon et al. 2011: 5), but not a great deal else. These views tend to emphasize the pedagogic opportunities for attracting students to the development of narrative construction skills through the use of bright shiny buttons and graphics, without emphasizing the revolutionary potential for interactive applications of these technologies.

## CRITICAL INTERACTIONS

There appear three key specificities to digital narrative: the potential for multimedia functionalities (as discussed above); interactivity (dialogue, collaboration and user-generated content); and the ease of publication and response (speed, space, multiplatform dissemination and independence of institutional association). Ferrer (2011) has supposed that digital narratives are balanced between their potential for sensual immersiveness (a corollary of those multimedia facilities) and their potential for interactivity. The former, we might note, gives the illusion of participation; the latter offers actual opportunities for participation. (We shall return to the issue of publication and response at the end of this section, as it is closely tied to the issue of interactivity.)

There are clearly some controversies in relation to the value of interactivity in narrative construction. Bolter and Grusin have responded sceptically to those cyberoptimists who have argued that 'when broadcast television becomes interactive digital television, it will motivate and liberate viewers as never before' and that 'hypertext brings interactivity to the novel' (Bolter and Grusin 2000: 59). They have indeed suggested that these claims appear merely the latest iteration in a flawed narrative of historical progress whereby 'each new medium is justified because it fills a lack or repairs a fault in its predecessor, because it fulfils the unkept promise of an older medium' (59). Koskinen adopts a similarly suspicious approach to 'the notion of interactive narratives' (Koskinen 2007: 125) proposing that 'no one in his right mind can write an alternative ending to the story of Jesus Christ. Or what is the point in taking *Romeo and Juliet* and attempting to improve its dialogue by making it interactive?'

Bubb notes that 'artists working on the internet' tend to 'see this space as flexible and unrestrictive...rather than focusing on issues of narrative' (Bubb 2012: 59). Yet the infinite flexibility of this space might contradict the structural demands of narrative. Elsaesser reports fundamental questions as to the compatibility of narrative and interactive forms (Elsaesser 2014: 302):

> Interactive narrative is most commonly understood as the use of digital technology to construct virtual environments within which to present stories interactively, that is, with input and feedback from the spectator. Here, one right away encounters a paradox: one widely held view is that, basically, there is no such thing as an 'interactive narrative'. The term confuses narratives with games, and interactivity with non-linearity.

Elsaesser, however, adds that 'faced with interactivity as the new disciplinary norm of the control society...the digital archive and the database would be the ambiguous ground of both compliance and resistance... The challenge in each case is to shape an actual out of the virtual and to retain or regain agency from interactivity' (310). Ryan similarly notes that critics have demonstrated diverse views upon the uses of interactive narratives, and argues that there are 'good and bad solutions, success and failure, entertainment and boredom on all layers of the interactive onion' (Ryan 2011: 60). What seems crucial is the textual development of these technologies to promote the development of user agency.

Roland Barthes famously argued that traditional texts represent what he called the *lisible* or readerly: fixed, final and finite products, rather than ongoing processes of interpretative production. Barthes' antithesis to this classic readerly text was the writerly or *scriptible* text. This textual ideal was founded upon the premise that the progressive function of literature is to transform the reader from a passive consumer into an active producer of meaning (Barthes 1974: 4). Barthes' writerly text (epitomized by the modernist experimentalism of such authors as James Joyce) resists semiotic closure and invites, embodies and requires cooperation and co-authorship: it understands that meaning is an act of interpretation rather than of intention or expression. As Barthes proposes, the semantic plenitude of the text originates where it is destined to end, in the mind not of its author but of its audience (Barthes 1977: 148).

But do those digital media texts which offer their 'produsers' (user-producers) the opportunity to generate their own versions of their narratives (from video games and hypertext-heavy news services, to blogs, vlogs, social media and Wikipedia) all invariably promote authorial collaboration, or do they merely sponsor the illusion of such empowerment? Manovich has argued that this 'myth of interactivity' offers its audience only an illusion of agency: 'interactive media ask us to click on a highlighted sentence to go to another sentence. In short, we are asked to follow pre-programmed, objectively existing associations' (Manovich 2001: 61).

The traditional video game, for example, affords its users the semblance of self-determination but it is one based, for the most part, upon an *illusion* of interactivity. Newman (2002) has argued that 'one of the most common misconceptions about videogames is that they are an interactive medium' and Arsenault and Perron have similarly challenged the popular notion that the video game is a predominantly interactive medium (Arsenault and Perron 2009: 119–120). They argue that in fact players are not active but reactive—that players respond to programmed structures within the game, structures designed to predict and react to the gamers' responses. The illusion of interactivity sponsors a sense of agency—but this agency has been externally predetermined or pre-designed. This illusion, however, remains central to the pleasure of the video game, a pleasure generated by a process whereby 'players regard themselves as the most important...causal agent in the environment' (Klimmt and Hartmann 2006: 138).

Yet does the evolution of multiplayer role-playing games in such virtual environments as offered by *World of Warcraft* afford opportunities for players to become authors who interact to construct their own narratives? The analysis of digital games has been caught since its beginnings between narratological and ludological approaches—the controversy as to whether these artefacts are to be seen primarily as texts or games. While Genvo suggests that 'narrative semiotics' may help to elucidate the processes of 'ludic mediation' (Genvo 2009: 139), we may be forced at this point to admit the limits of narratology. When a life is lived in cyberspace is it, after all, any more of a narrative than a life lived in the offline world? It may be a game (insofar as it involves interplay according to a set of rules and impacts extraneous to the material realm) but it is not a story. Stories are the tellings of lives, not the livings of lives. The livings of lives are just lives, offline or not.

Narrative construction takes place when one chooses to interpret or invent lived experience through repeated or recorded forms of storytelling (which may or may not be verbal): whether this be the novels of Tolstoy, the plays of Shakespeare, the films of Hitchcock, the paintings of Michelangelo or the diary entry, wiki contribution, vlog, blog or social media status update of any one of us. The process of writing comes to situate and define the writer. As de Man suggested, 'whatever the writer *does* is in fact governed by the technical demands of self-portraiture' (de Man 1984: 69). Our narratives transform existence into essential being; and the digital domain has afforded unprecedented opportunities to archive and disseminate such narratives.

The process of narrative construction is both introspective and extrospective. Digital storytelling (as an act of emancipation) is a process both of expressive liberation and of the self-disciplined acquisition (or indeed revolutionary seizure) of social and cultural capital. Much has been made of the internet's capacity to foster modes of interactive expression and publication from the point of view of the primary producer of meaning (the *author* of the digital narrative); and cybersceptics might suppose that this analysis reinforces the notion of the web as a site for narcissistic self-promotion. It might also be useful at this point to invoke the role and influence of the active *audience* in these processes of online interactivity—and in particular, in the process of narrative (self-)development, to explore how such interactivity might sponsor ways in which learner-writers (a category which should perhaps encompass *all* writers) can address their audiences by developing critical responses to the immediacy of reader feedback, and by exploring opportunities for ideational and aesthetic collaboration without sacrificing specificities of concept, perspective and voice—rather than merely shouting their unheard messages out into the long dark night of cyberspace.

Lawrence et al. point out that 'digital writing has enabled students to write for a variety of authentic audiences, both in and out of the classroom' (Lawrence et al. 2015: 201). The ease of online publication clearly impacts both upon students' enthusiasm for narrative construction and upon their own development of professional attitudes to those audiences (writing for those identified audiences rather than merely for themselves). In their own case study Lawrence at al. also emphasize the dialogical aspects of such practice: 'the peer audience in this study had opportunities to discuss, confront, and ask questions of peer authors (and from experience, students could expect their peers to read and provide feedback either in real life or via the forum) after posting their writing to the forum' (216). In a similar way the storytelling practices of both professional journalists and journalism students have been radically affected by the immediacy of audience and stakeholder feedback afforded by online publication; and one can witness similar developments in, for example, creative blogging and online filmmaking practices.

The contemporary journalism student can, for instance, therefore be encouraged to enhance their own professional standards through the real online publication of their work. This publication can take the form of their own blogging space: many students will of course already have their own blogs, and most should be familiar with the form. Such students can therefore learn, through the production of more audience-friendly content, to move from using the basic blog template to frame an obscure repository of their own personal opinions and anecdotes, towards the transformation of that space into a professionally structured and designed platform for proficiently sourced and narrated reportage. The journalistic blog can promote the development of traditional planning, research, writing, storytelling and design skills (producing a clearly themed and branded product offering original, crafted content to defined audiences), alongside skills in multimedia production (integrated text, graphics, animation, audio, video and photography), social media integration (parallel social media feeds, and opportunities for readers to post links thereto on their own feeds), hyperlink construction (including hyperlinks not only within the student's own blog archive but also to other organizations, and fostering reciprocal links from such organizations back to the student's blog) and audience feedback mechanisms and response processes (from the live moderation of comments within the blogging space, to reactions to comments in social media spaces—including ongoing revisions to original content and the addition of crowd-sourced materials).

This practice need not, of course, be limited to an individual student's journalistic (or creative) blog or vlog. Educators can establish (or support the establishment of) a hyperlinked and interactive network of such blogs branded within a consistent design and architecture as a badged classroom community. Such a network might take the form of a news website—one whose value to external audiences is founded not only upon the quality but also upon the specialist focus of its reportage (most commonly offering local, hyperlocal or institutional news, reviews, information and platforms for debate). Such sites can, of course, intra-institutionally, collaborate and amalgamate with sites produced by students of cognate academic disciplines (for example, in the convergence of journalism, filmmaking and creative writing sites). They can also enter into similar collaborative arrangements with related websites developed by community organizations and other educational institutions (including regional, national and international partners). Through the evolution of such networks of interaction and collaboration—with internal and external audiences, with stakeholders and local communities, and with their peers in diverse disciplines, institutions and cultures—students may develop competencies not only in storytelling but also in participatory citizenship.

## Hypertext

Jacques Derrida once described James Joyce's last two novels (*Ulysses* and *Finnegans Wake*) as comprising the last word in digital textuality—coalescing to form a '1000th generation computer' (Derrida 1984: 147). One might view this as setting the bar admirably high for what interactive or *scriptible* narrative might achieve: that self-styled 'letter self-penned to one's other, that neverperfect everplanned' by literature's greatest 'punman' (Joyce 1939: 489, 517).

Yet we might respond to Derrida that the text is not the computer but the software. The computer is the human brain—the amalgam of minds and memories, the culture—through which it runs. This is not to suggest that the human mind is an empty and passive vessel for the text; if it is a computer it is one which already has other programs—other memes, other cultural materials—interacting with it. Its hypertext links—its network of intratextual and intertextual allusions—are established through the memories of its readers. Its multimedia functionalities—its deployments of sound, form, image, movement, emotion and so many other sensory phenomena—are forged in their imaginations. Its capacity for interactivity is founded upon its readers' ability to engage in the creative interpretation of its ambiguities and obscurities. The proactive responsibility (response-ability) of the readership and the melding of audience and authorial authorities remain vital. This point might be borne in mind as we address the core issues exposed by these reflections.

There would appear three main challenges in the teaching of narrative development through digital media:

1. *The interactive, non-linear and ludic natures of digital platforms do not necessarily appear to lend themselves to traditional narrative structures. How can attempts at narrative interactivity simultaneously avoid the traditional video story-game's false interactivity and the online multiplayer life-game's false narrativity?* Some of our most sophisticated literary narratives—masterworks of modernism and postmodernism—are artefacts of playful interactivity and multi-linearity. If literary development is dependent upon the sophistication of the writing itself, rather than upon a reliance on the tools of the latest medium—which, as Bolter and Grusin (2000) reminded us, are just as flawed as such tools have always been—then that narrative software will discover that the prime site for semiotic collaboration is neither the computer interface nor cyberspace itself (these are mere facilitators of that collaboration) but the minds of its active audience-creators—its reader-writers, its *produsers*—themselves.

2. *The emphasis which digital media put upon self-expression is not necessarily conducive to classical structures of narrative communication. Narrative production becomes a mode of narcissistic self-promotion rather than a means to communicate and interact with (and empower) active audiences.* But insofar as our acquisition of this technological

capital is—as the likes of Underberg and Zorn (2013) suggest—paralleled by the acquisition of cultural capital, and insofar as our learning processes exploit the interactive potential of these media to deconstruct unidirectional hierarchies of knowledge and communication, we may therein develop the capacity not only to tell our own stories but to develop stories which—as Skouge and Rao (2009), Ching and Ching (2012) and Ranieri and Bruni (2013) propose—allow us to define our social situations and audiences, audiences with whom we can engage in dialogues which, as Anderson and Cook (2015) suggest, themselves underpin the development of broader civic participation and empowerment.

3. *Many of the promises which these media forms have made in relation to narrative advances have not been realized and are perhaps unrealizable.* If, however, we recognize that technologies are tools rather than solutions—if, as Lawrence et al. (2015) suggest, we take responsibility for our own stories, for our own narratives of situation, participation and emancipation—then we may eschew that illusion of agency which, Manovich (2001) warns, these technologies may offer us, an illusion which dilutes the desire for, and therein the possibility of, such empowerment—and instead develop that nascent social autonomy or *proto-agency* envisaged as resulting from digital narrative learning by Clark et al. (2015). Communicational interaction remains an interpersonal activity. Digital technologies are not in themselves interactive but facilitate interactivity with other people.

Though the pedagogic panacea once anticipated by such early educational cyberoptimists as Tiffin and Rajasingham (1995, 2003) may not as yet have materialized, the questions which these technologies pose as to how we teach narrative open up possibilities as to the development of both educational and narrative structures, practices and modes of reception which may inscribe, enhance and transcend blogging and citizen journalism, Wikipedia, social media, virtual worlds and video games. Digital storytellers may outstrip the amateurishness of so much of today's user-generated content in order to seize the opportunity—by prioritizing sophistication of content over the influence of technological forms, by learning to listen to audiences and by transforming audiences into active participants in literary, cultural, educational civic and social processes—to promote a late postmodern incarnation of Barthes' *scriptibilité*.

Writers, in short, become better writers when they are also better readers, and when their readers become writers too. Digital narrative developments offer vast capacities for interactive listening, as well as massive temptations to scream alone into the ether. The evolution of writing and reading might best be served when those two practices become indistinguishable. While digital technologies may play some part in the facilitation of that process, what really counts will be the evolution of content, of the textual matter itself, an evolution only made possible by learning, listening and interaction.

We return, finally, then to the parable of the old fabulist and his literary sons. But if the moral of the story is that we must choose between those different creative options, then why, we might reasonably ask, should we? The realm of textual possibilities is indescribably large, contradictory and contains multitudes. Let us have them all.

What do you mean, that's not what that story meant at all? Let's leave it open then. You are, after all, most keenly entitled to your own interpretations.

## WORKS CITED

Alleyne, Brian. 2015. *Narrative Networks: Storied Approaches in a Digital Age*. London: Sage.

Anderson, Kim, and Jonathan Cook. 2015. Challenges and Opportunities of Using Digital Storytelling as a Trauma Narrative Intervention for Children. *Advances in Social Work* 16 (1): 78–89.

Arsenault, Dominic, and Bernard Perron. 2009. In the Frame of the Magic Cycle: The Circle(s) of Gameplay. In *The Video Game Theory Reader 2*, ed. Bernard Perron and Mark Wolf, 109–131. London: Routledge.

Barthes, Roland. 1974. *S/Z*. Translated by R. Miller. New York: Farrah.

———. 1977. *Image-Music-Text*. Translated by S. Heath. London: Fontana.

Bolter, Jay, and Richard Grusin. 2000. *Remediation*. Cambridge, MA: MIT Press.

Bradbury, Kelly. 2014. Teaching Writing in the Context of a National Digital Literacy Narrative. *Computers and Composition* 32: 54–70.

Bubb, Jeremy. 2012. Back to the Future: Multi-Image Screen Narrative in a Digital Age. *Journal of Media Practice* 13 (1): 45–60.

Charles, Alec. 2014. *Interactivity 2*. Oxford: Peter Lang.

Ching, Kory, and Cynthia Ching. 2012. Past is Prologue: Teachers Composing Narratives About Digital Literacy. *Computers and Composition* 29: 205–220.

Clark, Wilma, Nick Couldry, Richard MacDonald, and Hilde Stephansen. 2015. Digital Platforms and Narrative Exchange: Hidden Constraints, Emerging Agency. *New Media & Society* 17 (6): 919–938.

Conrad, Marc, Alec Charles, and Jo Neale. 2011. What Is My Avatar? Who Is My Avatar? In *Reinventing Ourselves: Contemporary Concepts of Identity in Virtual Worlds*, ed. Anna Peachey and Mark Childs, 253–273. London: Springer.
Couldry, Nick, Hilde Stephansen, Aristea Fotopoulou, Richard MacDonald, Wilma Clark, and Luke Dickens. 2014. Digital Citizenship? Narrative Exchange and the Changing Terms of Civic Culture. *Citizenship Studies* 18 (6–7): 615–629.
Curran, James, Natalie Fenton, and Des Freedman. 2012. *Misunderstanding the Internet*. Abingdon: Routledge.
de Man, Paul. 1984. *The Rhetoric of Romanticism*. New York: Columbia University Press.
Derrida, Jacques. 1984. Two Words for Joyce. In *Post-Structuralist Joyce*, ed. Derek Attridge and Daniel Ferrer, 145–159. Cambridge: Cambridge University Press.
Dreon, Oliver, Richard Kerper, and Jon Landis. 2011. Digital Storytelling: A Tool for Teaching and Learning in the YouTube Generation. *Middle School Journal* 42 (5): 4–9.
Elsaesser, Thomas. 2014. Pushing the Contradictions of the Digital: Virtual Reality and Interactive Narrative as Oxymorons Between Narrative and Gaming. *New Review of Film and Television Studies* 12 (3): 295–311.
Emert, Toby. 2014. Hear a Story, Tell a Story, Teach a Story: Digital Narratives and Refugee Middle Schoolers. *Voices from the Middle* 21 (4): 33–39.
Fenty, Nicole, and Elizabeth Anderson. 2016. Creating Digital Narratives: Guideline for Early Childhood Educators. *Childhood Education* 92 (1): 58–63.
Ferrer, Raquel Herrera. 2011. Proposal of Strategies to Develop a Taxonomy of Digital Narrative. *Hipertext.net*, 9. http://www.upf.edu/hipertextnet/en/numero-9/taxonomy-digital-narrative.html
Flottemesch, Kim. 2013. Learning Through Narratives: The Impact of Digital Storytelling on Intergenerational Relationships. *Academy of Educational Leadership Journal* 17 (3): 53–60.
Gazarian, Priscilla. 2010. Digital Stories: Incorporating Narrative Pedagogy. *Journal of Nursing Education* 49 (5): 287–290.
Genvo, Sebastien. 2009. Understanding Digital Playability. In *The Video Game Theory Reader 2*, ed. Bernard Perron and Mark Wolf, 133–149. London: Routledge.
Joyce, James. 1939. *Finnegans Wake*. London: Faber and Faber.
Kajder, Sara. 2004. Enter Here: Personal Narrative and Digital Storytelling. *The English Journal* 93 (3): 64–68.
Keen, Andrew. 2008. *The Cult of the Amateur*. London: Nicholas Brealey Publishing.
Klimmt, Christoph, and Tilo Hartmann. 2006. Effectance, Self-Efficacy and the Motivation to Play Video Games'. In *Playing Video Games: Motives, Responses*

*and Consequences*, ed. Peter Vorderer and Jennings Bryant, 133–145. New Jersey: Lawrence Erlbaum.

Koskinen, Ilpo. 2007. The Design Professions in Convergence. In *Ambivalence Towards Convergence*, ed. Tanya Storsul and Dagny Stuedahl, 117–128. Göteborg: Nordicom.

Lawrence, Joshua Fahey, Melissa Niiya, and March Warschauer. 2015. Narrative Writing in Digital Formats: Interpreting the Impact of Audience. *Psychology of Language and Communication* 19 (3): 201–221.

Lotherington, Heather. 2011. Digital Narratives, Cultural Inclusion and Educational Possibility: Going New Places with Old Stories in Elementary School. In *New Narratives: Stories and Storytelling in the Digital Age*, ed. Ruth Page and Bronwen Thomas, 254–276. Lincoln, Nebraska: University of Nebraska Press.

Manovich, Lev. 2001. *The Language of New Media*. Cambridge, MA: MIT Press.

Newman, James. 2002. The Myth of the Ergodic Videogame. *Game Studies* 2 (1). http://www.gamestudies.org/0102/newman/

Nilsson, Monica. 2010. Developing Voice in Digital Storytelling Through Creativity, Narrative and Multimodality. *Seminar.net–International Journal of Media, Technology and Lifelong Learning* 6 (2): 148–160.

Ohler, Jason. 2006. The World of Digital Storytelling. *Educational Leadership* 63 (4): 44–47.

Papacharissi, Zizi. 2010. *A Private Sphere: Democracy in a Digital Age*. Cambridge: Polity Press.

Pedersen, E. Martin. 1995. Storytelling and the Art of Teaching. *English Teaching Forum* 33 (1): 2. http://dosfan.lib.uic.edu/usia/E-USIA/forum/vols/vol33/no1/P2.htm

Ranieri, Maria, and Isabella Bruni. 2013. Mobile Storytelling and Informal Education in a Suburban Area: A Qualitative Study on the Potential of Digital Narratives for Young Second-Generation Immigrants. *Learning, Media and Technology* 38 (2): 217–235.

Robin, Bernard. 2006. The Educational Uses of Digital Storytelling. In *Proceedings of Society for Information Technology & Teacher Education International Conference 2006*, ed. C. Crawford, R. Carlsen, K. McFerrin, J. Price, R. Weber, and D. Willis, 709–716. Chesapeake, VA: Association for the Advancement of Computing in Education.

———. 2008a. Digital Storytelling: A Powerful Technology Tool for the 21st Century Classroom. *Theory into Practice* 47 (3): 220–228.

———. 2008b. The Effective Uses of Digital Storytelling as a Teaching and Learning Tool. In *Handbook of Research on Teaching Literacy Through the Communicative and Visual Arts*, ed. James Flood and Shirley Brice Heath, 429–440. New York: Routledge.

Ryan, Marie-Laure. 2011. The Interactive Onion: Layers of User Participation in Digital Narrative Texts. In *New Narratives: Stories and Storytelling in the Digital Age*, ed. Ruth Page and Bronwen Thomas, 35–62. Lincoln, Nebraska: University of Nebraska Press.

Sadik, Alaa. 2008. Digital Storytelling: A Meaningful Technology-Integrated Approach for Engaged Student Learning. *Educational Technology Research and Development* 56: 487–506.

Skouge, James, and Kavita Rao. 2009. Digital Storytelling in Teacher Education: Creating Transformations Through Narrative. *Educational Perspectives* 42 (1/2): 54–60.

Tendero, Anotonio. 2006. Facing Versions of the Self: The Effects of Digital Storytelling on English Education. *Contemporary Issues in Technology and Teacher Education* 6 (2): 174–194.

Tiffin, John, and Lalita Rajasingham. 1995. *In Search of the Virtual Class*. Abingdon: Routledge.

———. 2003. *The Global Virtual University*. London: Routledge.

Underberg, Natalie, and Elayne Zorn. 2013. *Digital Ethnography: Anthropology, Narrative, and New Media*. Austin, TX: University of Texas Press.

CHAPTER 11

# Empowering Students as Researchers: Teaching and Learning Autoethnography and the Value of Self-Narratives

*Jess Moriarty*

## INTRODUCTION

> Good autoethnography is...a provocative weave of story and theory. (Denzin 1992: 25)

Creative writing workshops can and must provide safe ground for developing the imagination and the sharing of stories. In my own teaching, I have always tried to encourage students to view the discipline of Creative Writing as a craft, an arts-based practice that can (and should) be informed by research. They should be encouraged to play and take risks and not damage themselves with vicious self- (or even peer or tutor) critique but they should also recognize that it is a discipline, as important as any other, and that research can (and will) inform and enrich their study and process. The process of making is central to developing knowledge (Knights 2008; Charney 2011) and this needs to be acknowledged and celebrated in our teaching of creative writing. Equipping students with the skills to hone and craft their ideas into evocative texts in a variety of genres is an essential

J. Moriarty (✉)
University of Brighton, Brighton, UK

part of any writing course, but it is also important that students have the confidence to draw on their lived experiences and consider ways to bring their autobiographical narratives (back) to life.

When I started as a creative writing tutor on undergraduate and postgraduate modules at the University of Brighton in 2006, I discovered a tension between asking students to engage in a process of developing self-narratives whilst simultaneously suggesting that they remove the 'I' when they discuss their writing practice in their academic essays. It was a tension I experienced in my own work when completing a doctorate—why must we deny a personal link to our writing? Why must we pretend to be objective when how we view and experience the world and the narratives we develop are often inextricably linked? My research into autoethnography helped me to identify a methodology that allows me to talk about my own experiences and for this be a valued component of my academic work. I now regularly adopt an autoethnographic approach to my research and writing and have used it to argue that creative and evocative writing, including autobiographical narratives, should be viewed as a rich research tool and a way of accessing insider accounts as to what things can be and are like. My own work has explored experiences with academic writing via a script that drew on my experiences and interview data from academics at varying stages of their career (Moriarty 2015a); adopted a splintered narrative that merged script, poetry and memoir to detail my experiences of completing a creative PhD (Moriarty 2015b); and a study of the effects of neo-liberalism using autoethnodrama (Moriarty 2016). Having been told that any creative writing I produced would not be deemed worthy for the Research Excellence Framework (REF), the framework used for judging academic's success in terms of academic writing (Canagarajah 2002), it has been an absolute revelation to discover a methodology that permits creative work in academic research. In this way, I can allow research to inform my practice and present my findings via academic books, journal articles and chapters and also at conferences and in my teaching too. Instead of feeling fraudulent when I talk about writing in workshops and seminars, I now feel I can balance the expectations of my institution for publishable academic work with my own desire to write creatively and share what that experience and process is like with my students. It has brought me some balance in my academic life, and at a time of increasing pressure to do more for less and a shift towards a more neo-liberal audit culture in HE (Docherty 2012), this balance is not merely desirable, it is vital. In this chapter I explore the potential benefits of working with students on autoethnographic work and how it can inform and enhance their life writing, their confidence with their studies and also with themselves.

The benefits of linking my autobiographical experiences with the material I was studying via evocative and creative writing and research was transformational. But what I was advocating was so contrary to the style of traditional journal articles, chapters and handbooks that even as a doctoral student, I had been advised that my work might not be viewed as rigorous or 'academic' enough. Even now, I still receive rejection letters from journals dismissing creative writing in scholarly work. Undergraduate and postgraduate students are often resistant to explicitly research-led practice, preferring just *to do* creative work (Cardell and Douglas 2016). This coupled with the introduction of fees which has changed and intensified the pressure to do well at university means that persuading already reticent students to gamble their increasingly expensive degree by employing a methodological stance that is 'other' to dominant conventional academic practice can be a challenge. Legitimizing creative writing as an academic discipline by enhancing its epistemological status and engaging students with ways of conducting research that are potentially more democratic and inclusive make this challenge not only welcome but necessary. How, then, to bring emerging research methodologies that link research and writing practice to my teaching of self-narratives and encourage students to engage with research methods that resist the established, conventional practices of academic writing that dominate academic discourse at almost every level?

## AUTOETHNOGRAPHY

The study of the researcher as subject of investigation is evident in many social science disciplines including anthropology (Reed-Danahay 1997), sociology (Denzin 1997; Lucal 1999), communications (Ellis 1995, 2004; Ellis and Bochner 2000), education (Clough 2002), sport and physical education (Sparkes 2002) and mental health (Grant 2010a; Grant and Zeeman 2012). Autoethnography is a methodology that legitimizes academic research where the writer details their personal experiences, often through stories and autobiographical narratives, that situate them in the social world or culture under study (Reed-Danahay 1997). To this end, autoethnography is a process of research but it is also concerned with the product of that process. Reed-Danahay (1997) defines autoethnography as 'research (graphy) that connects the personal (auto) to the cultural (ethnos), placing the self within a social context' (Reed-Danahay 1997: 145). Autoethnographers story their lived experiences via emotionally rich texts that seek to actively resist and challenge dominant academic discourse. Autoethnographies explore messy and complicated *real* lives that are never just one thing or just another, which goes against the traditional, objective and omnipotent style of traditional research texts. Autoethnographers ask the reader to think with stories rather than about them (Frank 2005) which is why it is synonymous with creative work and artist practice. The artist doesn't tell you what to think about their work, they have ideas, carry our research and have an informed process. They produce and then they wait to see what the effects are. And this can be likened to processes in autoethnographic work.

In autoethnography, the writing up of data can be descriptive-realistic, confessional-emotive, analytical-interpretive, creative-imaginative and so forth, and draws on short stories, memoir, scripts, poetry and other forms of creative and personal writing that help the researcher to locate themselves in the society or culture they are investigating and connect with the reader on an emotional and personal level whilst also contributing to intellectual debate. These stories are predominantly written in the first person and use emotional and self-aware accounts that demonstrate how the writer has been affected by the social group and/or culture under investigation (Ellis and Bochner 2000). Autoethnographers challenge conventional and objective presentations of research data where the researcher's voice is usually absent and encourage empathetic readings that contribute to an enhanced social understanding (Sparkes 2002). Writing in this way provides a useful tool in teaching creative writing that seeks to engage students with the process of telling their autobiographical stories in a range of styles and genres which is linked to a rigorous research process of data collection and analysis.

With autoethnographic work, autobiographical and biographical stories about a particular social group or culture or experience can help the reader understand or better understand what or who it is under study, but also help the researcher to better understand themselves. Laurel Richardson describes this writing as a method of inquiry (Richardson 2000). In this context, stories can be told in the spirit of social justice by interrogating and critiquing potentially (or actually) repressive cultural institutions, norms, values, practices and logics (Grant 2010b). By engaging with a text on an emotional and theoretical level, it is hoped that the reader will make better sense of their own lives by considering themselves in relation to what they have read (Frank 2011). This process enables students storying their autobiographical experiences to take an objective stance and this detachment is often necessary when critiquing and editing their raw autobiographical material. Creative writing students, as with all writers, can struggle to distance themselves from their autobiographical writing and this can result in them producing work that whilst emotional and moving, lacks the technique and crafting of 'good' writing. Writing for therapy is an important and useful strategy for coping with difficult or traumatic experiences but creative writing courses in HE are also concerned with producing skilled writers who can create texts they feel confident to share with their peers, tutors and submit for assessments, competitions, performance and so forth. It is important to make the distinction between writing that is for therapy and writing that employs literary techniques and skills that also has implications for well-being and positive transformation. Autoethnographic teaching and practice should, in my opinion, adhere to the latter. While self-narration can be cathartic, 'the classroom is not a clinic' (Cardell and Douglas 2016). When working with students on their own auoethnographies, the emphasis is on transformational writing that employs skill and retains a sense of technique and craft. In this way, the process can empower students to develop as writers and as people and this can help them to see themselves more clearly as writing practitioners. This can be useful for how they envisage themselves and their discipline in the world outside the classroom once they graduate.

## Teaching Autoethnography

> I expressed some long felt and deeply felt emotion. And in expressing it I explained it and then laid it to rest. (Woolf 1989: 90)

Despite my ambivalence about our current political climate and the implications it has for HE, my feelings regarding what a privilege it is to work with students have not changed since I first joined the University of Brighton in 2006. Working with students to develop their confidence with ideas and helping them to understand storytelling in a range of genres is a pleasure that continues to challenge and develop me in parallel with their own evolution as writers, thinkers and people. And perhaps this is at the core of what the writing and sharing of our stories is all about. It is an act that helps us to consciously or subconsciously think about our humanity and what it means to be human. And of course there is a compelling argument that to some extent all writing is autobiographical or at least draws on our lived and imagined experiences of the world. With this firmly in mind, one of the first things I tell my students is 'don't feel you have to share the most difficult thing that has happened to you'. It is my responsibility as a tutor to create a dynamic space for the students to work in but it must also feel safe and supportive. Students are asked to share their writing with their peers every week and we discuss strategies for making this a constructive and positive experience including guidelines on things to look out for in each other's writing and appropriate responses. We also talk about why it is important to help each other to develop confidence with writing whilst simultaneously offering constructive criticism that will ensure our writing improves, otherwise there is no trajectory for the students to go on, their work will flat line and their sense of what 'good' writing is will not broaden and enrich, making the entire module pointless or certainly less productive. Even after the warning that no one should feel overly exposed or unnecessarily vulnerable by writing about traumatic and painful autobiographical events, some students often choose to disclose and story things that have been difficult. The writer is advised to mine those events and journey to those places that are still troubling for us, because it can make for rich storytelling and also because there are therapeutic dimensions to this process that can be healing and transformative (Hunt 2000). My thesis contains a script that details my own experiences with trauma following stress at work, health issues and the breakdown of a long-term relationship. The process of researching and writing the script was of huge benefit to my own well-being and helped me to feel differently about work, home and my writing. And so while asking students to venture into autobiographical writing about trauma is always with a cautionary precursor, it is also important that I use my own experiences and understanding about life writing in my teaching, in the hope that it will be empowering and positive for the students too.

Coffey (1999) criticizes autoethnography for having narcissistic and naval-gazing properties and, naturally, any study of self runs the risk of being indulgent or overly self-interested. When I teach autobiographical writing to undergraduates, we discuss issues of why one should write their autobiography, the aesthetics of autobiographical narratives (Nalbantian 1994) and editing their work so that the focus remains on writing well and not just exposing themselves on the page. They are also given examples of autobiographical texts to digest and discuss within their peer group. This

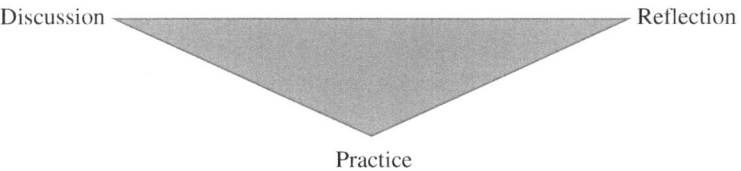

**Fig. 11.1** Triangulation of practice

process of reading, thinking and discussion enables students to connect their writing to the ethics of what they write and how and why they write it and this conscious layering between themselves and their writing develops knowledge, techniques and the confidence to apply these to their own writing, thus reducing any narcissistic tendencies and instead helping them to produce evocative and absorbing work. Whilst they must remain present in their autobiographical narratives, a process of attachment and detachment is important to all writers and can be developed and increased using autoethnography as it is a methodology that seeks to connect the individual to their social/cultural worlds. Instead of using autobiographical writing to just look in, autoethnographers have to look up and out as well. Autoethnographers engage in a cycle of reflection and action, often triggered by wanting to find something out about themselves in relation to the wider world and this critical process of self-analysis and understanding in relation to cultural and social discourses can help to make sense of their own lives by reconceiving their perspectives in relation to others (Fig. 11.1).

Engaging students in a triangulation of discussion–reflection–practice can help them to 'make new sense of situations of uncertainty or uniqueness' that they might experience (Schon 1983: 61) and these are crucial research skills that have the potential to help them make sense of their academic studies and lived experiences whilst at university. Not only can this help them to feel surer about their writing and their studies but it may also impact on their well-being (Moriarty and Reading 2012).

Once students have been introduced to writing autobiographical narratives, I then offer examples of auoethnographies and we explore the notion of employing self-narratives to examine the situatedness of self in relation to others in a social construct (Reed-Danahay 1997; Spry 2001). We look at examples of autoethnography as a social process whereby individuals come to greater understanding of themselves and others

(Schubert 1986: 33) as a result of their writing (Carless and Sparkes 2007; Grant 2010a; Moriarty 2015a, b). I ask the students to consider how their own writing and research might illuminate readers by engaging them in a vivid and evocative narrative that is 'ethnographical in its methodological orientation, cultural in its interpretive orientation, and autobiographical in its content orientation' (Chang 2008: 1). But this can still make it difficult for students to develop connections between lived experiences, academic study and their social worlds. This lack of clarity can be damaging for their confidence with their research and so, inspired by the work of Carless and Sparkes (2007) and Sikes (2000), I have devised the following guiding questions that I recommend students practising autoethnography ask themselves and their readers/audiences:

- Does the story hold together in an intelligible and coherent manner?
- Do the characters and events seem plausible?
- What might readers/audiences learn from the writing—about the social world under study and also about themselves?
- Did the writing affect the reader/audience emotionally and/or did it resonate personally?
- Can the reader empathize with any of the characters or not?

It is a series of questions I have used in my own work and it can help to refocus or motivate the work at stuck points in the research. While supporting the students to become independent researchers and thinkers, guiding questions such as these are useful. They provide criteria that students can return to in their assessed work at university but also when they graduate and use their writing in postgraduate or professional work.

Guba and Lincoln (1989) advanced five authenticity criteria essential in autoethnographic study: fairness, ontological authenticity, educative authenticity, catalytic authenticity and tactical authenticity. The fourth criterion, catalytic authenticity, is 'the extent to which action is stimulated and facilitated by the evaluation process' (Guba and Lincoln 1989: 249) where the purpose is some form of action or decision-making. Lather (1991) argues that research that has catalytic authenticity should have a 'reality altering effect and channel impact so that participants gain self-understanding and, ultimately, self-determination through research participation' (68). This sense of transformation as a result of self-study and of feeling differently about oneself as a result of the research process is particularly useful for students about to graduate from university and develop a sense of themselves and their discipline of study in the world outside the classroom. This is a potentially intense process that can benefit from one-to-one supervision away from the classroom and peer support that may increase feelings of vulnerability for any student engaging in an autoethnographic process. For these reasons, I have found it particularly useful to work with final-year and postgraduate students on autoethnographic approaches as these can evoke a range of emotions and feelings that the student does not fully begin to make sense of until the work is underway or even complete. In this way, the writing becomes a method of enquiry, a notion that is supported by Richardson (2000) who suggests that 'writing is also a way of knowing—a method of discovery and analysis. By writing in different ways, we discover new aspects of our topic and our relationship to it. Form and content are inseparable' (923).

In 2010, one of my third-year students approached me and asked if he could do a creative dissertation. Luis (not his real name) had taken other creative writing modules and while his work had been sound, it was safe. He had worked as a fashion model and was popular with the other students, whilst maintaining an aloof separation that only increased his kudos. I had watched him take part in writing exercises without giving much away about what he thought or felt which I assumed was because the degree was just a stepping stone and an experiment in how much socializing you could do and still pass. He struck me as the sort of student who coasted but was bright enough to do well. I had judged him and deemed him to be taking the creative dissertation route because he thought it was the easy option. Slightly cynically, I tried to warn him off. And then he told me what he wanted to do. And he told me why. And I realized I had been utterly wrong about him. He explained that he had been holding onto difficult autobiographical experiences that he had buried deep within himself but were beginning to affect him in ways that were taking over his life. When we finished talking he said, 'I don't want to feel like this anymore. I want the happy ending.'

Of course, I could not and did not promise him that, but I gave him some articles where the researchers had employed autoethnography and asked him to think about what his project might be like. We also talked about the ethical implications of storying traumatic experiences and how this might impact on him and what he might consider to help with this. It soon became clear that he had no interest in producing a conventional dissertation. I also gave him my own writing and explained why I had felt an urgency to story my experiences with working in HE and how the process had helped me to feel differently and more positive about my role as an academic but also as mother, daughter, friend, partner, colleague, sister and woman too. Luis decided that he wanted to use his critical and creative work to hold up a mirror to his life and experiences with mental health issues and reflect what it had been like for him. He was not seeking any kind of truth or definitive solution to how he had been feeling, he simply hoped that by merging his research and evocative writing, it would help to facilitate positive changes in his life and that it might trigger an enlightened response in those who read his work. Denzin and Lincoln (2008) describe qualitative researchers who are interested in interpretive, narrative, theoretical, political and cultural techniques as 'bricoleurs' or quilt-makers as they seek to offer a patchwork montage of their research experiences, drawing on a range of skills, techniques and genres to project a version of the research that is evocative, messy and openly imperfect. Luis identified this model as being appropriate for his research as he argued that mental health issues (much like any life experiences) are not experienced in a linear format or only in one way. By employing different genres, he wanted to create a split narrative drawing on poetry, memoir and script to tell a story that was messy, that was complicated, that was lived. It might not be deemed perfect by the people marking his dissertation but it was how it had to be done in order for it to maintain its importance and transformational potential for Luis himself and he hoped that anyone reading his work would respect and engage with this. We started to explore what the different sections of his patchwork would look like, the tools he would need to create them and how he might stitch them all together.

He worked incredibly hard, absorbing articles and books and sending me his writing for critique and discussion. Tutorials were intense as different emotions and awarenesses emerged as he worked. He simultaneously engaged with a counselling service, recognizing that the writing process and aspects of the therapy might overlap at times but that they were also separate. Whilst we both accepted that there was an undeniable therapeutic dimension to the process, we were both clear that I am not a counsellor and that, in this context certainly, he was not a patient: our focus was on the writing. I worried if he was going to hold everything together or if the pressure of completing his final year together coupled with unlocking this Pandora's Box of how he had been feeling and living would be too much, but when we discussed the ethical implications on his own well-being, he was resolute: 'I just can't feel like this anymore.' And he kept going.

**2AM**
My mind wanders hopelessly.
I tend to think about
Something that happened
4 years ago, or something
That happened 1 hour ago,
My mind takes me to the future
And somewhere 10 years from now.
Bleak.
My mind is like a hurricane,
Wreckage.
It's full of beautiful yet
Horrible things.
Loss of breath joins
My wandering mind,
The storm is sucking me in.

By the time Luis handed in his dissertation, the storm had passed. The present and the future stopped seeming like desolate and tortured places and he started to talk about his life after graduation with optimism and relief. The process of writing about trauma had helped him to see his experiences in a new way and he felt differently about them and also about himself. Instead of feeling happy for him, I panicked. What if it didn't get through the marking process? Or what if it did but achieved a mark that failed to reflect his blood, sweat and tears? What if I had encouraged him to write in a way that was deemed too personal and/or creative? Of course, I did not reveal these fears to Luis. I just waited for the marker's report with a growing sense of dread that the system he had believed in might ultimately let him down.

When Luis graduated with a first and was also awarded a prize for his outstanding dissertation, it was a moment of joy and of hope. He has stayed in touch and I am honoured to hear about the English teacher he is becoming and how motivated he is to work with his pupils, to hear their stories and to try and help them to see the value in their own processes of writing and reflection. He has even written a chapter for a collection of narratives from teaching that I am co-editing where he talks about his writing and how it has helped him to encourage his own pupils to use their own work to develop their writing skills and self-confidence. I often talk about how he came to write his dissertation and what it meant—to him but also to me. Watching students be brave, be vulnerable and their commitment to the process of developing their craft and evolving as writers, academics and as people, remains the biggest inspiration to my own teaching. Through our writing and sharing of stories, our interpersonal exchanges accord us subject positions, and these serve to guide the moral direction of our individual and social lives (Davies and Harre 1990; Harre 1991). Writing in this way can help some students to evolve and recover from traumatic experiences, to feel better prepared for their professional and personal lives post-graduation and more confident about what is to come. And if and when the storm returns, they can feel surer about finding a way through.

## Conclusion

I have slowly come to believe that no story is true for all time and space: we invent our stories with a passion, they are momentarily true, we cling to them, they may become our lives and then we move on (Plummer 1995: 170).

I have worked with students on their auoethnographies for several years now and the processes are always slightly different but on each occasion the practice of creation and crafting has been transformative, uplifting, life affirming. For the student, but also for me. I will always be grateful to each one of them for allowing me some insight into their individual practice and change. By using their research and writing to understand and make meaning about themselves and their social, cultural, political, emotional worlds, students can evolve past notions of themselves as just learners and begin to accept themselves as writers with something personal and academic to say about the humanities and about creative writing. I have found this of particular use with dissertation students and on a module with MA students where they become artists in residence and have to work with a group/organization on a co-devised creative brief that employs their research skills and creative writings. Students often pick residencies that have a personal relevance and resonance and working in this way can help them to navigate through their residencies and produce work that is personal and social.

But using autobiographical narratives in research is hard and students can and should be supported with this process. A set of criteria I suggest they are given for developing autoethnographic work would include the following:

Students should:

1. Be clear about what they want to write and why;
2. Be able to identify literary techniques that they have employed to make their writing vivid;
3. Be actively engaged in a process of crafting and critique;
4. Be clear about how this connects to the social world
5. Be willing to engage in a transformative process.

Working in this way can support students to make sense of the world and to let their sense of it become vivid through their craft of writing. In this way they can use their writing to reflect and shape their lives as they enter post-graduation. They can develop as better researchers, writers and thinkers and use this to help them fulfil their personal ambitions. I have found that working in this way can help them to develop their technique and craft, enhance their self of self, help them to recover from traumatic experiences, feel more confident about their place in their discipline of creative writing and the place that their discipline has in the world outside the lecture hall. They realize their writing matters. And it really does.

## WORKS CITED

Canagarajah, S. Athelstan. 2002. *Geopolitics of Academic Writing*. Pittsburgh: University of Pittsburgh Press.

Cardell, Kylie, and Kate Douglas. 2016. Why Literature Students Should Practise Life Writing. *Arts and Humanities in Higher Education*. https://doi.org/10.1177/1474022216635825

Carless, David, and Andrew Sparkes. 2007. The Physical Activity Experiences of Men with Serious Mental Illness: Three Short Stories. *Psychology of Sport and Exercise* 9 (2): 191–210.

Chang, Heewon. 2008. *Autoethnography as Method*. Walnut Creek, CA: Left Coast Press.

Charney, Daniel. 2011. *The Power of Making*. V&A.

Clough, Peter. 2002. *Narratives and Fictions in Educational Research*. Buckingham and Philadelphia: Open University Press.

Coffey, Amanda. 1999. *The Ethnographic Self*. London, UK: Sage.

Davies, Bronwyn, and Rom Harre. 1990. Positioning: The Discursive Production of Selves. *Journal for the Theory of Social Behaviour* 20 (1): 43–63.

Denzin, K. Norman. 1992. The Many Faces of Emotionality. In *Investigating Subjectivity: Research on Lived Experience*, ed. C. Ellis, 17–30. London: Sage.

———. 1997. *Interpretive Ethnography: Ethnographic Practices for the 21st Century*. London: Sage.
Denzin, K. Norman, and S. Yvonne Lincoln. 2008. *Strategies of Qualitative Inquiry*. 3rd ed. Thousand Oaks, CA: Sage.
Docherty, T. 2012. Research by Numbers. *Index on Censorship* 41 (3): 46–54.
Ellis, Carolyn. 1995. *Final Negotiations: A Story of Love, Loss, and Chronic Illness*. Philadelphia: Temple University Press.
———. 2004. *The Ethnographic I: A Methodological Novel About Teaching and Doing Autoethnography*. Walnut Creek, CA: Mira.
———. 2000. Autoethnography, Personal Narrative, Reflexivity: Researcher as a Subject. In *The Handbook of Qualitative Research*, ed. K. Norman Denzin and S. Yvonne Lincoln, 733–768. Thousand Oaks, CA: Sage.
Frank, W. Arthur. 2011. What Is Dialogical Research and Why Should We Do It? *Qualitative Health Research* 15: 964–974.
Grant, Alec. 2010a. Autoethnographic Ethics and Rewriting the Fragmented Self. *Journal of Psychiatric and Mental Health Nursing* 17: 111–116.
———. 2010b. Writing the Reflexive Self: An Autoethnography of Alcoholism and the 'Impact' of Psychotherapy Culture. *Journal of Psychiatric and Mental Health Nursing* 17 (7): 577–582.
Guba, Egon, and Yvonne Lincoln. 1989. *Fourth Generation Evaluation*. Beverly Hills, CA: Sage.
Harre, Rom. 1991. The Discursive Production of Selves. *Theory & Psychology* 1 (1): 51–63.
Hunt, Celia. 2000. *Therapeutic Dimensions of Autobiography in Creative Writing*. London and Philadelphia: Jessica Kingsley Publishers.
Knights, Ben. 2008. Teaching and Writing as Complementary Processes. In *Duet Encounters*, ed. Maria Gregorzewska and Aniela Korzeniowska. Warsaw: Wydawnictwo Uniwersytetu Warszawskiego.
Lather, Patti. 1991. *Getting Smart: Feminist Research and Pedagogy with/in the Postmodern*. New York, NY: Routledge.
Lucal, Betsy. 1999. What It Means to Be Gendered Me: Life on the Boundaries of a Dichotomous Gender System. *Gender and Society* 13 (6): 781–797.
Moriarty, Jess. 2015a. *Analytical Autoethnodrama*. Rotterdam, Boston, and Taipei: Sense.
———. 2015b. Leaving the Blood in: Experiences with an Autoethnographic Doctoral Thesis. In *British Contemporary Autoethnography*, ed. Nigel Short, Laetitia Zeeman, and Alec Grant. Rotterdam, Boston, and Taipei: Sense.
———. 2016. Autobiographical and Researched Experiences with Academic Writing: An Analytical Autoethnodrama. *NAWE* 2 (1).
Moriarty, Jess, and Christina Reading. 2012. Linking Creative Processes with Personal, Vocational and Academic Development in Cross-Disciplinary Workshops. *International Journal for Cross-Disciplinary Subjects in Education*

*(IJCDSE)*, Special Issue, 1 (2), ISSN: 2042 6364 (Online). http://www.infonomics-society.org/LICEJ/Published%20papers.htm

Nalbantian, Susan. 1994. *Aesthetic Autobiography: From Life to Art in Marcel Proust, James Joyce, Virginia Woolf and Anais Nin*. Basingstoke: Palgrave Macmillan.

Plummer, Ken. 1995. *Telling Sexual Stories: Power, Change and Social Worlds*. London: Routledge.

Reed-Danahay, Deborah. 1997. *Auto/Ethnography: Rewriting the Self and Others*. New York, NY: Berg.

Richardson, Laurel. 2000. Writing: A Method of Inquiry. In *The Handbook of Qualitative Research*, ed. K. Norman Denzin and S. Yvonne Lincoln, 2nd ed., 923–948. Thousand Oaks: Sage.

Schon, Donald. 1983. *The Reflective Practitioner*. New York: Basic Books.

Schubert, H. William. 1986. *Curriculum: Perspective, Paradigm, and Possibility*. Ann Arbour, MI: Macmillan Publishing Company.

Sikes, Pat. 2000. Truth and Lies Revisited. *British Educational Research Journal* 26 (2): 257–270.

Sparkes, C. Andrew. 2002. *Telling Tales in Sport and Physical Activity: A Qualitative Journey*. Leeds: Human Kinetics.

Spry, Tammy. 2001. Performing Autoethnography: An Embodied Methodological Praxis. *Qualitative Inquiry* 7 (6): 706732. http://www.nyu.edu/classes/bkg/methods/spry.pdf

Woolf, Virginia. 1989. Sketch of the Past. In *Moments of Being*, 72–173. London: Grafton Books.

CHAPTER 12

# Narrative and Narratives: Designing and Delivering a First-Year Undergraduate Narrative Module

*Richard Jacobs*

## 1

It may well be, as it was the case with me, that lecturers teaching in Higher Education for the first time are asked to take over, or start from scratch, a module designed to help first-year literature students make the transition from secondary or college education into HE. Such modules might typically be centred on theory (if the aim is to make transition something of a jolt) but perhaps more sensibly might be centred on narrative. This may be sensible because narrative (unlike theory) is 'natural' and pervasive at all the levels of education to which students have previously been exposed. They 'know' narrative and they certainly 'know' lots of narratives. The most effective way of allowing students the opportunity to develop a self-aware and reflective approach to literary study (to think about and examine what they 'naturally' know) is to start from what it is they know and where it is they are. Thus the crucial role that a narrative module can play in (ideally) the first part of the students' first-year work.

R. Jacobs (✉)
School of Humanities, University of Brighton, Brighton, UK

Accordingly, this chapter has the practical aim of describing such a module as it has evolved over the years I have been leading it at a university in the south-east of England, a university which takes students from a wide range of academic and social backgrounds. As well as its important role in transition to literature at university, the module also encourages students to integrate their own creative work with their critical work on narrative. This emphasis on the creative and the critical as mutually enhancing practices is a distinctive feature of the single-honours literature course at this university, though students are not obliged to choose any of the creative writing options.

The module outline for 'Narrative Literary Texts' highlights its transitional role, describing it as 'a bridge from students' earlier experiences of reading narrative texts' which 'encourages them to reflect on those early experiences', including with forms such as fairy tales and myths. Students are introduced to a variety of narrative texts and genres (texts 'selected for the specific nature of their narrative techniques and problems') and to some key issues in narrative theory. The module 'offers students an awareness of narrative as central to being human and allows them scope to explore narratives in creative and personal as well as critical ways in a reflective journal'. The three stated aims of the module are to give students opportunity to:

1. Reflect on their earlier experiences of narrative;
2. Study a range of narratives, including early forms such as fairy tales and myths; and
3. Study narratives in the context of a broader consideration of narrative discourse, structure and theory, and in the light of the importance of narrative in social and cultural life.

The end-of-module assignment (one or more shorter tasks during the module are preparatory) is a journal which students are encouraged to approach in a reflective and personal way and to make it very much their own in terms of design and presentation. Typically two thirds of them handwrite it and often illustrate it. The task is,

> A reading journal of reflective work, which may include creative as well as analytic material, which may be handwritten and which may include multimedia elements. It should contain about 3000 words and represent the student's own selection and reflective discussion of ideas, issues and narratives

(which can include media narratives) encountered during or outside the module, in any mix of taught and non-taught texts.

For new students used to formal essays this is a potentially intimidating brief in its open specifications and invitation to be independent in their approach. So we always bring into early classes good and widely varied examples of previous years' journals (a mix of those with some or with no creative work) and we also keep reminding them that they need to make sure that their own journals meet the stated assessment criteria. Students need to:

1. Show understanding of narrative forms, structures and some aspects of narrative theory;
2. Show awareness of the functions and cultural significance of narrative;
3. Demonstrate familiarity with a range of narratives from a variety of sources; and
4. Show engagement with narrative form and functions in a completed reflective journal.

Over the years this narrative module has changed and evolved, usually reflecting student feedback. It also changes over the years according to staff availability. Typically a team of four tutors deliver the module to between 150 and 200 students in the form of a weekly 90-minute lecture followed by a 90-minute seminar in a group of no more than twenty students. What follows is an indicative list of what a teaching schedule might look like.

- Week 1: Narrative in our lives. Fairy tales and folk tales: sociopolitical, psycho-therapeutic, structuralist approaches
- Week 2: Myths, mythologies, myth-theorists
- Week 3: Some narrative theoretical ideas: author/narrator/reader; openings and closure; 'story' and 'discourse'; free indirect style
- Week 4: Narrative form, desire and the death-instinct: why we read on
- Week 5: Dreams and crises of interpretation: Lewis Carroll's 'Alice' books and Freud's case study of 'Dora' (*A Case of Hysteria*)
- Week 6: Herman Melville, *Bartleby*
- Week 7: Henry James, *The Turn of the Screw*
- Week 8: Joseph Conrad, *Heart of Darkness*

- Week 9: Thomas Mann, *Death in Venice*
- Week 10: James Joyce, 'The Dead'
- Week 11: Katherine Mansfield, 'Bliss' and Jean Rhys, 'Goodbye Marcus, Goodbye Rose'
- Week 12: Detective stories by Conan Doyle and Raymond Chandler
- Week 13: 'Disneyfication' debate; assignment tutorials
- Week 14: Journal deadline

Lectures, the first three especially, include opportunities for new and potentially diffident students to talk to each other and to the lecturer. Thus the first lecture, following some simple propositions about narrative in our lives (the way we make sense of our lives and ourselves, the way we negotiate our relations with time and mortality, narrative's power to coerce as well as liberate), has included two short group exercises, in the first of which the students tell each other everything they can remember about the Red Riding Hood story and the lecturer helps them articulate the many differences they come up with. Those differences can then be mapped onto the Perrault and Grimm versions (to be looked at in detail in the seminar) which in turn can themselves be sharply contrasted with the reconstruction of the medieval oral version known as 'The Grandmother' (Tatar 1999: 10–11). This allows for a simple demonstration of Jack Zipes' socio-cultural approach to the evolution of folk tales (Zipes 1993), in this case from the matriarchal celebration of female cunning over her male aggressor (in the oral version) to the woman internalizing the blame for her own rape (in the Grimm).

In the other mid-lecture exercise, after Bettelheim's therapeutic approach (Bettelheim 1976) has been introduced, the students are asked to talk to each other about which childhood anxieties or traumas might be served by the narratives of fairy tales like Cinderella, Snow White, Sleeping Beauty, Hansel and Gretel, and Jack and the Beanstalk. Connections can be made between the older sisters' self-mutilated feet in the Grimms' version of Cinderella ('Ashputtel') and foot-binding (as well as FGM), and between their tale 'All Kinds of Fur' (studied in the seminar in terms of its rich narrative ambivalence—are there two kings in the tale or just one?) and contemporary issues of incestuous child abuse. These make for a lively chance for students to see the broader cultural ideas and issues on to which these apparently 'innocent' texts open out.

Close reading in the seminar of the differences between the Perrault and Grimm Red Riding Hood/Little Redcape stories (in Maria Tatar's translated edition; Tatar 1999: 11–16) affords opportunities to discuss many aspects of narrative. (And students are invited to test out Propp's thirty-one functions (Propp 1968) on one of these or indeed any narrative of their choice.) The different target audiences (the Perrault more clearly aimed at titillating its courtly adult readers) allow students to consider the so-called invention of childhood. The more subtly characterized little girl in the Grimm (more vain, gullible and disobedient) and the potential to read that narrative symbolically and intertextually (her wandering deeper and deeper into the forest; the Wolf as Satan); the hardening of gender hierarchies in the introduction of the patriarchal policeman figure who rescues the women; the multiple consciousnesses in the narrative of the Grimm ('the wolf thought…'; 'the huntsman thought…')—these give students the chance to think about the impact of the early rise of the European novel, evident in these features of the Grimm.

This is most evident in one particular feature of the Grimm version. When Redcape arrives at her grandmother's after the wolf has eaten her and got into her bed, the text reads, 'she went to the bed and drew back the curtains. Grandmother was lying there with her nightcap pulled down over her face'. Later when she in turn is eaten and the wolf is snoring in bed, the huntsman 'walked into the house and when he got to the bed he saw that the wolf was lying in it'. This serves to enforce the gendered distinction between the naïve girl who can't see behind the disguise and the clever man who can, but it also plays the subtle narrative device of momentarily slipping into the consciousness of both characters in a way that anticipates free indirect style.

The most fruitful differences pertain to the endings. The Perrault ends like a joke with a good punchline: 'Upon saying these words, the wicked wolf threw himself on Little Red Riding Hood and gobbled her up.' This is followed by a rather knowingly sexy 'moral' pointing out that 'perfectly charming' wolves follow young ladies 'into their chambers'—or in Zipes' edition the even sexier 'into their alcoves' (Zipes 1993: 93). With the introduction of the huntsman who rescues the women from the belly of the wolf the Grimm version allows for carefully differentiated closures, with the huntsman and the grandmother receiving physical rewards (the wolfskin; cake and wine) while Redcape's reward is the internalized moral lesson (not tacked-on as in the Perrault) which allows her to 'grow', thereby affording her the illusion of the 'deeper' characterization that distinguishes the protagonist in classic realist fiction.

With myths the starting point is on how they differ from fairy tales and the emphasis is on myths as aetiological, their power to relieve anxiety and resolve contradictions in symbolic terms and retrospectively by 'guessing backwards'. (Students are encouraged to write, for their journal, their own myth, starting from the anxiety which their myth will resolve but not mentioning it in their final product.) Answering more immediate needs in pre-scientific times (what is thunder?) myths today still have powerful cogency, especially at times of inflamed social anxiety, such as that stoked by right-wing media outlets over immigration. Creation myths are offered as particularly pure forms of anxiety relief ('where did we come from?') with the notion that, in David Leeming's words, 'a myth is to a culture what a dream is to an individual' (Leeming 1994: vii), and the Genesis myth of the Fall affords another interactive group exercise.

After hearing it read out (including the punishments), the students are introduced to the notion of how myths can be over-determined and asked to come up with as many questions or anxieties which the myth 'answers' (such as, why do we have to die, why do we wear clothes, why is childbirth painful for the woman, why do men assume superiority over women and so on). Creation and Fall myths from various cultures are looked at in the seminar, one particularly interesting example being from Russell Hoban's dystopian post-apocalypse novel *Riddley Walker*, the passage with the myth 'Why the dog won't show its eyes' (Hoban 1980: 17–20). Students are encouraged to consider the cultural reach and power of the Fall myth by seeing it as intimately connected with (in effect the same story as) the story Lacan told of how the infant, at first identifying the totality of the world as the unitary infant+mother, has to negotiate a series of wounding separations and losses: we are all exiles from that Garden.

As in the first lecture, key theorists in the field are briefly introduced, in this case Frye, Eliade, Burke, Freud and Barthes. The importance of Barthes' notion of myth as history mystified as 'nature' (Barthes 1973: 142–159) is emphasized in its continuingly urgent political relevance (a chance to define ideology) and students are offered online links to Peter Conrad's updating of Barthes' *Mythologies* in his Radio 4 series of brief broadcasts on contemporary myths, from the Selfie and the Apple icon to the Kardashians (now a book: Conrad 2016).

## 2

The following two weeks address some aspects of narrative theory in the hope that the range of narrative issues and ideas in the first two weeks will have prepared students for the potential challenges inherent in the concepts that we now explore. After some preliminary distinctions made in the week 3 lecture between the various roles played by author, narrator and reader we look quickly and by way of accessible introduction (in the form of a group exercise in the lecture) to the openings of *Jane Eyre* and *Catcher in the Rye*.

This comparison serves to bring out some broad distinctions between (largely) explicit and (largely) implicit meaning in the two texts, the role of the reader as (largely) passive and (largely) active, respectively, having to 'fill in the gaps' in the case of the latter text (this is to introduce 'reader-response' or 'reception theory' criticism) and the way those distinctions correspond loosely to 'realist' and 'modernist' fiction and to Barthes' 'readerly' and 'writerly' texts (Barthes 1990: v). (A usefully complete very short 'writerly' story is Hemingway's 'Cat in the Rain'.) Students are encouraged to note the way Jane is 'characterized' through difference (introducing the notion that meaning is a product of difference), especially when she refers to her 'physical inferiority to Eliza, John, and Georgiana Reed'. The narrative there immediately suggests all the other ways in which Jane is clearly not inferior to the other three children who, here and in the following sentence ('the said Eliza, John, and Georgiana'), by only being named collectively, in effect highlight and isolate Jane's privileged uniqueness and thus enhance the reader's attentive engagement with the first-person narrative.

Students are also encouraged to compare the way they are, as readers, addressed or positioned or included (or excluded) in the two texts, in the first by the way Jane's reading of her book about birds in comfortably wrapped and enclosed seclusion duplicates (in a consoling and flattering way) what the reader is doing with this novel, whereas in *Catcher* the reader is forced, without choice, into the role not only of confidant but of Holden's intrusively inquisitive psychiatrist, so that his opening words ('if you really want to hear about it') imply 'our' unspoken inquisitorial question. (For 'it' see Bennett and Royle 2009: 19–20.) This in turn allows Holden to pretend that he doesn't want or need to unburden and is only being forced to by 'us', a pretence that allows him to sound more in charge, less vulnerable and less in need of help than he actually is. He wants to unburden but can't allow himself to admit it.

The emphasis in the lecture shifts to the way narrative comprises two halves of a relation where one half is a kind of abstract impossibility: this is the difficult relation between what is (confusingly in the case of the first term) usually called 'story' and discourse or *fabula* and *sjuzhet* or crime and inquest: the following week's lecture emphasizes crime fiction as exemplary for narrative and week 12 of the module is devoted to the genre. (See Sue Kim and Will Norman's chapters in this volume for fine discussions of teaching *fabula* and *sjuzhet*.)

This relation is between the 'what' of narrative, conceived as an abstract and impossible 'log' of the totality of 'content', and the 'how' of narrative, the actual text that we read, with all its decisions made as to order and selection of events, cast of characters, dialogue, point of view, tone, genre and the rest. The two parts of the relation are necessary but the first is unavailable—and there is doubt as to whether it is even prior to the second, in what Jonathan Culler explores as the double logic of narrative (Culler 1981)—or available only by artificial means.

I have found it helpful to devote most of the seminar to an exercise designed to demonstrate the crucial 'story'–discourse relation, as well as the artifice needed to bring 'story' into view. In advance the students are given a grossly simplified 'story' version of Nabokov's brilliant short story 'Signs and Symbols' (a text which at this stage they are told not to read). They are also told how artificial it was of me to produce this 'story', especially as they are going to be asked to treat it, without theoretical warrant, as 'prior' to any 'later' discourse. They are then asked to come to the seminar with an outline treatment of such a discourse, that is an outline of their own short story, with some passages written, having carefully considered and chosen between the various options open to them as to point of view, narrative perspective, dialogue, sequence of events and so forth.

Here it is:

*Signs and Symbols*
   'Story' as shadow or raw material behind 'discourse' which is the narrative you will outline and write part of. Artificially generated from Nabokov's 'discourse'.

- Unnamed Russian Jews born *c.*1885 and live in Minsk
- Married *c.*1905
- He a fairly successful businessman *c.*1905–1917
- His brother Isaac emigrates to USA *c.*1910
- Russian revolution 1917
- They move around/living in Europe: Leipzig, Berlin, Leipzig 1917–*c.*1938
- Only son born *c.*1928

- Son's early life shows unusual symptoms/talents
- They emigrate to USA *c*.1938, financially dependent on brother Isaac
- Aunt Rosa and many friends/relatives killed in concentration camps
- Son in special school *c*.1938–*c*.1945: humiliations and difficulties
- Son in sanatorium from *c*.1945: he has advanced persecution ('referential') mania
- His three birthdays in sanatorium 1945–1947: what presents would be safe to give him?
- He attempts suicide at least twice
- Today's birthday visit: they choose as a present a jar of brightly coloured fruit sweets
- They can't see their son because of another suicide attempt
- They return home, consider moving him into their flat and look at their present
- They receive phone calls some or all of which are wrong-number calls

In groups students compare their efforts—the point of course being to demonstrate the infinite variability, the plasticity of 'discourse', the 'how' of narrative in its complex relations with the (in effect) monolithic 'what' of 'story'. Their efforts are indeed so startlingly various in treatment, point of view, tone, choice of when to start their story and whether to use flashback, which episodes to dramatize and which to pass quickly over and the rest as to take us all aback. They are then issued with and read the Nabokov treatment (Nabokov 1996: 598–603). It's not unusual for us all to notice some perhaps awkward or bumpy aspects of what he does, despite the brilliance of the short story.

Free indirect style is more easily demonstrated. We look at extracts from *Emma* (very arguably the first novel in English to use it as a pervasive narrative rhetorical strategy) and *Madame Bovary* (where it perhaps reaches its apogee in terms of rhetorical power) and students are encouraged to 'translate' such passages into more orthodox third-person narrative or dialogue. As with the Nabokov exercise, of course, these creative or re-creative exercises could go straight into their journals.

The fourth week is devoted to narrative and desire, the relation in Freud's 'Beyond the Pleasure Principle' between desire and the death-instinct and the relevance of that struggle to the way plots unfold and why and how we read them. Of course, the crucial critical text here is Peter Brooks' excellent *Reading for the Plot* and the key chapter 'Freud's Masterplot' (Brooks 1992 ed.: 90–112; see the Introduction to this volume for more on Brooks). Here is a simple summary of some of the ideas as mediated during the lecture (part of a larger summary document posted online for the students):

- Walter Benjamin argues that what we seek for in narrative fiction is the knowledge of death, a knowledge denied to us in our own lives. In our lives we can never know the death that writes 'the end' to a life that thereby confers coherence and meaning to that life. We seek that in narrative.
- Benjamin thus argues for the *necessary retrospectivity* of narrative: only the end can finally determine and confer meaning.
- Thus the end writes the beginning and shapes what comes between. Prior events or 'causes' can only be so retrospectively, reading back from the end.
- *Anticipation of retrospection* is our chief tool in making sense of narrative: we read on in confident dependence on the idea that what remains to be read will end in restructuring the provisional meanings of what we've already read.
- Detective stories are exemplary narratives: plots as the production/creation/working out of 'crime' ('story') mediated in/by 'inquest' ('discourse').
- The end of the plot restores the possibility of transmission (handing the story on): at the moment of death life becomes transmissible. At the end the claim to understanding merges with the claim to transmissibility.
- Thus the prevalence of framed narratives in which tellers and listeners dramatize the problem of transmission.
- The reading of plot is a form of desire that carries the reader forward, telling us about desire (the protagonist's) and simultaneously arousing desire (in the reader) as a dynamic of signification and of making sense.
- Plots therefore *dramatize* the protagonist's desire and at the same time *manipulate/incorporate/appropriate* the reader's desire. The narrative of desire merges with the desire for narrative.
- Desire is always present at the start of a narrative whether in initial arousal or at a state of intensity requiring action for change.
- Desire in this sense is Freud's Eros which always seeks to combine substances into ever greater unities. Desire, for Peter Brooks, is a totalizing textual erotics.

- For Freud there is a permanent battle within the psyche between Eros, the pleasure-principle, and Thanatos, the death-instinct. We read in and through desire but that desire is subtended by the drive to return to quiescence, the organism at rest. Plot for Brooks dramatizes the interplay between forward momentum, totalizing and dilating (generating subplots and apparent diversions), and closure in death/peace/quiescence/return. This interplay structures what Brooks calls the *erotics of narrative*.

The lecture goes on to connect these ideas with larger issues of desire and death in narrative texts, as exemplified in the very different work of Jonathan Dollimore and Denis de Rougemont (Dollimore 1998; de Rougemont 1983), especially the—on the face of it bizarre—romantic notion that death is desirable (Hamlet's third soliloquy; Keats' *Nightingale* ode) and that the only true love is that which is consummated in death. De Rougemont argues that the founding myth for love in the Western world, the Tristan and Isolde story, presents desire as nourished by and thriving on obstacles. The lecture suggests that a novel like *Wuthering Heights* is compelling evidence that the 'purest' love is (as well as pseudo-incestuous) constituted in and structured by loss, driven by obstacles and validated in death.

The seminar text is another fairy tale, Wilde's *The Happy Prince*, chosen as a bridge between the earlier fairy tales and the short novels in the second part of the module, and as a simple demonstration of the notion that love is best served in death, and also because a number of technical narrative features, especially concerned with form, make it a useful place to take stock before the module turns to more substantial texts.

Students start by considering the way this fairy tale differs from those in the Perrault–Grimm classic tradition (realist rather than symbolic setting; socially mixed 'cast'; dimensionalized protagonists; politicized satire and so on) and thinking about how this reflects the impact of classic realist novels, especially Dickens and his sympathy for children in poverty. (Anderson's tales are specifically referenced twice in this story.) The very unusual ending (God telling an angel to bring him the Prince's broken heart and the dead swallow) makes many students suspect a kind of institutional pressure to end in this 'tacked-on' way. In that light students experiment with trying on alternative endings which proliferate in the last page of the story, all of which 'work' (though some are signally bleak and blackly comic); together they make students realize how different closures in effect rewrite the whole tale.

In terms of form students are introduced to the idea of reader-competence when they note that the second sentence of the tale ('he was gilded all over with thin leaves of fine gold, for eyes he had two bright sapphires, and a large red-ruby glowed on his sword-hilt') is a brilliant snapshot of the plot, backwards, so that once the ruby is given away the alert reader 'knows' the rest of the plot. A related point is that when we first hear the Prince say 'Swallow, Swallow, little Swallow…' we 'know' he'll say that several times, in this instance because of the heightened, lyrical language that we have the competence to know will be repeated, as in refrain.

Revisiting the notion of meaning being a product of difference students are asked to list all the binary opposites that structure the tale (like drab European city–exotic Egypt, an opportunity to consider Said's Orientalism), of which one of the most telling is the horizontal–vertical axes on which the swallow is journeying. He thinks he's on his usual horizontal migration; he's actually on a vertical journey of self-discovery from which (like Redcape) he learns, changes and internalizes wisdom and compassion. In contrast, the Prince has already done his 'growing up', in the back-story when he dies and sees poverty for the first time.

Sexuality and gender are deliberately represented against the grain of typical fairy tales. Heterosexual relationships are shown to fail (if only by the fact that all the families are one-parent), clearly in the Swallow–Reed relationship (and it's her fault), and most sharply in the young couple on the palace balcony where the man is the romantic dreamer and the woman is cruelly selfish and materialistic—and actually wrong, as she fulminates against the 'lazy' seamstresses, one of whom we've already met, working on this woman's dress with her sick son. A point about form again: Wilde has manipulated our anger towards this young woman by sequencing the plot in that order. In contrast homo-erotic love is privileged (not very subtly in the case of the playwright with all the usual fairy-tale princess visual descriptors and the sugar-daddy friend) and of course validated in the death of the homo-erotic couple, sanctioned at the end by God. It's an intertextual mix of a gay Romeo and Juliet (the Swallow's evolving love life is exactly analogous to Romeo's; the Tristan myth is behind both texts) and the sacrifice of Christ on the Cross. A heady mix and students are quick to relate the story to what they know about Wilde who seems in the fairy tale to have anticipated his own martyrdom.

The week that follows brings together, in what is perhaps an innovative way, Carroll's 'Alice' books and Freud's early case study of 'Dora'. The contrast here is between narrative as freedom and release and narrative as oppression and coercion. Despite the potential for coercion and even abuse in the case of Carroll with Alice, and the potential for restorative or at least palliative care in the case of Freud with Dora after her trauma—and despite the fact that the trauma in the case of the 'Alice' books is Carroll's and not Alice's—the texts are in a deeply paradoxical relationship with each other in terms of the uses to which they put narrative. Carroll, despite and because of his love, uses narrative to set Alice free; Freud forces Dora into a prison-house of narrative (Freud 2013).

After sketching in the immediate founding contexts for these texts that concern relations between older men and girls (and attempting a neutral summary of the debate around the nature of Carroll's interest in Alice and other young girls), the lecture notes that the texts deploy narrative in a variety of contrasting ways: as dreams and nightmares; as complex mediations of fantasy and truth; as modes of freedom and oppression; as therapy and self-therapy; as responses to trauma; as personal love-gifts and as cultural critique.

The lecture deals with the 'impossibility' of the Alice books: the impossibility of remembering or summarizing the 'plot' of the books, particularly *Wonderland*, as they are far from the logicality and consequentiality of realist fiction but instead have the illogical randomization of dream fragments that blur into each other, as if in Freudian 'free association' for Carroll in a kind of self-therapy, for the imminent loss of Alice. (In the seminar students are invited to test this idea of self-therapy by looking at characters who are conscious or unconscious self-representations, like the Dodo, the Mock-Turtle, the White Knight and, most poignant of all, the invisible insect in the train-carriage.) But there is one clear thread to the plot: Alice's desire to get into the beautiful garden and her shock when she at last gets there to find it full of cardboard cut-outs and a murderous mother. This is connected with the (Lacanian) work in the second week: the idea that we are exiles, that the desire to return to the garden/mother can never be fulfilled and that what we think we desire will always be elsewhere.

The books also stage an impossible crisis about time which is both cyclical and linear, a distinction offered in the first lecture (Nikolajeva 2000). The two collide in a neat moment in the mad tea party when Alice, learning that it's 'always tea-time', that there's 'no time to wash the things' and that's the reason they keep moving round the table (a pure demonstration of cyclical time), very pertinently asks, 'but what happens when you come to the beginning again?' The crisis (the incursion of linear time: no clean plates left) is averted in the March Hare's curt reply, 'suppose we change the subject'.

More generally, linear time is suggested by the emphasis in both texts on growing (becoming a queen on the chess board in *Looking-Glass*) and by the number of death jokes, and cyclical time is suggested by not just growing but shrinking and the return to the riverside at the end of *Wonderland*; there we have the painful sense that Alice will forget the whole experience. There are also impossibly varied ways of reading the opening sequence of *Wonderland* (from the fall down the rabbit hole to the emergence from the pool of tears): as classical myth (voyage to the underworld); as the Christian Fall and wish to return to the garden/mother (as just mentioned); in terms of biology (the birth canal, amniotic fluid); as psychoanalytic dreams of falling and flying (orgasm/death); as rite of passage, the child becoming adult (the classic trope of fairy tales); in terms of evolution (the animals emerging from the sea); and as a joke at the expense of school-room history teaching: the story of 1066 (when English history 'started') is used to 'dry' them all off.

The books are also impossibly ahead of their time, as well as impossibly radical critiques of conventional pious mid-Victorian notions about childhood. They anticipate modernism in their refusal to assign stable meanings to anything, their refusal to let the author control and hold sole responsibility for meanings, making the reader do the work instead—as Barthes said of modernist or writerly texts, to return to the work in week 3 (Barthes 1990). They are also modernist in their fragmentary and contradictory plots, their illogicality and inconsequentialities, and the frequent language games which expose the randomness with which words and meanings are meant to be connected. The surprising critiques of Victorian childhood ideas centre on the absence of morals and even the satire on the very notion of drawing morals for children, as well as the parodies of famous moralistic poems which were force-fed to children. In a sharp ironic reversal Alice is the only adult among unruly animals/children, a reminder of Juliet Dusinberre's idea that the 'Alice' books are not just for the child in every adult but the adult in every child (Dusinberre 1987: 36).

The lecture ends contrasting the free 'modernist' space into which Carroll released Alice (and, in his self-therapy, himself—as well as releasing Alice from himself) with Freud, despite writing much later and much closer to mainstream literary modernism, oppressing Dora and imposing on her a narrative as if from a realist novel of his making, the depressing story of a teenage girl actually desiring the older man who assaulted her and whom she ends up marrying—which is, amazingly, what Freud thought Dora and Herr K should do. (Freud's case studies of men impose no such closure-fixated narrative on to their protagonists.) Carroll knows that Alice will grow up and forget him and the 'love-gift' of his or rather her narratives (the starting point for what must be the most moving and brilliant of all the by-products in the 'Alice'-industry: Dennis Potter's wonderful film *Dream-Child* (1985), in which multiple narratives are layered together in an extraordinary and indeed modernist way); Dora, in a very pointed moment in cultural history, simply walks out on Freud, terminating the treatment: a refusal to be in his narrative.

In the seminar students are given a number of materials on the Dora case, including her two dreams analysed (rather coercively) in the treatment (the 'Alice' books are in effect long dreams that refuse analysis) and a reproduction of the Raphael Madonna in front of which she stood for hours and of which Freud made surprisingly little. He also made little of Dora's family being Jewish in an anti-Semitic Vienna. Some of the best journal-entries that have come out of the Alice/Dora week have started from those materials, in some fascinating and creatively startling cases transposing Alice and Dora.

## 3

The literary texts that comprise the rest of the teaching weeks on the module have changed regularly over the years, though the intention, as mentioned at the outset, is for the choice to focus on texts 'selected for the specific nature of their narrative techniques and problems'. It will be seen that the emphasis is on proto- and early modernist texts and students are asked to consider and debate the gender imbalance among texts of those kinds. Opportunities are also found for discussion of the realism–modernism 'divide' (we saw that the 'Alice' books and Freud's 'Dora' reverse the usual polarity.) The week on detective stories gives an opportunity to return to Brooks' *Reading for the Plot* in his analysis of 'story' and discourse in Conan Doyle's 'The Musgrave Ritual' (Brooks 1992: 23–29; see also Jacobs 2010: 54–65). In relation to the iconic short novels or stories by Melville, James, Conrad, Mann, Joyce, Mansfield and Rhys there's no need here to spell out in detail the nature of the techniques and problems they embody, though these would self-evidently include issues of framing, unreliability or limited point of view of narrator, allegories (but allegories of what?), the limitations of narrative expressibility, imitative and transgressive desire as narrative motor (Girard 1966; Tanner 1979), the encodings of history and ideology in narrative and so on. But I wish to dwell on the case of *Bartleby*, as it is such a special case for any larger treatment of narrative.

The lecture starts by thinking about Dickens' *Bleak House* (published just before 'Bartleby') as the kind of typical big fat Victorian novel that Brooks had in mind when he wrote about how the plots of novels, like Freud's Eros, bring together multiple strands of story and apparently disparate characters into larger and larger unities and how readers, impelled by desire, enjoy the process of negotiating apparent digressions and subplots in the knowledge that the end will bring a totality of meaning. *Bleak House* is again typical in setting up mysteries in order to serve the reader's pleasure in reaching solutions, answers and meanings. Mysteries in plot are only there in order to be solved—why does Lady Deadlock faint? Who is the mysterious law-copyist Nemo whose handwriting she recognizes before she faints, and so on. We read on to find out.

*Bleak House* has more pointed connections with 'Bartleby' and the suggestion is that Melville, very conscious of Dickens' massive popularity compared to his own (which was at a low point at this time), was consciously 'playing' with Dickens and *Bleak House* in particular, subverting them, when composing 'Bartleby'. Its opening, with its comically self-satisfied and complacent narrator and his elaborate description of his comically named copyists, seems designed to fool the reader that she or he is reading a story in Dickens' lighter vein. ('The Dead' also generically fools the reader, in fact twice: first we're fooled into thinking we're reading a lightly ironic treatment of a death at a party; then towards the end into thinking it's a warmly romantic treatment of reignited sexual love between husband and wife.) We soon enough realize that we're reading a very different sort of text—but what sort?

The focus is on 'Bartleby' as a radically subversive text—subverting, in a very far-reaching way, the usual conventions of the mid-Victorian novel. The lecture lays out the subversive tactics of the story in relation to character and characterization, plot and to the reader's urge or rage to interpret. We discuss the usual modes of characterization in mainstream fiction: characters who are 'characterized' by exhibiting a limited number of 'traits' and doing/performing those and nothing else; and those (the protagonists) who grow and develop in more or less predictable ways, as if on moral or spiritual journeys of self-discovery (like Wilde's Swallow). Turkey, Nipper and Ginger-Nut clearly belong in the first category; the lawyer in the second—though his transformation is certainly not predictable.

But Bartleby himself can't be put in either of these boxes—or in any box, and that's the point. For he's not a 'character' in any sense of the word. He is radically unknowable and he and his actions (or preference not to act) are radically inexplicable—and the key point here is that in those respects he's most unlike textual characters and most like us—in our unknowabilities, to others and to ourselves. This is the deepest paradox of the novella: the least 'knowable' character, the 'weirdest' or 'oddest' in nineteenth-century fiction, is the most human, the most like you or me. Because how we see and what we most value in ourselves is, paradoxically, what is least knowable to others: that we, and Bartleby, are mysteries that can't be 'solved'. In effect what we—and the lawyer—are confronted with is the challenge of realizing the painfulness of actually treating other people as unknowable mysteries. Mainstream nineteenth-century novels do the opposite: they cheer us up with the notion that 'characters' (and plots) can be explained (explained away).

We consider the complete absence, with Bartleby, of those usual indicators of 'character plausibility': a recoverable back-story, notions of ambition and aspiration (crucial to Brooks' sense of desire), motivation and goals, the 'depth-effect' of character development and so on. And we look in detail at the way Melville writes about him, using language not to 'fill out' the 'character' but to empty it out—suggesting the paradoxical and impossible. We look at his voice and his movement: his 'singularly mild', 'flute-like', 'mildly cadaverous' voice, the way he 'noiselessly slid into view' and 'gently' or 'mildly disappeared'. Bartleby's own language, his dialogue (if that's the word) is in the same way gesturing at impossibility, emptying out, mere echo and repetition: 'At present I would prefer not to be a little reasonable.' Bartleby is referred to as 'a little luny' and 'a little deranged'. But we explore the opposite, paradoxical idea: perhaps he's the only 'sane' one in the text. The others are 'mad' because, like us, they're playing the social game, getting through life by the 'mad' conventions that structure our world. Bartleby refuses.

In terms of plot, most novelists populate a field that gets bound into a totality (Brooks on Freud's Eros): Melville depopulates the field, simply dropping Turkey, Nippers and Ginger-Nut out of the narrative, 'stripping' the text right back to the dynamic between Bartleby and the lawyer—whose language, very movingly, is transformed from the complacent and self-satisfied legal jargon at the start to the charged, poem-like simplicities at the end. After which is tears, and then silence. What we confront is the idea that 'normal' plots give us revelation and knowledge, but not here.

As readers we have the urge, the rage to explain and interpret. This astonishing text frustrates us at every point, as it does the lawyer. All attempts to 'explain' Bartleby and 'this little narrative' are really only clutching at straws, playing the critical/interpretive game. For a text published in 1853 at the height of Victorian realism this is unprecedented and a prefiguring of the 'anti-novels' of postmodernism. The text is like a hand grenade tossed into the conventions and complacencies of the nineteenth-century novel. Above all, all attempts to explain Bartleby are really no more than an affront to his dignity, an intrusion into his privacy and his silence. Not for nothing is the best book on 'Bartleby' (which surveys the whole 'Bartleby' critical industry) entitled *The Silence of Bartleby* (McCall 1989; see also Royle 2011: 151–168).

The module ends with a 'Disneyfication' debate in which colleagues from literature and related disciplines give short presentations debating the impact of Disney on the narratives in the fairy-tale tradition, after which students join the debate. This returns everyone to the beginning of the module and, in listening to different critical voices debating films they all know from their childhood, students are given an opportunity to reflect on those narratives in the light of what they've learned on the module as they address the journal assignment.

## Works Cited

Barthes, Roland. 1973. *Mythologies*. Translated by Annette Lavers. London: Granada.

———. 1990. *S/Z*. Translated by Richard Miller. Oxford: Blackwell.

Bennett, Andrew, and Nicholas Royle. 2009. *An Introduction to Literature, Criticism and Theory*. 4th ed. Harlow: Pearson.

Bettelheim, Bruno. 1976. *The Uses of Enchantment*. New York: Knopf.

Brooks, Peter. (1984) 1992. *Reading for the Plot*. Cambridge, MA: Harvard University Press.

Conrad, Peter. 2016. *Mythomania*. London: Thames and Hudson.

Culler, Jonathan. 1981. *The Pursuit of Signs*. London: Routledge and Kegan Paul.

De Rougemont, Denis. 1983. *Love in the Western World*. Translated by Montgomery Belgion. Princeton, NJ: Princeton University Press.

Dollimore, Jonathan. 1998. *Death, Desire and Loss in Western Culture*. London: Allen Lane.

Dusinberre, Janet. 1987. *From Alice to the Lighthouse*. Basingstoke: Palgrave Macmillan.
Freud, Sigmund. 2013. *A Case of Hysteria*. Translated by Anthea Bell. Oxford: OUP.
Girard, Rene. 1966. *Desire, Deceit and the Novel*. Translated by Yvonne Freccero. Baltimore: Johns Hopkins University Press.
Hoban, Russell. 1980. *Riddley Walker*. London: Jonathan Cape.
Jacobs, Richard. 2010. Republicanism, Regicide and "The Musgrave Ritual". *The Victorian Newsletter* 118: 54–65.
Leeming, David. 1994. *A Dictionary of Creation Myths*. Oxford: OUP.
McCall, Dan. 1989. *The Silence of Bartleby*. Ithaca, NY: Cornell University Press.
Nabokov, Vladimir. 1996. *The Stories of Vladimir Nabokov*. London: Weidenfeld and Nicholson.
Nikolajeva, Maria. 2000. *From Mythic to Linear*. Lanham, MD: Scarecrow Press.
Propp, Vladimir. 1968. *Morphology of the Folktale*. Translated by Laurence Scott. Austin: University of Texas Press.
Royle, Nicholas. 2011. *Veering*. Cambridge: CUP.
Tanner, Tony. 1979. *Adultery and the Novel*. Baltimore: Johns Hopkins University Press.
Tatar, Maria. 1999. *The Classic Fairy Tales*. New York: Norton.
Zipes, Jack. 1993. *The Trials and Tribulations of Little Red Riding Hood*. London: Routledge.

# Index[1]

## A

Abbott, H. Porter, 2, 129, 131
Abel, Elizabeth, 45–48
Ali, Monica
   *Brick Lane*, 141
Amis, Martin
   *Time's Arrow*, 31
Anachrony, 15, 40, 48, 49, 52
*Anagnorisis*, 35
Analepsis, 32, 48, 49
Antiracialism, 41
Archive, 18, 25–27, 29, 36, 87, 88, 90, 107, 123, 163, 165, 167
Aristotle, 16, 35, 56, 57, 63, 66, 73, 75
Augustine, 27–29
Austen, Jane, 2, 3
   *Emma*, 5–8, 199
   *Mansfield Park*, 4, 7
   *Pride and Prejudice*, 78

## B

Baldick, Chris, 6, 7
Barnes, Julian
   *The Sense of an Ending*, 35
Barthes, Roland, 3, 19, 20, 164, 169, 196, 197, 204
Benjamin, Walter, 20, 200
Bergson, Henri, 16, 77
Berlin, Isaiah, 103, 104, 111, 117, 198
Bettelheim, Bruno, 2, 20, 194
Booth, Charles, 143, 144, 149–152
Bowen, Elizabeth
   *The Heat of the Day*, 141, 142
Brecht, Berthold, 59, 60
Brooks, Peter, 3, 8–11, 13, 14, 20, 89, 147, 199–201, 205–207
Brown, Sterling, 16, 82, 83
Butler, Marilyn, 6

## C

Carroll, Lewis, 193, 202–205
Chandler, Raymond, 17, 89, 90, 101n4, 101n5, 194
   *The Big Sleep*, 93–96
Cheng, Anne, 43

[1] Note: Page numbers followed by 'n' refer to notes.

© The Author(s) 2018
R. Jacobs (ed.), *Teaching Narrative*, Teaching the New English,
https://doi.org/10.1007/978-3-319-71829-3

Chiang, Ted, 49, 50, 52
  'Story of Your Life', 15, 40, 48–53
Closure, 1–4, 6, 8, 10, 11, 164, 193, 195, 201
Coetzee, J. M., 35
  *Slow Man*, 33, 34
Collaboration, 142, 161, 162, 164, 166–168
Conduct books, 18, 127, 131
Connor, Steven, 8, 9
Conrad, Joseph, 20, 147–152, 158, 193, 196, 205
  *The Secret Agent*, 19, 141, 147
Context, 3, 14, 16, 24–27, 71, 72, 76, 78, 80, 81, 83, 90–92, 95, 97, 123–138, 151, 156, 158, 160, 161, 178, 184, 192
Culler, Jonathan, 198
Cultural Studies, 42, 123–127, 137
Cyclical time, 203, 204

**D**

De Rougemont, Denis, 201
Derrida, Jacques, 25, 36, 167, 168
Desire, 1, 5, 6, 9, 10, 13, 14, 84, 94, 114, 119, 126, 169, 176, 193, 199–201, 203, 206, 207
Dickens, Charles, 2, 5, 9, 123
  *Bleak House*, 4, 206
  *Great Expectations*, 8
Disneyfication, 20, 194, 208
Dollimore, Jonathan, 201
Doyle, Arthur Conan, 90, 91, 194, 205
Duration, 27, 28, 31

**E**

Eagleton, Terry, 36, 64, 67
Eliot, George, 2, 129, 136
  *Middlemarch*, 124, 128, 135
Empowerment, 158, 160, 161, 164, 169

Entanglement, 17, 89, 93–101
Epoch, 26, 36, 51

**F**

*Fabula*, 16, 31, 48, 49, 52, 88–92, 94, 100, 197, 198
Fairy tales
  Grimm, brothers, 194, 195, 201
  Perrault, Charles, 194, 195, 201
Fan, Christopher, 52
Faulks, Sebastian
  *A Week in December*, 141
Felluga, Dino, 49
Felski, Rita, 60, 126
Fitzgerald, Penelope
  *Offshore*, 141
Flaubert, Gustave, 151
  *Madame Bovary*, 3
Focalization, 15, 40, 43, 44, 148
Fontane, Theodore, 146, 153n4
Frequency, 31
Freud, Sigmund, 10, 11, 20, 74, 75, 196, 200, 201, 206, 207
  'Beyond the Pleasure Principle', 199
  '*Dora*', 3, 20, 193, 202–205

**G**

Genette, Gerard, 15, 27, 31, 32
George, Sheldon, 135
Girard, Rene, 12, 13, 206
Goldberg, David Theo, 41
Gothic, 98, 100, 101

**H**

Hale, Dorothy J., 5, 9
Haney Lopez, Ian F., 42
Harris, George W., 66, 67
Harvey, David, 24, 25, 29
Heterogeneity, 127

Hobbes, Thomas, 73–75
Holbein, Hans, 115–117, 120n5, 120n6
Holsinger, Bruce, 106, 107
Husserl, Edmund, 28
Hypertext, 161, 163, 167–170

**I**

Icelandic saga, 140, 146
Integration, 47, 50, 158, 167
Interiority, 17, 105, 111
Ishiguro, Kazuo
 *Never Let Me Go*, 35

**J**

Jameson, Fredric, 3, 36, 125
Joyce, James, 164, 205
 'The Dead', 194, 206
 *Ulysses*, 139, 167

**K**

Kureishi, Hanif
 *Gabriel's Gift*, 141

**L**

Lethbridge, Emily, 140
Linear time, 204
Literacy, 2, 114, 159, 160
Locke, Attica, 16, 101
 *Black Water Rising*, 96, 99, 100
Logocentrism, 161
Lukacs, Georg, 110, 111

**M**

MacCulloch, Diarmaid, 112, 113, 119n2
Mantel, Hilary, 103–119

*Wolf Hall trilogy*, 17, 105, 116
Mapping, 18, 89, 139–146, 148, 152
McEwan, Ian, 143
 *Saturday*, 141
Melville, Herman, 20, 205–207
 *Bartleby*, 193
Miller, D.A., 3–6
Modernism, 3, 168, 204
Moore, Alan
 *From Hell*, 141
Moretti, Franco, 17, 88–93, 95, 97, 100, 101, 111
Morrison, Toni, 43, 45, 46, 48
 'Recitatif', 15, 40, 43–48
Morson, Gary Saul, 30, 32, 34
Multimedia, 156, 161–163, 167, 168, 192
Musselwhite, David, 5, 7, 10
Myths, 20, 155, 192, 193, 195, 196

**N**

Nabokov, Vladimir, 199
 *Pale Fire*, 79
 'Signs and Symbols', 198
Narratability, 1–4
Negotiation, 42, 43, 131, 132
Nuttall, A.D., 56, 65, 66

**O**

Oedipus, 30, 32, 59, 77
Omi, Michael, 15, 40, 42
Omniscient narrator, 109
Order, 3, 13, 15, 18, 31, 40, 42, 48, 49, 51, 88, 90, 94–97, 100, 101, 134, 140, 142, 145, 156, 159, 161, 169, 184, 198, 202, 206

**P**

Palimpsests, 141

Paretsky, Sara, 16, 97–99, 101
  *Blood Shot*, 96
Performativity, 43, 52
*Peripeteia*, 35
Plato, 15, 16, 56, 57, 59, 72
Poe, Edgar Allen, 16, 87, 90–92, 94
Postracialism, 41, 42
Praxis, 159
Prince, Gerald, 44
Prolepsis, 31, 32, 48, 49
Propp, Vladimir, 20, 195

**R**
Readerly, 3, 164, 197
Realism, 3, 4, 72, 146, 208
Repressed, 41, 75, 100, 101
Retrospection, 9, 26, 29, 32, 200
Ricoeur, Paul, 27, 28, 127
Romance-epic, 147

**S**
Scriptedness, 35, 52
Shelley, Mary, 5
  *Frankenstein*, 7
Simultaneity, 24, 25, 29, 30, 51
*Sjuzhet*, 16, 31, 48–50, 52, 88, 89, 91, 100, 197, 198
Smith, Ali, 34
  *Hotel World*, 33
Smith, Erin, 94
Smith, Zadie
  *NW*, 141
Spark, Muriel, 177, 178
  *The Driver's Seat*, 31, 34
Stiegler, Bernard, 25
Stoppard, Tom, 16, 84
  *Arcadia*, 77, 83
Surprise, 14, 23, 24, 35, 36, 80, 100
Swift, Graham
  *Waterland*, 31

**T**
Talib, Ismail, 40, 44, 49
Tanner, Tony, 12, 206
Tatar, Maria, 194
Teacher-training, 159
Temporality, 15, 23–27, 30, 32, 36, 94, 127
Tense, 15, 27, 32
Todorov, Tzvetan, 16, 17, 27, 31, 32, 88–92
Transition, 14, 17, 20, 53, 131, 160, 191, 192
Trollope, Anthony, 124, 129, 130, 132, 133
  *The Way We Live Now*, 136

**U**
Uncertainty, 23, 24, 36, 45, 58, 181

**V**
Visualization, 18, 139, 141–145

**W**
Waters, Sarah, 141
  *The Night Watch*, 142
Wilde, Oscar, 84n1, 201, 202, 207
Williams, Joanna, 61, 63
Williams, Raymond, 60, 65, 118
Winant, Howard, 15, 40, 42
Woodruff, Paul, 57
Woolf, Virginia, 2, 16, 143, 179
  *Mrs Dalloway*, 141, 142
  *Orlando*, 80, 81
Writerly, 3, 164, 197, 204

**Z**
Zipes, Jack, 20, 194, 195

The manufacturer's authorised representative in the EU is Springer Nature Customer Service Centre GmbH, Europaplatz 3, 69115 Heidelberg, Germany. If you have any concerns regarding our products, please contact ProductSafety@springernature.com

Printed and bound by CPI Group (UK) Ltd, Croydon, CR0 4YY
23/03/2026
02076666-0005